The Ink Trade: Selected Journalism 1961–1993

ANTHONY BURGESS (1917–1993) was a novelist, poet, playwright, composer, linguist, translator and critic. Best known for his novel *A Clockwork Orange*, he wrote more than sixty books of fiction, non-fiction and autobiography, as well as classical music, plays, film scripts, essays and articles.

Burgess was born in Manchester, England and grew up in Harpurhey and Moss Side. He was educated at Xaverian College and Manchester University. He lived in Malaya, Malta, Monaco, Italy and the United States, and his books are still widely read all over the world.

WILL CARR is Deputy Director at the International Anthony Burgess Foundation, and has previously held senior roles at the Poetry School, Arts Council England, the Wordsworth Trust and the National Association for Literature Development. His edition of Anthony Burgess's novel *The Pianoplayers* is published by Manchester University Press.

Also available from Carcanet Press

Anthony Burgess
Revolutionary Sonnets and other poems

The Ink Trade

Selected Journalism 1961–1993

✳✳✳ ANTHONY BURGESS ✳✳✳

edited by

WILL CARR

CARCANET

First published in Great Britain in 2018 by
Carcanet Press Ltd
Alliance House, 30 Cross Street
Manchester M2 7AQ
www.carcanet.co.uk

A CIP catalogue record for this book is available from the British Library.
ISBN 978 1 78410 392 7

The publisher acknowledges financial assistance from Arts Council England.

Typeset in England by XL Publishing Services, Exmouth
Printed and bound in England by SRP Ltd, Exeter

Contents

Introduction

ANTHONY BURGESS'S newspaper career was a long one, and began when he was twelve years old. A drawing in the *Manchester Guardian* on 21 November 1929 by John Burgess Wilson (as he then was) of 261 Moss Lane East, Manchester was a winning entry in the Christmas 'Fathers and Mothers' competition, and depicted his father Joseph Wilson sleeping in his armchair next to a bottle of whisky and a pipe. Poems in *Electron* – the school magazine of Xaverian College, Rusholme – followed; and his earliest book and theatre reviews were written while studying English literature at the University of Manchester between 1937 and 1940, where they appeared in *Serpent*, the student newspaper.

Burgess was conscripted into the army in December 1940 and served in the Royal Army Medical Corps and as musical director of a dance band. He was eventually posted to Gibraltar in 1943, where as well as his work as a teacher in the Royal Army Educational Corps he reviewed films for the *Gibraltar Chronicle* until his demobilisation in 1946. After shuttling between unfulfilling teaching jobs in England, Burgess and his first wife Lynne lived in Malaya and Brunei between 1954 and 1959 where he taught for the British Colonial Service, and it was then that he began to publish his first fiction. His career as a journalist began to flourish once again after they had returned to England and Burgess became a full-time writer.

From 1960 Burgess contributed regular articles to *Country Life* and the *Listener*, as well as anonymous reviews to the *Times Literary Supplement*. This work took place alongside the task of writing novels: by 1962, Burgess had published ten, including *The Malayan Trilogy*, *The Right to an Answer*, *The Doctor Is Sick*, *The Worm and the Ring*, *Devil of a State*, *One Hand Clapping*, *The Wanting Seed* and *A Clockwork Orange*.

From May 1963 Burgess was also the fiction critic of the *Yorkshire Post*, writing a fortnightly column on new novels. He had joined the paper in 1961, and in his time there contributed more than sixty articles about several hundred different books. One morning a book called *Inside Mister Enderby* by Joseph Kell appeared on the doormat of his house in Etchingham along with the regular parcel of five or six that Burgess was called upon to review, and he led with a not entirely positive notice of it in his next article. As quickly became apparent, *Inside Mister Enderby* was in fact by Anthony Burgess himself, writing under a pseudonym, and his mischievous review of it in retrospect could have been judged as a private joke invisible to all except Burgess's publishers. However, his subterfuge was discovered and reported in the diary column of the *Daily Mail*, and the *Yorkshire Post* promptly sacked him.

It does not seem that Burgess's review of himself was the product of arrogant hubris. In the second volume of his autobiography, *You've Had Your Time*, he makes clear that he was under the impression that the books editor at the *Yorkshire Post*, Kenneth Young, was in on the joke as Burgess had warned him earlier that year that a pseudonymous novel was about to appear; indeed, Burgess had already been revealed as the author of *Inside Mister Enderby* a month before in a review in the *Daily Telegraph*, so his cover had long since been blown. The remarks he makes about *Inside Mister Enderby*, reprinted here as the first review, 'Poetry for a Tiny Room', are in any case hardly very complimentary about the qualities of the novel. Gore Vidal remarked at the time that the response of the *Yorkshire Post* was somewhat humourless: 'at least, he is the first novelist in England to know that a reviewer has actually read the book under review'. Burgess later retold the story many times, as did others; a version appears in the final piece in this book, 'Confessions of the Hack Trade'.

This notorious sacking was not the end of his journalistic career, of course. Dismissal from the *Yorkshire Post* did nothing to slow his prodigious output. Continuing his association with the *Listener*, he became its television critic; he continued to review books and write commentaries for the *Times Literary Supplement*; he began to contribute reviews to the *Guardian* from 1964, and later for the *Observer*, for which publication he wrote almost continuously until the end of his life. He became the theatre critic of the *Spectator* in 1965, and broadened his remit to include book reviews for that publication as well. He wrote for the *Hudson Review*, *Encounter*, *American Scholar*, the *Times*, the *New York Times*, and the *Los Angeles Times*.

Burgess's literary stature increased throughout the 1960s, with his journalistic writing taking place alongside the production of more novels (*The Eve of St. Venus, Nothing Like the Sun, Tremor of Intent, Enderby Outside*) and, increasingly, commissioned screenplays (some original, some based on his own novels, none of which went into production). His first television appearance was on the BBC in 1962, and he contributed to many radio programmes, including *Woman's Hour, Children's Hour* and *The World of Books*; his *Desert Island Discs* interview was broadcast on 28 November 1966. Burgess was perhaps one of the first writers to embrace television and radio as a way of establishing a public persona and communicating his ideas to a mass audience, and he would continue his media activities for many years to come.

As his reputation grew, and especially after the adaptation of his novel *A Clockwork Orange* into a film by Stanley Kubrick in 1971, Burgess's journalistic activities expanded still further as he defended his book on air and in print. As well as producing many pieces of writing about youth culture and violence, he commentated on almost all aspects of contemporary culture for publications across the world, including *Rolling Stone, Le Monde, Corriere della Sera, Playboy, El País* and many more. The breadth of the subjects that he covered was astonishing, going far beyond his areas of immediate knowledge and expertise to include writing about food, anthropology, jazz, the evils of taxation, architecture, feminism, Islam, and whatever else was demanded by the editor of the day. His greatest loyalty was perhaps to the *Observer* ('my paper', as he called it), to which he contributed more articles than to any other single publication – but Burgess would write for almost anyone, about almost anything.

This makes Burgess's journalism sound like the worst kind of hack work, knocked off quickly and clumsily for the money. Some of his pieces on more populist subjects, such as pieces on the royal family, the Moors Murderers or football hooliganism for the *Daily Mail*, on first reading seem slighter than his writing about literature – but even here there are references to Shakespeare, Beethoven and Catholic theology that make the approaches taken entirely distinctive. It seems clear that Burgess's ability to write high-quality copy for many different readerships, while always combining sober judgment with a characteristic style and flair, contributed to the unending demand for his work from newspapers.

Nonetheless, Burgess was often anxious not to contradict the impression that his journalism was merely the work of a pen for hire. He made many claims that reviewing and other journalistic writing were subliterary activities and a distraction from the real business of writing novels; but how seriously to take these claims is not always clear, especially when they themselves are contained in articles for the newspapers. In a 1973 'Viewpoint' column for the *Times Literary Supplement* Burgess complains at length about the injustices visited upon journalists – non-payment of fees by villainous editors, last-minute spikings of copy innocently sweated over by the naïve and luckless writer – and finishes by saying:

> I quit now, while I'm still enjoying it. No more 'Viewpoint' from me. […] If one happens to be a novelist, one has really very little to give in the way of ideas, new literary theories, scholarly assessments […] The business of being a novelist entails the shedding of intellectuality, the ability to think in general terms, even the capacity to read anything but proofs. The alternative to indulging in literary expatiation is grunting about the woes of the professional writer or feeling compelled, as I do more and more these days, to engage in long public acts of self-defence or renewed recrimination.

While Burgess did abandon this particular column (though not the *Times Literary Supplement* altogether, for whom he continued to write for another twenty years), it is by no means clear that he really believed much of this. By 1973 he had completed seventeen novels and three works of literary criticism (as well as working on film scripts, music, translations and many other creative activities) so it was not as if he had been completely distracted by his writing for periodicals. Further, his journalistic writing, especially that directly concerned one way or another with literature, offered him space to reflect on his own practice, to explore new areas of fiction and culture, to check out the competition, and to develop his theories of the novel itself. Especially after 1968, when he left England for good to live variously in Malta, Italy and ultimately Monaco, journalism and the mass media more generally seems to have offered Burgess the opportunity to participate in contemporary literary and artistic culture in England and the United States that his self-imposed physical exile otherwise denied him.

It is also clear that Burgess's journalism lies behind many of his book projects, and is reworked into his more permanent statements about literature. His extensive reviewing and literary commentaries certainly laid the foundations for his surveys *The Novel Now* (1967) and *Ninety-Nine Novels: The Best in English Since 1939* (1984), and there were also substantial non-fiction works on D.H. Lawrence, Ernest Hemingway and James Joyce. Clive James, replying to Burgess's anti-journalism claims in his book *The Metropolitan Critic* (1974), remarks that 'if Burgess's literary journalism was meant to be such an inherently inferior activity he might have done us the grace of being worse at it, so that we could have saved the money it cost to buy *Urgent Copy* and the time it took to enjoy it.'

Urgent Copy (1968) was the first collection of Burgess's journalism to be published in his lifetime, and is the model for this new selection insofar as its focus is squarely on substantial literary studies of his contemporaries and predecessors. It remains a fascinating entry point to his literary preoccupations during the first extremely productive part of his career. In the introduction to *Urgent Copy*, Burgess is mildly and unconvincingly apologetic that these commissioned and apparently relatively insubstantial pieces have been captured in book form, and expresses an anxiety that he has been rather too kind to some of the writers whom he has commented on. This is evidently due to sympathy:

> Book-writing is hard on the brain and excruciating to the body. It engenders tobacco addiction, an over-reliance on caffeine and dexedrine, piles, dyspepsia, chronic anxiety, sexual impotence. Behind the new bad book one is asked to review lie untold miseries and very little hope.

It is true that Burgess would often look for the positive in making his judgments, but he could also be very direct. Many writers receive stern appraisal, and there are some examples in this new selection; but these appraisals are not made in the service of scoring cheap points. Any disappointment felt at a shortcoming of a new work is genuinely felt. The main feeling that Burgess's literary studies engender is a sense of excitement at meeting new writing, devouring it greedily and presenting an invitation to his readers to experience it too.

Burgess's second collection of journalism is *Homage to QWERT YUIOP* (1986), which is a huge selection of pieces written between 1978 and 1985 taken from the *Times Literary Supplement*, the *New York Times* and the *Observer*. There are nearly three hundred essays, which Burgess estimates in his introduction to represent approximately a third of his total output in this period. His total output of journalism, at least: novels published during this period included *Earthly Powers*, *Abba Abba*, *The Pianoplayers*, and several more. Rather more wide-ranging than *Urgent Copy*, *Homage to QWERT YUIOP* includes – as well as a large volume of book reviews – essays on the world of the cinema, critical assessments of particular authors, and pieces on linguistics and music. This new selection aims to represent at least some of these preoccupations.

By the time of *Homage to QWERT YUIOP* Burgess no longer pretended to undervalue his literary journalism, writing that:

> I do not mind doing this work; indeed, I enjoy it. It is a means of keeping in touch with a public that does not necessarily read my or anybody else's fiction. The reading and reviewing of books keeps my mind open to fresh ideas in both literary creation and criticism. And the need to keep within the limit of a thousand words or so is, as with the composing of a sonnet, an admirable formal discipline.

As HIS vast output shows, Burgess was disciplined, formidably so, and this quality was of immense value to literary editors: he could be relied upon time and again to produce a lively and critically acute reading of a new book, to length and to deadline. Burgess was fond of emphasising the authentic labour inherent in writing. In *Urgent Copy* he compares himself to a carpenter, for example, making a table or cupboard of a specified size as quickly as is consistent with efficiency; and the title of *Homage to QWERT YUIOP* refers to Burgess's main tool as a novelist and journalist, the manual typewriter. 'When you hear your own clatter you know you are at work, as a blacksmith is. More, the rest of the household knows you are at work and does not suspect you of covertly devouring a *Playboy* centrefold.' The title of the present volume is in this mode, reflecting Burgess's own sense of himself as a worker engaged in honest and blameless industry.

A third selection of Burgess's journalism was made after his death by Ben Forkner and Burgess's widow Liana. *One Man's Chorus* (1998) captures some of Burgess's range, with a sample of his travel writings and reflections on contemporary world events; there are also pieces marking anniversaries of particular writers and musicians, and again a selection of literary studies. Taken together, the three books of Burgess's journalism reveal but a fraction of the enormous and largely invisible whole, and it is a great sadness that all of these selections are now out of print. As part of the Irwell Edition of the Works of

Anthony Burgess, a major series published by Manchester University Press, it is likely that a critical edition of *Urgent Copy* will be made available in the coming years, and this will be welcomed by a new generation of readers: Burgess's journalism is both an important document of the twentieth century in its own right, and critical to a full appreciation of his fiction and other creative work.

The Ink Trade brings into view a number (albeit a relatively small number) of Burgess's works that have not been seen since their first publication, or which have never been published in any form before. The definition of 'journalism' has been stretched slightly to include pieces given as talks or lectures and written up for publication, but which have for one reason or another never appeared; the main body of the selection is taken from periodicals, some of which will have had only very small readerships. The essays span Burgess's entire journalistic career, from an example of his fiction reviewing for the *Yorkshire Post* to his more expansive work for the *Observer* at the end of his life. Rather than grouping the articles by theme, as was attempted to an extent in *Urgent Copy* and *Homage to QWERT YUIOP*, the arrangement is almost completely chronological, with a minor adjustment at the very beginning and end to enable the selection to start with Burgess's ill-starred review of his own book, and to conclude with a reflection on his own journalistic practice many years later.

Readers will find that themes emerge in any case as the book progresses: certain names reappear, occasionally unexpectedly, as do certain preoccupations. There is a sustained engagement with language and how it is used, especially in the pieces on slang and translation. There is an anxiety about television and the mass media, balanced by a fascination with cinema. The business of writing, and how it interacts with literature itself, is often there; popular fiction sometimes gets a kicking, though not necessarily just because of its popularity. Obscenity; Irishness; American culture; European identity; the question of what a novel actually is: all these questions and many more are wrestled with in different ways as Burgess confronts a new subject. At times the list of his subjects reads like a roll-call of an Anglocentric canon of literature – and it may in fact be that Burgess's journalism and other critical writings have contributed more to the creation of that canon than has previously been acknowledged. Always in place are Burgess's touchstones of Gerard Manley Hopkins, T.S. Eliot, Somerset Maugham, Ford Madox Ford and others, who are invoked in surprising contexts, both to offer insights into the importance of a particular set of ideas or a particular piece of writing, and to articulate something about Burgess's own artistic work.

The most important figure to loom behind this selection, and perhaps behind all of Burgess's writing, is that of James Joyce. Burgess's early experiences of reading Joyce as a schoolboy were so profound that they shaped his later output in fundamental ways, and his engagement with Joyce and his works became the main artistic challenge of his life. Joyce appears in these pieces as one who opened up the possibilities of modern fiction, but also as a monitory presence whose *Ulysses* casts a shadow over the century. 'Joyce as Novelist', published here for the first time, presents a detailed and extended personal account, late in life, of the ways in which Burgess measured himself against his great inspiration.

Where available, full bibliographical details of each piece are provided as footnotes to the main text. The titles of the pieces are those used when they were first published, or, where there has been no previous publication, are taken directly from the manuscripts. In *Homage to QWERT YUIOP* Burgess changed a number of the titles from the published texts to his own original preferred titles, but in the interest of assisting possible future bibliographers this practice has not been followed here. On a very few occasions no title has been provided either by the author or anyone else, and for ease of reference a title has been invented using a brief phrase from the piece itself – this has been clearly noted throughout. Undated pieces have been assigned a place in the volume based on internal evidence, and this again has been noted.

Editorial intervention has been kept to a minimum, especially as a number of these pieces have already been edited by others before publication by a newspaper or journal. Where a published version of an article exists, this is the version preferred; previously unpublished pieces take the text from the typescript. Like the typescripts of his novels, Burgess's typescripts of his journalism are largely free of corrections, with the text being presented clearly and unambiguously: in this respect the editor's role has been a straightforward one, and Burgess's copy has been left as it is. However, minor spelling errors have been silently corrected, and instances of repetition have in a few cases been deleted. Like most journalists, Burgess was not above reusing material on occasion, particularly for publications in different countries – though given the volume of what he produced it is surprising that there is not far more of it, accidental or deliberate.

There are of course some gaps in this selection. There are no pieces specifically about music, yet Burgess's journalism about composers and musicians could easily fill another volume. It would be a hugely valuable volume too, giving greater understanding of Burgess's own musical writing and how it relates to his literary output. Similarly, there is little directly about religion, and material drawn from Burgess's writings on this subject would provide new angles on an important concern of his fiction, quite apart from being a fascinating collection in its own right. While television appears from time to time in these pieces, there is none of Burgess's television criticism proper here: a shame, or perhaps an opportunity for another project, as his *Listener* reviews from the 1960s constitute an intriguing and illuminating document of a particular cultural moment. Looking beyond newspaper reviews and criticism, there is of course a wealth of print and broadcast interviews, documentaries, radio programmes and much more which remains uncollected. There is no complete catalogue – while Paul Boytinck's bibliography remains a monumental achievement and a vital resource, it does not cover all the periodicals for which Burgess wrote, and ends in 1982 – and despite the recent renewal of scholarly interest in Burgess's life and work it is unlikely that one will be created in the immediate future. Given the scale and challenges of the task, a collection of complete journalism remains a distant prospect.

The potential value of such a collection is not in doubt, especially in the interest of reappraising Burgess's wider contribution to twentieth-century fiction. Indeed, many of Burgess's essays connect directly to the materials and preoccupations of his novels. The title of the present selection is in fact taken from the piece 'By-products of the ink trade', reprinted here, which is a review of the fifth series of the *Paris Review* interviews with leading writers. In Burgess's own wide-ranging 1972 interview with the *Paris Review* he describes the benefits of book-reviewing to a novel-writer:

> It's good for a writer to review books he is not supposed to know anything about or be interested in. Doing reviewing for magazines like *Country Life* (which smells more of horses than of calfskin bindings) means doing a fine heterogenous batch which often does open up some areas of value in one's creative work. For instance, I had to review books on stable management, embroidery, car engines – very useful solid stuff, the very stuff of novels. Reviewing

Lévi-Strauss's little lecture on anthropology (which nobody else wanted to review) was the beginning of the process which led me to write the novel *MF*.

Quite apart from the idea that reviewing books and writing about them presents useful ways of finding out about the world, the example given here shows a way in which the novels and the journalism directly interact. Burgess's positive review of *The Scope of Anthropology* by Claude Lévi-Strauss appeared in 1967, and was later collected in *Urgent Copy* as 'If Oedipus Had Read His Lévi-Strauss'. The approaches to mythology and linguistics ultimately outlined in Lévi-Strauss were already of interest to Burgess, as can be seen in his 1963 piece 'The Corruption of the Exotic', collected here, and in the novel *MF* (1970), which Burgess would later describe as one of his favourites. Similarly concerned with linguistics and anthropology, Burgess's 1965 essay 'Word, World and Meaning' appeared first in the *Times Literary Supplement*, reappeared in *Urgent Copy* and then is presented as a lecture delivered by a character in the 1980 novel *Earthly Powers*. Other examples of journalism and novel-writing overlapping in surprising ways include Burgess's writing about translation, which illuminates his novel *Abba Abba* about the Roman poet Belli; or his essay on Shakespeare 'Getting the Language Right', again reprinted here, which offers an understanding of his use of Elizabethan language in *Nothing Like The Sun*; or 'The Anachronist Strikes Back', which articulates his technique in writing the historical novel *The Kingdom of the Wicked*.

Because of the many different forms in which Burgess worked – fiction, poetry, film scripts, classical music, as well as journalism – he is often described as a polymath, excelling in disparate fields. However, this does not fully capture the way in which different types of artistic production are closely linked in his work: books such as *The Pianoplayers* combine prose, song lyrics and sheet music; lectures (such as 'Can Art Be Immoral?', a previously unpublished piece that is collected here) contain verse; narratives are driven using stage musicals or comic songs, such as in *End Of The World News* or *Napoleon Symphony*. Journalistic forms are used in the same way: fictions are paired with lengthy critical essays, such as in *A Dead Man in Deptford*, and dialogue is turned into an interview in *1985*. These techniques again show the ways in which Burgess's journalistic writing is very much part of his creative process.

Altogether it is clear that Burgess's journalism operates not least as a way of working through ideas and approaches that also emerge in novels and other works. Bringing some of Burgess's journalism back into view in this selection will offer new perspectives on his literary career. It is hoped too that this selection will have an appeal beyond students and researchers, and have something to offer to a new generation coming to Burgess for the first time: a disparate general readership, surprised and delighted to find writing of such quality and interest in the unpromising surroundings of newsprint. In recent years Burgess's journalism has fallen into neglect. *The Ink Trade* provides a way in to this vast storehouse, and demonstrates that it can be as rewarding as the best of his novels.

Acknowledgments

ANTHONY BURGESS'S journalism is scattered around the world, and working with it would be impossible without the support of very many people. I would like to acknowledge in particular the Trustees of the International Anthony Burgess Foundation, whose archives in Manchester have provided the bulk of the material in this book; I would also like to acknowledge L'Institut Mémoires de l'Edition Contemporaine in Caen and the Harry Ransom Center at the University of Texas at Austin, both of which house important Burgess collections.

I would also like to thank Harry Gallon, who has done an excellent job of transcribing these articles into a usable form; and Michael Schmidt and Luke Allan at Carcanet Press for taking the project through to its conclusion. My colleagues at the Burgess Foundation have assisted me a great deal: Amelia Collingwood has provided valuable technical assistance, Anna Edwards has aided me many times in navigating the complex Anthony Burgess archives, and Graham Foster has always provided valuable advice and help of all kinds. I would especially like to thank Andrew Biswell, whose knowledge of Burgess's life and work, and especially of his journalism, is unrivalled, and for whose generosity and encouragement I am extremely grateful.

Poetry for a Tiny Room

Joseph Kell's first novel *One Hand Clapping* was a quiet and cunning female monologue that fell from the presses almost unnoticed.

One Australian periodical acclaimed its virtues in a two-page review that, giving a thorough synopsis of the plot, must have made purchase of the book seem supererogatory. For the rest, reviewers had other things to think about. That little book now thinly stalks the bookstalls as a paperback, its bright eyes quietly watching the reception of its successor.

Whatever readers may think of the content of *Inside Mister Enderby*, they are hardly likely to ignore the cover. This shows a lavatory seat (wood, not plastic), entwined with ivy. It is Mr Enderby's lavatory seat, wherefrom he blasts his poetry at the world. (Mr Eliot said recently – and in the *Yorkshire Post* too – that poetry is a lavatorial or purgative art.)

If the world takes no notice, Mr Enderby will not worry. He has rejected the world: he has retreated to the smallest room in the house; there, scratching bared knees, he writes the verse that his Muse dictates to him.

But the world will not leave him alone altogether. It drags him out of his lavatory to receive a poetry prize and a proposal of marriage from Vesta Bainbridge, a *chic* vision from a woman's magazine. Soon, Enderby is on his honeymoon in Rome. The eternal city is the antithesis of the toilet: here is the Church, here is the State, here, in lapidary form well-preserved, is the meanest history known to man. Here, too, is treachery, for Rawcliffe, a jealous fellow-poet, has stolen a poetic plot from Enderby and persuaded Cinecittà to turn it into a bosomy horror film. Enderby, appalled, flees.

But his Muse flees also. He can no longer write. He attempts – unhandily, as with everything except his craft – a suicide which the State tut-tuts over. He is turned into a useful citizen, normal and unpoetic. There is a middle way between greatest Rome and smallest room – the way of the decent job and the decent life. Enderby is cured.

This is, in many ways, a dirty book. It is full of bowel-blasts and flatulent borborygmus, emetic meals ('thin but over-savoury stews', Enderby calls them) and halitosis. It may well make some people sick, and those of my readers with tender stomachs are advised to let it alone.

It turns sex, religion, the State into a series of laughing-stocks. The book itself is a laughing-stock.

Yorkshire Post, 16 May 1963
Review of *Inside Mister Enderby* by Joseph Kell [pseudonym of Anthony Burgess] (London: William Heinemann, 1963)

Spring's Fruits in Autumn

SALLOW AUTUMN fills our laps with leaves, folios rather. Heavy fruits (Sillitoe, Aragon, Barth; Uris to come next week) drop in the silent autumn night. Season of lists, etc.

Paradoxically a transatlantic gust comes smelling of spring and one's (meaning my) youth when all literature was exciting and none more so than the work of the prose experimenters – Joyce, Stein, Hemingway, John Dos Passos.

Dos Passos's trilogy *USA* once haunted me like a passion. It is a measure not so much of one's own approaching autumn as of the way in which Dos Passos has been absorbed by a whole generation of writers (Norman Mailer, Budd Schulberg, etc.) that the spring thrill is a mere ghost in *Midcentury*. Here you will find all the techniques of *1919* and *The Big Money* – potted biographies (Freud, Eleanor Roosevelt, James Dean), newsreels with headline-montages, italicised prose-lyrics, slabs of bald narrative, typography having a field-day. But you will also find no change in the story-line – there is still the Marxist dichotomy, the worker's fight.

Blackie Bowman, Terry Bryant, Frank Worthington emerge from the Second World War to resume the patterns of their 1919 proto-types. They copulate, earn, brawl, are bewildered by the big world of headlines, but they remain faceless, charade or morality figures, grim in the face of the capitalist villains.

It is old drama in new costumes, and the Dos Passos techniques seem only viable for that, incapable of development. They sprang to life fully armed in the early days, cognate with the gimmicks of expressionist playwrights like Toller and Georg Kaiser. Gimmicks soon look old-fashioned. It is embarrassing when one has to use the glass of 'historical perspective' to read what the cover calls 'a novel of our time'.

The other breath of spring and youth blows in with Anita Loos, already a classic, a writer whom one would describe – if it did not sound pretentious – as one of the minor shapers of the modern sensibility. *No Mother To Guide Her* is as sharp and digestible as a good asti spumante: Hollywood-in-its-heyday has never been so well lampooned. Bliss (a columnist of amazing innocence, worshipper and knight of the sadly set-upon star Viola Lake), a character to compare (the only one I can think of) with the shamefully neglected Augustus Carp, is just that. Bliss, I mean.

Key to the Door is Alan Sillitoe's attempt at a big *Bildungsroman* – the first 21 years of a new Seaton (Brian not Arthur), shuttling between depressed pre-war life in Nottingham and disaffected RAF other-rank down-with-the-bleddy-boggers grousing in Malaya. The Nottingham parts (boozing, swearing, courtship, marriage) we have already met in *Saturday Night and Sunday Morning*, in its way a seminal work. Mr Sillitoe writes vividly and aromatically of proletarian life, though one becomes a little tired of the self-pity.

The Malayan sections chilled me. Young Brian seems to grouse through a dripping and frightening jungle-and-mountain-scape completely without (if we except his grousing mates) human figures. We hear of Malayans, and wonder which of the Malayan races he means. Occasionally a Malay, clad for some reason in a sari, glides through. There is an unconvincing Chinese dance-hostess and 'keep' called Mimi. It is the complete lack of concern or even minimal interest in people other than the ingrown group of working-lads that appals.

But one is also appalled morally. Brian cannot see the Chinese Communists as enemies. His failure to kill off a terrorist who eventually snipes at his own mate meets no condemnation. The political naivety of the book is incredible. But to be just, there is life and a certain poetry: nobody is going to doubt Mr Sillitoe's talent. He needs more than talent now: he needs to grow up.

'She was like a picture that one sees in an art gallery that makes you feel sad because it is painted.' V.S. Pritchett has lost nothing of the image-maker's gift, nor that micrometrically delicate ear for the fall of speech of ordinary people. Yet I was not always happy with this volume of short stories, *When My Girl Comes Home*. The title-piece is 73 pages long, and feels like it. It is the minor characters (Jack Draper, for instance, to whom war itself is the enemy, so that he lumps the combatants of both sides together) who carry more life than the major.

There is a certain flatness and plotlessness not normally associated with this brilliant writer: the expected seems to happen a little too often. Too often, too, one cannot really care about what happens to the characters: our sympathies are not engaged. But there is so much to be thankful for – keen observation, exact notation of contemporary manners, and always that marvellous ear.

The Sot-Weed Factor is a good title, even if it only means 'The Tobacco-Estate Manager'. This immensely long novel is a pastiche of old-time picaresque, in an honourable and best-selling American tradition, telling of an obdurately virginal poet, Eben Cooke ('virgo' being male in medieval Latinity) and his exploits at sea and in the New World. It owes everything to the episodic booze-and-bawdry boys, and is none the worse for that. It must have been great (though laborious) fun to write.

Yorkshire Post, 19 October 1961. Reviews of:
Midcentury by John Dos Passos (London: André Deutsch, 1961);
No Mother To Guide Her by Anita Loos (London: Arthur Barker, 1961);
Key to the Door by Alan Sillitoe (London: W.H. Allen, 1961);
When My Girl Comes Home by V.S. Pritchett (London: Chatto & Windus, 1961);
and *The Sot-Weed Factor* by John Barth (London: Secker & Warburg, 1961)

The Corruption of the Exotic

MY FIRST attempts at writing fiction were made in response to an exotic stimulus, and I have often wondered since whether this was right. I was living in Malaya in 1955, working for the Government and, in my spare time, carrying on with what I thought was my true artistic vocation – the composing of music. One morning I woke to hear the muezzin calling – 'There is no God but Allah' – and, as often happens when one first wakes, to find the names of my creditors parading through my mind, together with what I owed them. Something like this:

La ilaha illa'la
Lim Kean Swee $395
Chee Sin Hye $120
Tan Meng Kwang $250
La ilaha illa'la

And so on. Here obviously was the beginning of a novel: a man lying in bed in the Malayan dawn, listening to the muezzin calling, worrying about his debts. So, out of this little *collage*, I began to write, with suspicious ease, my first published work of fiction.

The *collage* started things off; it helped to establish a rhythm and also a technique of juxtaposition. I found a line from Clough which pleased me: 'Allah is great, no doubt, and juxtaposition his prophet'. Juxtaposition of races and cultures was the underground stimulus, the thing that wanted to be expressed. I really wrote this novel, and the two that followed, because I wanted to record Malaya. In other words, my motive for starting to write fiction was an impure one. One should always be inspired by an aesthetic impulse and not by subject-matter which is intrinsically strange, fresh, and glamorous.

It is significant that the novels I wrote about the East and Africa sold far better than anything I wrote about England in the past, present, or future. The novel of impure motive always sells best – the book that pretends to be didactic about sex or violence but is really pornographic; the book that is really didactic when it pretends to be merely entertaining; the book that tells of something strange instead of doing something strange. People want to be moved or instructed; they rarely want that static thing that is art.

The exotic, then, is a dangerous and corrupting thing for the novelist to write about. Bemused by its glamour, he will too often think he is writing better than he is. If it is one of the novelist's tasks to glorify the commonplace, in the exotic novel the commonplace is already half-glorified for him; he gains credit from his reader's ignorance. A novel may open like this: 'I was drinking a bottle of flat and gassy light ale in a dingy little pub off Cross Street, Manchester. The rain was pelting down outside'. Any self-respecting novelist would want to regard that as a mere first draft; he would want to work some strangeness into it, to infuse that bit of shock which is essential to art. But supposing the novel opens like this: 'I was drinking a bottle of *samsu* in a *kedai* off Jalan Sultan in Kuala Kangsar. The Sun' – or, if you like, the monsoon – 'was raging down outside'. Any attempt at rewriting would be regarded as supererogatory; the shock of glamour and strangeness resides in the subject-matter itself. This is dangerous and corrupting.

One wonders sometimes about the 'exotic' novels of the great established novelists. My favourite book of D.H. Lawrence used to be *Kangaroo*, but I am pretty sure I liked it for the wrong reasons. First, the *tour de force*: Lawrence seems to have created a whole continent out of a few scraps of Australiana picked up on a two-day visit to Sydney. One admires the magic, but the magic is irrelevant to the book – the artist's, or his biographer's, affair. Second, the fascination of juxtaposition: blue-eyed cockneys in a world of marsupials. Yet as a book it is a mess: ill-written, full of interpolated matter from newspapers, the endless Lawrence-Frieda struggle, a political gestation flown over from Fascist Italy, all mixed up anyhow. The setting saves it: Australia is doing most of Lawrence's work for him. *The Plumed Serpent* is similarly saved by Mexico and that eponymous Quetzlcoatl. I do not think many would doubt that Lawrence's best novel is *Sons and Lovers*, where the writer, or his daemon, has to work hard, infusing the magic of myth into the commonplace. His later, sicker work leans too hard on exotic props.

For lesser writers like myself, the most dangerous temptation of all when writing about the exotic is to trade on the reader's ignorance and to falsify. Everything one observes – the Tamil workers drinking toddy, the snakes among the canna leaves, the jungle orchids – is unknown to the average sweet-stay-at-home reader. One is taking a faithful photograph for his benefit. No, not a photograph: that is the job of the travel-book writer. One is painting a faithful picture in full colour. Why, if the reader is so ignorant, should not one go a stage further than faithful reproduction, introduce imaginary colours? The next stage is the introduction of imaginary flora and fauna and imaginary tribal customs. It becomes easier sometimes to invent than to copy. Transfiguration leads to lies.

I return to that word 'juxtaposition'. One of the most difficult problems that faces the artist in any medium is the problem of presenting transition. A character is good and becomes bad; a character is ignorant and becomes enlightened. When does the change take place, where does the watershed start? It is rarely possible to point to the moment of initial transformation in real life, and art should, in this connection, imitate life. St Paul's sudden conversion, when he sees that he may no longer kick against the pricks, is miraculous or traumatic – a stroke, a fit. It is apt for religious, but not for secular, drama. God may do these things but an artist not. But a writer on life in the tropics is apt to bring about godlike transformations. He will pretend that Malays or Chinese or Indians are different from Anglo-Saxons and are capable of sudden changes of personality. He will juxtapose a 'before' state and an 'after' state; he will justify his unwillingness or incompetence to present subtle transition by saying, in effect, that there is a great gap between the Eastern and Western psyches. We are back to Elizabethan travel-tales and men who have three heads and a foot as big as a tea-tray. Allah is great and juxtaposition his prophet.

The Russians, as well as the peoples of the Far East, are a godsend to the novelist who is poor on psychological transition. For the Russians are well-known to be all manic-depressives – up one minute and down the next. It is delightfully easy to portray Russian characters: knives followed by kisses; sudden drunkenness, sudden sobriety; war and peace. But serious English readers of English novelists writing about Russians have a vast Russian literature available for checking-up purposes. The Russians are, alas, not quite exotic enough. It is best to stick to Eastern peoples, who have attempted few self-portraits. They will not betray the British novelists whose inability to present consistency in character or probability of motivation or action is blandly explained away by the magic words 'a different world'; 'an *exotic* world'.

For the honest writer about this world, however, there are definite problems of communication. How much should one explain, how much dare one take for granted, when writing about Malaya or Africa for a home-keeping audience? Should one explain that Sikhs do not smoke, that Chinese women get together in lesbian sororities, that Malays regard the head as sacred? I think not. It is the job of the travel-book to explain; it is the job of the novelist to take what he is given and use it honestly and without apology or surprise. You do not want footnotes in a novel. But I have been hurt at the incredulity of critics, especially when I have been recording fact or personal experience in an exotic novel. In my first book, *Time for a Tiger*, I made my four main characters, one of them a woman, go on a pleasure trip through country infested with communist terrorists. At the time when the novel was set, one did this sort of thing often. It was perhaps foolish, but one had to take the chance. One went on an amateur anthropological excursion or to the cinema in a town fifty miles away, and if one were sniped at or found an ambushing log laid on the road, it was fate; one could not live for ever. Some critics said that nobody would ever do this, that this sort of improbability marred the novel. On the other hand, I was taken to task for pretending that Muslims drink brandy. This, I was told, was never done. Reviewers are good at ignorance and half-knowledge. They are also good at confusing the improbable with the inadvisable. I am a reviewer myself.

The subject-matter of all novels is people, and how they affect other people. The *mise en scène* is a matter of indifference; travel and residence abroad persuade me that people are not very different from each other. A novelist who sets his novel in foreign parts ought, I think, to write the sort of novel that – all things being equal – a native novelist of those parts might write, at least as far as the background is concerned. There should be no such thing as an 'exotic novel'. If the content of the novel about Egypt or Malaya seems strange to the British reader, then let it remain strange until that reader is able to verify it for himself. One of the jobs of art is to deep-freeze emotions against the time of their being needed. The impact of the exotic, the initial shock that ends Conrad's *Youth*, is properly not a part of the exotic novel at all, but of the home-based novel: it does not come into this context. One only really *smells* a foreign country on one's first day in it – Singapore, for instance, with its hot wet dish-rags, cat-piss and turmeric. The first day abroad is the last day at home. With it you can end a home-based novel or begin a novel about readjustment to the exotic. But you will not write *Malaisie* or *A Passage to India*.

The more I read British novels, which is another way of saying 'the older I get', the more I become convinced that the British novelist's job is to write about here and now. This was not always my view. I used to believe that the area of available subject-matter should be as wide as possible – covering the whole of geography and those imaginary countries conjured by drugs. One may term this the heresy of width. It is a truism to say that depth is the important thing, but we tend to forget what is meant by depth. If, as with the Greek tragedians, the subject-matter is myth, then depth means mining under the myth till the individual consciousness is reached. If, as with most of us, the subject-matter is the individual consciousness, then depth means digging for the mythical.

Here I can approach deep waters – the deepest. Shall I take a chance and commit a general statement about the novelist's real function to a mere parenthesis? I think I will. In the nineteenth century there were few allomorphs of the art of fiction: drama was trivial till Robertson came along; alleged poems like *Aurora Leigh* and *The Princess* were only novels or novellas in prosy verse. The novel itself was the only way into fictitious worlds peopled with fictitious people. And novelists like Thackeray, Dickens, Bulwer Lytton, fulfilled not only the novelist's task but the dramatist's. More – they were also moral essayists, epic poets, preachers. In our own day we see that two main kinds of fiction function side by side. There is, first, that *immediate* fiction called drama – a form in which characters and events are presented directly, without the intermediacy of their creator: the author does not get between us and the story, commenting, describing, judging. Then there is the novel itself, in which we expect to meet the author and to sustain the impact of his personality – a personality inevitably stronger than that of any of the personalities he has created.

But the most vital forms of drama today are found not on the stage but on the screen – small or large – and they are capable of a greater plasticity than has ever been possible on any stage after 1642. Film and television have learnt a great deal from the novel: the swift change of scene, the visual or tangible symbol, dream and fantasy, even the interior monologue and the linking narration have been incorporated with ease into the new fluid drama. Devices of which the novelist had the monopoly have been taken over and are exploited with skill by the new race of dramatic writers. What is there left for the novelist to do?

The answer, I would say, lies in the related fields of myth and language. He must either revivify old myths or create new ones. James Joyce slammed old myths on new matter, thus freeing himself from the need to be his own plot-maker, and then used the myth to exploit language. The point about myth is that everybody already knows the story, and hence the movement and interest proper to a film-plot are automatically transferred to what is done with the myth – and what is done is done through language. Dialogue will be less important than those inchoate pre-articulatory levels which can only be treated through experiment in language, and drama, relying on dialogue, cannot reach here. New myths can be achieved through either the cross-fertilisation of old myths or a direct act of creation. But the myth must never be an end in itself. I fear that in William Golding's *Lord of the Flies* or Iris Murdoch's *A Severed Head* the content is more important than the technique. The content has certainly been neatly filleted out in, respectively, a first-class film and an interesting stage adaptation. Beware of a novel that transfers too easily to another medium. Golding seems to be doing the novelist's real job in *The Inheritors*, where language has to suggest a world before language existed. This work is itself, as Beethoven's Ninth Symphony is itself: no adaptation to another medium seems possible.

What this question of depth amounts to, then, is how far the resources of language can be stretched to clarify the springs of human motivation. I am not advocating a literature of the pre-conscious solely and simply, but in those crepuscular regions of the mind there is at least a field that the other fictional art-forms find it hard to reach. In a moment, if I am not careful, the magic name of Jung will make its appearance, and that I must avoid. We are concerned with art, not science, however poetic the science of the mind seems in the work of Jung and his followers. And we are immediately concerned with this question of the distraction of a highly seasoned subject-matter. Whatever depth means, it cannot be achieved with exotic butterflies distracting the eyes and the purpose.

What I am really trying to say is that subject-matter is not all that important to art. The more banal, commonplace, everyday, the subject-matter of the novel is, the more the novelist is compelled to work hard at his craft. In effect, the novelist can never know whether he is capable of doing a good job until he has stripped his subject-matter of whatever glamour – whether conventional or inverted – it may possess. This may seem a somewhat puritanical view of the novelist's art, but I do not see why the stringencies that enable us to find the true and the good should not also apply to the search for the beautiful. Impure motives, whether in science, ethics, or art, quietly wreck a civilisation.

All this sounds portentous, but all I mean is that we ought to take the novel seriously and not attribute the excitement or beauty of the subject-matter to the novel itself. I am not advocating an extension of the modern provincial novel which, sadly, is developing its own set of conventions and stock responses indicative of a morbid concern with content more than form. I am suggesting rather that we should just take what we are given – here and now – and spend the resources of our art on it.

Unfortunately, from one point of view, 'here and now' is beginning to mean 'foreign parts' to some novelists. The exodus to Tangier, Mallorca, Switzerland, the Isles of Greece, goes on, the formation of exiled writers' colonies, writers caught between the native life of the country and the remembered life of home. These writers know too little of the real 'here and now' to write about it with the authority of native authors; they have to fall back on 'there and then' – volumes of reminiscences, novels set in the near-present, but full of subtly wrong nuances and overtones, historical novels, thrillers. One wonders how much true devotion to his art form is shown by the novelist who expatriates himself because of income tax, disillusionment with English society, climate, or in search of greater sexual tolerance. It is the novelist's task to stay here and suffer with the rest of us. He can, through his art, lessen that suffering.

Listener, 26 September 1963

Why, This is Hell

CHRISTOPHER ISHERWOOD's creative dilemma is an excruciating one. He wants to demonstrate that hell, like love, is not hereafter; it is a portable void that exists in time. But can a novelist properly deal with a state of alienation? His job is to record the multiplicity of the world and even perhaps seem to rejoice in it. Mr Isherwood's solution is to see the multiplicity as a set of disguises; a viable fictional aim is the stripping off of these to show the one great tired face. Chrissie, Herr Issyvoo, Bradshaw – all these have been allomorphs of a recording eye, though the novelist's trick – despite the 'I am a camera' disclaimer – was to flash the illusion of a genuine identity. In *Down There on a Visit* trickery becomes irony. 'Down there' is 'down here', and we cannot visit where we already are. The circumference is crammed with characters; sink a shaft from each, though, and you arrive at a common centre – the hell of isolation, universal and single.

In *A Single Man* Mr Isherwood concentrates openly on this hell and calls on the unities of time and space to help hold the lamp. The rich variety of the world shrinks to the freeway and the supermarket. Here is a day in the life of George, a middle-aged Englishman who lectures at a Californian university. He lives alone, since Jim, whom he loved, is dead. Jim meant the whole of life, symbolised in the small menagerie they had, now dispersed. The bridge that connects George with his two-car bar-and-barbeque neighbours is sagging. Mr Strunk, more charitable, a reader of popular psychology, says, in effect: 'Here we have a misfit, debarred for ever from the best things of life, to be pitied, not blamed'.

But George's aloneness doesn't go far enough. Nor does the fact that he belongs (as the Jews and Negroes and Commies belong) to a minority necessarily ennoble him. At the end of his lecture on *After Many a Summer* he tells his students that persecution makes the minorities nastier, hating not only the majority but the other minorities. 'Do you think it makes people nasty to be loved? You know it doesn't! Then why should it make them nice to be loathed?'

The minorities put on protective, apotropaic clothing, and it is Mr Isherwood's grimly humorous task to strip George naked. He sits on the john after breakfast and carries his bared buttocks to the ringing telephone. In the gym, where he goes for his daily work-out, he find comfort, a sense of community, in the common stripped condition: the pot belly and the athlete's muscles enter a democracy rather than an agape. At night he swims naked with one of his students, Kenny. Kenny puts him to bed, drunk, in clean pyjamas, but he wakes to throw them off and, the alcohol itching in his groin, masturbate. He masturbates to the image of 'the fierce hot animal play' of two students he has seen earlier on the tennis court. 'George hovers above them, watching; then he begins passing in and out of their writhing, panting bodies. He is either. He is both at once.'

Even know the nakedness is not complete. After the metaphorical death of the orgasm, the sham death of sleep, comes the true, hypothetical, death of the body. This trilogy of deaths is the final ritual of stripping. Isherwood has told his entire story in the present tense, which lends itself to hypothesis. The day itself is a ritual covering an emptiness. Jim is dead and cannot be replaced. Charlotte, another British expatriate, offers herself, but George doesn't want a sister; Kenny, an Alcibiades with towel-chlamys slipping from his shoulder, flirts at offering himself, but George doesn't want a son. The hell of isolation can accept no palliatives.

What sounds like an intense book is, as we must expect from Isherwood, tense only in its economy. The language makes no big gestures, and some of the most telling effects are produced by ellipses. But, as in *The World in the Evening* and *Down There on a Visit*, one sometimes has a feeling that one is being deliberately put at one's ease: Quakerism may embarrass, and so may homosexuality; let us make no protestations; let us neither raise nor lower our voices. Not that I think the homosexuality of this novel is one of its main issues: the love for dead Jim is the love for dead anyone; the particular loneliness may serve as an emblem for the loneliness of all single men, those smallest of minorities. And yet, since much of Isherwood's reputation rests on his skills at finding a shorthand for rendering the external world, and since no observer of that world can really be a camera, we sometimes find our taste assaulted. When Kenny's blanket slips, we are told: 'At this moment he is utterly, dangerously charming'. He is not. Isherwood sometimes forgets to suffer dully the wrongs of which *all* men are capable. His job is to probe at the cavity which sleeps, unsensed, in even the most comfortable member of the majority. In other words, we don't want a limited hell. But that we so rarely stand outside and twitch our noses at a man who is George, and not a George who is a man, is a testimony to Isherwood's undiminished brilliance as a novelist.

Listener, 1 October 1964
Review of *A Single Man* by Christopher Isherwood
(London: Methuen, 1964)

On the End of Every Fork

IT'S AMAZING how little is needed to slake the thirsts of the pornography-hounds, the prurient sniggerers, the protectors of public morals. From the title of William Burroughs's masterpiece they will be led to expect something illicitly agapoid, a sort of phallic Laocoön, and they will be disappointed. What they will find, on the other hand, is a palimpsest of obscenity so emetic that no amount of casuistry will be able to justify a charge of inflammation and corruption. This, God help us, is no *Fanny Hill* or *Lady Chatterley's Lover*. It is a picture of hell, and hell is not corrupting. The obscenity is not of Mr Burroughs's devising: it is there in the world outside. We're all sitting grinning at a ghastly meal which he suddenly shows us to be cannibalistic. The meat on the end of every fork is revealed as the guts and blood of our fellow-men. It is a revelation which will please nobody and may spoil a few appetites, but it has to be made, though few have the courage to make it. Mr Burroughs joins a small body of writers who are willing to look at hell and report on what they see. The body is, in fact, so small that I can think of only one other writer with whom he may be compared. This is Jonathan Swift.

I suppose there is a sense in which Swift's 'Modest Proposal' may be regarded as obscene, or perhaps the final book of *Gulliver's Travels*. But only a corrupt world will be disgusted by *saeva indignatio*. Swift's starting-point was a sense of outrage with the world that the corrupt may still regard as insane. Burroughs's vision is that of a man who has escaped from the agony of drug-addiction and regards the inferno with the cleansed eyes of the remembering artist. His introduction is autobiographical and clinical: he appends a long article from *The British Journal of Addiction*. Some of his more charitable readers, too weak-stomached to take the art, may wish to look on the whole work as a snakepit record, a terrible but necessary thesis on the nature of the life of the damned, a piece of unusually frank didacticism. They will be wrong, since Burroughs is demonstrating that his difficult subject can only be expressed through the static (that is, neither didactic nor pornographic) shaping of the artistic imagination.

Naturalism is not enough here, nor is the euphemistic or peri-phrastic. There are flights which some will glibly categorise as surrealistic, fantasias of violence which are cognate with those in the 'Journal of an Airman' of Auden's *The Orators* but which serve no mere schoolboy rebelliousness. There are fugues which derive their themes from the everyday symbolism of rage – the processes of sex and excretion, developed into perversion and coprophagy. The creation of new and horrible worlds, as in the same author's *The Ticket That Exploded*, is as necessary to Burroughs's vision as it is to Dante's. There is no device which seems to me to be purely fanciful or gra-tuitous; I can think of no other way in which a book like this could possibly be written.

As in any important piece of literature (and *The Naked Lunch* is very important) one ends by admiring the art which is able to trans-mute such terrible subject-matter into the pretext for a kind of joy (compare *King Lear*). It is the mystery of art which enables us to read Swift again and again and emerge not harrowed but elated. Mr Burroughs's art is highly individual. He has in his time admired both Gertrude Stein and James Joyce, but he has developed techniques which seem to betray very little of the influence of that mistress and that master. For that matter, he admires Sterne and Jane Austen. His concern is with art first and last, and it is doubtful whether the cries of outrage which his book will undoubtedly provoke in this country will disturb him much. The making of this particular work of art was part of an ineluctable vocation. It demands to be read.

Guardian, 20 November 1964
Review of *The Naked Lunch* by William S. Burroughs
(London: John Calder, 1964)

Into the Mass Mangle

THE DENTIST (or stomatologist, as he would perhaps now prefer to be called) knows exactly where he stands – on his surgery floor, looking into mouths. The writer knows all too haemorrhoidally where he sits, but where he stands hardly at all. The blessed delimitation that applies to writers in the Navy – the narrowing-down of the medieval 'clerk' – is something all dry-land writers long for: they want, be it ever so humble, the pride of the specialist. For no man can call himself a novelist or a poet any more: he is a writer who writes, among other things, novels or poems. The response to the public-bar disclosure ('And what do *you* do for a living?' – 'I'm a writer') always follows the same pattern: 'What sort of things do you write?' – 'Books.' – 'Have you published a book yet?' – 'I've published twenty.' – 'What kind of books? *Dirty* books?' – 'No, not those either' (The man in the street can accept the pornographic or the didactic, but never the stasis of art). And then comes, in this society full of writers, the odd dropping of a name: 'So-and-so lives just round the corner – he writes for television', or, if one's interlocutor is a woman, 'he writes for *Queen*'.

The true writer nowadays is, unless he is a pornographer or didact or both, not the book-writer but the journalist. This is altogether appropriate in a society that regards itself as dynamic and puts a great value on the new, meaning usually the ephemeral. No writer of books will despise the quick returns of journalism, and the lure of reviewing or the odd thousand words of topical comment is not solely that of the sure small cheque at the end of the month. His audience is immediate and often very large; he is not cut off, facing a long architectonic agony alone; there is none of the neurosis of wondering about sales or the depression of not finding his work on the bookstalls; stylistic sloppiness and factual errors are not much noticed and, anyway, soon forgotten; if he is Cyril Connolly he is amassing a book as well as earning his bread and butter.

But the temptation to write nothing but journalism is one to which too many brilliant writers have yielded – especially those round about thirty. It would be possible to reel off a long list of names of young men who should be writing books but who, having tasted the pleasure of being known – and by a much bigger audience than the mere book-writer can expect – are likely to push on till cancer of the lung gets them, doing television criticism in this paper, literary reviewing in that, the occasional longish sociological-aesthetic study in *Encounter*. It is a living, it is writing; more, it is what is known as being a writer.

But there is a new field of a para-literary endeavour which is more tempting, and much more corrupting, than journalism. There was a time when television promised to be to young contemporary writers what the stage had been to the university wits of the first Elizabethan age. Television drama was to be the great popular fictional medium, and its analogue was to be found less in the stage-play than in the novel. Clever young men tend to write novels rather than stage-plays; many novels appear every week; there are few professional play-wrights; television drama borrows its fluidity from the novel. It was, then, to the novelist that television applied in the days – not so long ago – when it aspired to a new art of drama. It seemed to offer a *deuxième métier* to the writer of books.

Some novelists will remember well an evening early in 1962 when, after a conducted tour round the BBC Television Centre, they were harangued over a fork-supper and told that it was their duty to write for television. Great names in BBC television – some now heard no more, a few exalted to further greatness – lent the occasion not merely lustre but a quality of top-level urgency. The response of the nov-elists to the harangues was predictable: 'If I write a novel and have it rejected by my publisher, there are other publishers to try, scores of others. If I write for a television play there are only two possible organisations to send it to. If I succeed in placing it, I receive an outright sum – no royalties, no subsidiary rights. I fear cuts, emenda-tions, tamperings, last-minute bannings.' And so on. The assumption was that the novelist would be approaching his television play seri-ously, expending on it the care appropriate to a novel; more than that, his play would probably use material that – with free develop-ment and more elbow-room – could be made into a full-length novel. The air is not crammed with themes and plots and characters; every novel – however inferior – has the seed of something precious in it. One performance of your television play: a Tyburn glory, a dramatic occasion which ends in an execution. What would the fee be? Some-thing in the region of £500.

No novelist can predict what his new novel will earn. It will often be much less than £500, but even the unsuccessful can go on to the end of their careers sustained by the hope of global bestsellers and cables from Hollywood. Fees are in order for casual journalism, but not for works of literature. The payment of a fee, however generous, for a work of literary art seems to blaspheme against it to the status of a mere thing to be used. If a thing can be bought for use, it can also be bought for non-use. The fee paid for a portrait or piece of sculpture seems to justify a sort of consignment to oblivion – withdrawal from a public gallery to a private place. Pay for a piece of literature and your private place may as well be an attic or a locked drawer.

This has happened far too often with commissioned television plays, as most authors know. The procedure is something like this: the telephone call from the producer with an idea; the lunch; the formal briefing; the composition of the work; the submission of the work; the wait; the acceptance, with payment of half the total fee; the conference, with requests for cuts and emendations; the retyping; the further changes; the receipt of an official typed copy, with further requests for cuts; the silence of apparent satisfaction; the balance of the fee; the vain wait; the author's resignation as an interim silence is protracted beyond hope. He has received his fee – generous enough for a few weeks' work – but he is not content. Money is not everything.

It is evident to anyone who makes a habit of watching television drama that the literary artist has been deemed incapable of bringing much to it. There are a few exceptions, but it is safe to assume that the art, such as it is, has settled contentedly at a level of mere craft, and that its most acceptable practitioners are journalists. In a form which takes so much of its style and colour from the director, perhaps it was inevitable that the strongly individual voice of the literary artist should jar. The great expectations of 1962 will now never be fulfilled. What is required for television drama is a hackable block of material for the director to work on. Even the name of the television dram-atist has ceased to have much importance in trailer or credit list. It is not style or individual vision that is wanted (those qualities which proclaim the artist) but rather the solidity of topical, surprising or controversial content – the sort of thing the journalist is most con-cerned with. And not only the journalist but also the sort of man whom the journalist interviews – the philosophical taxi-driver, convicted homosexual, retired glasshouse NCO.

What applies to television drama applies also to the television documentary, except that the writing of the para-literature of a spoken commentary is more patently the kind of journalism the writer of books is used to. There will be no heart-burning over cutting, emending to fit the kind of film the director likes best, oversimplifying or even falsifying. The commentary is often in the service of the visual material. It is assumed, however, that the literary man is only to be called upon for a literary documentary (the old heresy of the hegemony of content), and there are not many of those.

From the point of view of television it would seem that the professional writer of books has little to bring except his own personality in the context of his own or other men's work. Both channels do shamefully little for literature – that is to say Independent Television and BBC One; BBC Two feeds so small a minority that it cannot yet be taken very seriously – but what has been done – in programmes like *Writer's World* and *Bookstand* – has been what the writer himself would want, and that is to give him a chance to address an audience that has the facelessness of a readership and to say those things which used to be said in prefaces. Addressing a camera represents an immediacy of contact which does not call for the histrionics of the stage or the lecture platform: many writers have a gift for this kind of communication, and it is a kind of communication which they hunger for and which the austerity of their art will not permit. Nevertheless, one would not call such rare television appearances anything more than the luxury of self-advertisement.

The author can do something for the publicising of literature in general, as BBC Two's programme *Take It or Leave It* has shown. There is a lucid element here – giving a name to an anonymous passage read by an actor – but there is criticism, too. And yet the true value of such a programme lies on the fringes that the audience never sees – the fact that authors meet and talk and have the sense (almost lost since Dr Johnson's time) of belonging to a club. The average reader will hardly believe how lonely the contemporary writer is becoming. Latent in all these television activities however, is – as has been said above – the danger of a subtle corruption. The writer's personality may become divorced from his function as a writer; he may be used to deliver opinions on non-literary subjects, even set up as a guest in a satirical show. Soon nothing will seem sweeter than the hot lights and the red eye. To be a television personality is easier than writing, even reviewing.

What then can the dedicated writer of books do, other than reviewing, to augment his income and to satisfy needs which are not met by the daily damnation of the typewriter? One answer is to stick to his secondary vocation (whether teaching or writing advertisement copy), but the danger is that the occupation that earns the more money can never be regarded as anything other than primary: this turns serious writing into a mere hobby. The alternative may be regarded as hackwork, but it was good enough for Dr Johnson. The writer of books should call himself that and get on with the job. The novelist cannot be writing novels all the time, but he has a great gift of being able to organise words into chunky battalions of 80,000 or so: he knows, which the journalist rarely does, how to write at length. There are many books to be written – 'small histories', language primers, travel guides, anthologies, volumes of comprehension exercises for schools. The important thing is to write books: Johnson saw that.

One may conclude that the position of the serious writer has not been greatly changed by the development of the new mass media: he is wanted rather less, if anything, than he used to be. The chameleon journalist, who is interested in everything so long as he is not called upon to write more than two or three thousand words about it, the script-writer, the television personality – these make money out of half-sincere verbalising. The dedicated author, who is concerned about words and the reality behind them, may take some of the crumbs, but the bulk of the cake is theirs. Still, one must not repine, as Mr Waugh would say, entrenched among the bestsellers. Write four books a year, and you will survive. And if authors survive they have done something for civilisation.

Times Literary Supplement, 29 July 1965

Bitter-sweet Savour

LONGEVITY IS rarely desired by artists, who are fearful of outliving their talent as well as their fame. Whether he desired it or not, Somerset Maugham achieved a productive old age, and his laying down of the pen seemed an act consonant with a sense of the proprieties: his achievement was large; it was time for the dignity of silence. There was certainly no sign of the diminution of strength or elegance in his latest writings: his Muse stayed with him until it was time for his superannuation. Posterity may say that a literary gift which is not of the greatest will last longer than a genius, which is all for explosions that waste the creative tissue, and that Somerset Maugham's lack of genius is best attested by a vast output whose quality showed little variation. Genius or not, Maugham had, up to the very end, the satisfaction of knowing that he was read, and read widely. It is likely that he will go on being read, and that his novels and stories – turned into films and television plays – will increasingly find audiences that have little time for books.

It is Maugham's popularity that tends to upset the highbrow critics (there is no place for him in such surveys of fiction as Walter Allen's *Tradition and Dream*), and students of literary style find magazine banality in his prose. In fact, Maugham's seeming artlessness was a very considerable art, starting as a reaction against Victorian opulence, refined – in the time of his maturity – till it became a supple and economical instrument closer to Maupassant than to Henry James. Maugham knew perfectly well what he was doing: *Cakes and Ale* is a textbook of literary criticism as well as a superb novel.

Perhaps I ought to modify that judgment and say 'a superb work of fiction', for *Cakes and Ale* reads like an inflated (but deliciously inflated) short story. The short story was Maugham's true *métier*, and some of the stories he wrote are among the best in the language. The form fitted a talent that was wide rather than deep, not (as with James) going over the same ground again and again till its possibilities were exhausted, but best nourished by travel, brief encounters with many human types, an anecdote swiftly jotted down between rubbers of bridge, a newspaper report, 'brunch' with a planter in Burma, a whisky *suku* in a Malayan club. The width of observation was something new in England fiction, as was the willingness to explore moral regions then regarded as taboo (as in *Rain*). The honesty of the reporter's eye rejected the total disguise of fictional re-creation and sometimes courted (as in *The Painted Veil* and some of the Malayan stories) the risk of wounding innocent people, which often meant the danger of libel. This was the penalty of being true to life.

Perhaps one of Maugham's finest creations was the first-person narrator who is almost, but not quite, the author himself. Here again was something that English fiction needed – the dispassionate commentator, the *raisonneur*, the man at home in Paris and Vienna but also in Seoul and Djakarta, convivial and clubbable, as ready for a game of poker as for a discussion on the Racine alexandrine, the antithesis of the slippered bookman. The chaperonage of this man-of-the-world was, and still is, a comfort to ordinary people who want to read but are frightened off by the image of the man-of-letters.

His plays – perhaps with the exception of his last, *Sheppey* – have not worn well but his books – though they, like the plays, deal with the surface of an age that is gone – are surprisingly undated. *Liza of Lambeth* still has power to shock, and *Of Human Bondage*, despite its inordinate length and its untypically clumsy prose, remains a viable, almost clinical, study of sexual obsessions. (A medical apprenticeship served Maugham better than it served Cronin.) The abiding flavour of his work is sharp and astringent. 'It tastes of tart apples. It sets your teeth on edge, but it has a subtle, bitter-sweet savour that is very agreeable to the palate'. Maugham is there describing Driffield's *The Cup of Life* in *Cakes and Ale*, but he might well have been describing his own stories, or at least the best of them. The best of them are going to live for a very long time.

Listener, 23 December 1965. The original piece is untitled.

The Big Daddy of the Beats

THERE ARE very few authors in whom personality triumphs over style; Jack Kerouac is one of them. It isn't, as with Victor Hugo, a matter of our aesthetic objections being overborne by brute strength: Kerouac conquers in a saintly way, by sheer goddam niceness. This character Jack Duluoz is one of the nicest cats you could ever meet, with his puppy-dog innocence tempered by moments of old-dog guilt, his enthusiasm for life not yet soured by the bad world.

Kerouac, perhaps frightened that we may be bored by the hipster sanctity, tries to paste on a bit of dangerous leanness, but it's not good. The old prelapsarian Adam beams out, literally incapable of harming a mouse and (when his pilgrimage brings him to London) blessing our filthy wicked city for its love of cats. Real cats that is, like with fur.

Desolation Angels calls itself a novel, but it is only that in a very Pickwickian sense. Nothing much happens except taking the road, listening to jazz, calling on old friends, laying some chick in the wholesomest way possible, going to somebody's pad for a beer and poetry. And the characters are real people wearing pseudonyms like dark glasses: Duluoz is Kerouac himself; Irwin Garden is Allen Ginsberg; Bull Hubbard is Bill Burroughs. The pretence that this is art should be laughed away gently: give the boy a ball of majoun to chew and send him off to read his nice Zen book. The thunderous portent of the title is only some cat sitting in on the drums. What this is is a record of the good quiet life, a pot session after a hearty breakfast, seeing a bit of the world man, doing no harm to nobody.

But one wonders sometimes if this niceness is not perhaps a kind of art. A beautiful glow turns Ginsberg into a great poet, not a hairy rhymester selling his Vaseline bars as fake holy relics. Burroughs becomes an all-American folk-hero, swinging and swaggering down the Calle Larache, rebuking his companions for walking too slow: 'Lard assed hipsters, ain't no good for nothing!' Kerouac's achievement has been to relate a kind of religiosity to the immediate small glamours of jazz, pot, and pop art. The Beat movement is being debased by its unkempt fringe – unwashed youths who think Zen is a cough-sweet – but it remains a genuine city-cult that can, over cheap wine and harmless drugs, mention God and Christ working out his karma and the ground of All Being without sanctimony or embarrassment.

And the Kerouac way of writing, though frequently deplorable, is occasionally to be seen as an analogue of the jazz solo, aleatoric, punctuable only with dashes like breath, capable of describing the banal (eating a cheap Chinese meal, catching a Greyhound bus) without tedium. Beat newspapers, like the *East Village Other*, employ the panting rhythms deftly: Kerouac has created a limited but viable idiom. In his apocalyptic moments Big Daddy – as when he is on Desolation Peak, waiting like Zarathustra to descend to the plain – mashes up a prose-poetry out of Whitman and Wolfe and Dylan Thomas. It goes down well enough, since this saintly man is not trying to show off: it is the way he wants to write, not the way he thinks he ought to. And he has, after all, a vision.

The vision, for this Catholic Canuck, resolves itself into the big American one. San Francisco may look west to the East but the wide God's land is the one the Beats want to wander: Zen on the move. In his European travels Kerouac yearns towards mother, cereals for breakfast, the pine trees outside the window. His philosophy is homespun American, and not bad either.

But then comes the exotic dressing which give Kerouac his flavour. 'Eternity, and the Here-and-Now, are the same thing.' Evil is negation; keep your palate clean for life, all of which (jazz, kif, Zen, poetry, Jell-O) is good. I rather dig this man.

Guardian, 22 May 1966
Review of *Desolation Angels* by Jack Kerouac
(London: André Deutsch, 1966)

The Seventeenth Novel

THIS ENGLISH summer has been cloudy, cold, thundery, and it
has matched the clinical bulletins about the British economic situation. The other night, after a painful session at the dentist's, I had
a painful session watching Harold Wilson on television. We have
been over-spending; we must retrench; we must restore confidence
in sterling. One of my few motives for trying to earn more money
must be the increase in the price of Scotch. I can think of no other
motive. Foreign holidays are, thanks to currency restrictions, out,
and I have no strong desire to holiday in Britain; the more I earn,
the closer I approach that precipice that tumbles me into paying 19
shillings out of every pound in surtax. Two years ago the Labour
Government promised us hard times; it seems to have been faithful
to that promise.

It is now midnight. This morning I climbed to my study to push
on with a comic novel I am trying to write. It is a great wonder to
the laity that comedians are able to go on with their routines while
suffering bereavement, an abscess or an economic recession. It is also
a great wonder to me. Writing a comic novel can be approached with
the same weariness and pain as writing a tragedy, and the weariness
and pain will, with a professional, never show.

Yet there is something showing in my work that I am far from
happy about, and perhaps it is only the general ambience of depression
that makes me willing to speak of it. I mean evidence of dissatisfaction with forms and tropes and vocabulary and rhythms that orthodox
English provides. I am now working on my seventeenth novel, and I
doubt if I can go on much longer in the same modes – straight narrative, naturalistic dialogue, bits of interior monologue, atmospheric
récit. I feel, as every writer must feel on his seventeenth novel, that I
am in danger of repeating myself.

The hero of this novel is a middle-aged poet who is working as
a bartender in an American-owned London hotel. The sixth line of
the first chapter described him washing glasses. I have written: 'He

burnished an indelible veronica of lipstick.' What I mean is that he polished a red smear that, like the imprint of Christ's bleeding face on the towel of St. Veronica (preserved to this day in Rome), seemed to be set there in perpetuity. There is no intention of facetious blasphemy: it is necessary to establish certain religious undertones as soon as possible, since these are relevant to the character and preoccupations of my poet.

Setting down the image, I was well enough pleased. It seemed sufficiently apt and original. And then came the doubt: Had I used it before? I searched through my published books – a very wearisome job – and found that I hadn't, but with no real sensation of relief. I had not used it before but, I thought, I might use it again.

The more fiction one writes, the more one sees a certain pattern of locales and situations. In my books, people drink in bars or pubs, and these are becoming more alike; worse, the drinkers are always behaving in the same way; worse still, I am more and more tempted to draw on the same kind of language for describing pub, people and behaviour. Two men will fight, and the fights are becoming more like each other. Faced with the need to describe a city street, I can find nothing to say about it that I have not previously, and more freshly, said.

I have created so many characters, major and minor, that I am in danger of completing the roster and having to go back to the beginning again. There is a limited number of ways in which a woman can be pretty and a man ugly, and an even more limited number of modes for the conveying of these qualities. One's readers may not notice, since they have mostly, thank heavens, rather poor memories, but one notices oneself and one does not like to cheat. A book may bore its reader, but it ought not to bore its author. One's 17th attempt at an orthodox piece of fiction ought to carry the same tremulous glamor as one's first.

It is because of this fear of self-repetition and, more than that, this dissatisfaction with the limitations of ordinary language that I begin to look with a sort of wistfulness at the fictional experimentalists. And I have become convinced that none of these undertakes a new approach to fiction to bring new enlightenment to his readers or to carve, with Flaubertian martyr's courage, new paths for other writers. The writer experiments because he is bored. He is like God, who, suffering with Alberto Moravia's hero from *La Noia*, has to create a new cosmos to become less *annoiato*.

Nabokov's *Pale Fire* is a little tedious to read, but it must have been very exciting to write. Some of the novels of the French *nouvelle vague* are, with their stasis, their concentration on things rather than people, more than a little tedious, but one can see that they had to be written to save their authors from the *ennui* or treading the worn path again. William Burroughs's cut-out and fold-in techniques, designed to give a 'new look' to language, perhaps give this new look only to their author. But their author must be allowed to protect himself from boredom.

It is the need to make language genuinely new, rather than merely look new, that drives James Joyce to create the pun-Eurish of a *Finnegans Wake*. One can understand Joyce's position very well. In *Ulysses* he had used up the resources of orthodox language, not only in the fabrication of portmanteau-words, pastiche, mimicry and mockery, but also in the exact notation of action and speech. What could his next book be except a new limitation or a tame repetition unless he broke language up and recast it? The author is told to think of his readers, but he must also think of himself.

Ideally, a novelist should be not just a polyglot but a panglot. Let him write his first novel in English, exploiting all the resources of the language; then let him shake French by the scruff of the neck and go on to demotic Greek. One can only be truly creative if one creates not merely a subject but the medium in which that subject moves. The most that the average novelist or poet can do is to fashion an idiom; sometimes this does not seem to go far enough. Neither Schönberg nor Picasso was content with an idiom; it had to be a new language or nothing.

I cannot create a new language, though I have found, by accident and with a shock, that, in my novel *A Clockwork Orange*, I made a transitory dialect for real as well as fictional teenagers. But I feel that I must, to counter my own weariness, do something new. The new fictional images that present themselves to me in the still summer watches, with the wind temporarily quiet, are fantastic. Will they work?

Before *The Times* changed, for the worse, its format, I dreamed of a novel in which the hero's life was presented in strict *Times* form, from opening advertisements to closing crossword. I am dreaming, more wakefully, of a novel presented as a mock-biography, complete with photographs and index. I have thought of telling one story in the text and a counterpoint story in footnotes. In delirium it occurred to me that I might recast one novel already half-written in the form of a small encyclopedia, so that the reader, armed with all the relevant information, might work out the plot for himself.

These things require a courage which perhaps very few professional novelists, faced with the need to earn a living, can really possess. A married woman can find this courage more easily than a married man. Sterne began *Tristram Shandy* from the fortress of a clerical living. Joyce at least had a patroness.

And yet, when one looks at some of the experimental novels that stem from Sterne or from Nathalie Sarraute, one is struck by the salutary realisation that the new shapes are not really enough. Sterne had Uncle Toby and Mr Shandy; Nabokov has Kinbote; Joyce had both Bloom and Earwicker. There are certain things that the novel cannot do without, and the greatest of these is character. Some of our young British experimentalists grumble because of lack of appreciation, but they have all the Shandeian tricks off pat, but they have none of the Shandeian grotesques.

The terrible daring of *Ulysses* comes off because Bloom and Dedalus are big enough to survive their torturing. Tell a young experimentalist to try something on the lines of the lying-in hospital scene in *Ulysses*, and he will produce a passable pastiche history of English literature, but he will not have the human tension of Bloom's first true meeting with Stephen. A novel should not be an evening of conjuring tricks; it should be a genuine play.

What I have said is obvious enough. The fact remains that, at least for myself, to make novel-writing a genuine intellectual stimulus I must impose on myself certain formal stringencies. The big secret perhaps will be the rendering of these so unobtrusive that the reader will think he is reading something very orthodox. The listener to Alban Berg's opera, *Wozzeck*, may not be aware that one act is in the form of a symphony and another in the form of a suite, but that does not invalidate Berg's sense of the need for such a subtle imposition. I have myself, perhaps overcautiously, followed Berg in certain novels, making one paragraph a Petrarchan sonnet set as prose, turning a whole opening section into a slavish simulacrum of Wagner's *Das Rheingold* (nobody noticed; in any case, the novel – for a quite different reason – got itself banned), identifying, in *Nothing Like the Sun*, the drunken narrator with the dying subject of his narration.

The reader may draw his own conclusions, and they will probably not be favourable. One conclusion may be that I should give up writing novels, but another may be that the traditional novel-form is no longer very satisfying to the novelist.

Having said all this, I feel a little better now. The night air is warmer, and tomorrow brings the task of pushing on with my comic novel. What I have already written may cease to seem pedestrian and become fresh, incisive, original; the new sheet in the typewriter may fill itself with all sorts of daring felicities which, pleasing the reader, shall not have bored the author. In any case, one must get on with the work one thinks one does best. The fact that one can have doubts about it may be a good sign, since doubt, as we know, is an intermission of faith. Only the very bad writer is always absolutely sure of the value of what he is doing.

New York Times, 21 August 1966

Here Parla Man Marcommunish

IT WAS, I believe, a certain M. Étiemble who devoted a whole book to the condemnation of what he called *Franglais* – the long-term debauching of French by commercial English (strictly speaking, commercial American). However such a liaison may be refused benefit of academy, nothing can prevent its becoming a common law marriage: languages only give house-room to foreign words when they can't get on without them. Nobody told the French to adopt *nouveau look* (new look), *rocanrole* (rock 'n' roll), *bestseller*, *kidnappé* and so on: they had to go into the language because their referents couldn't be named more succinctly out of the native word-stock. I can understand M. Étiemble's being annoyed that *brassière* – which has a basic denotation of 'shoulder-strap' – should threaten to take over the function of *soutien-gorge* (which does its job well enough), but generally speaking he has no right to denounce a linguistic process which is as old as speech itself. Languages in contact, as Mario Pei reminds us, are bound to mix.

English has become a great exporter of words, but this represents a kind of historical justice. After all, we've had – in the formative years of the language – a great mass of French and Italian dumped upon us. Grateful for loanwords which became an indispensable part of our lexicon, we've expected gratitude from Italy for *futbol* and *colcrem* and from Russia for *khuligan* (hooligan) and *loder*. This last word, which means 'lazybones,' comes from 'loaded': visiting Russians were greatly struck by the slowness of the stevedores on British docks. We're not sympathetic to 'pure language' slogans. But, if any foreign nation thinks we've foisted too many words on it, the time has come to show that English can still absorb an alien lexis with a good grace. The Common Market will give us an opportunity to start a new wave of Europeanising English.

But, before we think about words, let's think about the setting-down of words on paper. If the Arabs were to join the Common Market, I'd suggest that we follow them in doing without upper-case letters, thus saving much typing and printing time, as well as the expense of two different kinds of typeface. As it is, we can at least follow Romance usage by employing lower-case initials in proper-name adjectives – british, french, wilsonian, and so on. German, which – consulting majority usage in the Common Market – will have to throw away all its noun-capitals, nevertheless sets an example to English in its willingness to eschew hyphens and to make word-compounds into real words. If it can use *Grundbuchamt*, we ought to have 'landregistry,' and 'insurancebroker' need be no more eccentric than *Versicherungsmakler*.

Of course, it would help our german market-partners if we dug up germane wordroots, turning 'menstruation' into 'monthflow' on the analogy of *Monatsfluss*, and making a nipple a breastwart (*Brustwarze*). But the french spent centuries knocking latin into us, and 'education' is *éducation* to them, just as it is *educazione* to the Italians. 'Updragging' is altogether Nordic and has a coarse unupdragged quality about it. Besides, languages don't make that sort of deliberate adjustment. We take in loanwords because we need them. We need *ombudsman* and *sputnik* and *Autobahn* and, presumably, *discothèque*, *boutique* and *espresso*. 'The sweet life' means little, but *la dolce vita* means a lot. I, personally, should be happy to see terms like *bistro* and *Bierstube* absorbed into english, if the referents too could be absorbed with them. For neither *bistro* nor *Bierstube* is subject to british licensing laws. And though *minijupe* derives from 'miniskirt,' the french term implies elegance, while the quantian original suggests big knobbly clumsy british teenagers. A *brassière* could have been a 'bustholder' (german *Büstenhalter*), but it was right to regard bosoms as a french delicacy. Yet everything finds its own level: the vulgar 'bra' is a typically british compound of prudery and immodesty.

Mr Wilson, if it is he who is going to lead us into the Common Market, will no doubt be found equal to the linguistic demands of the inauguration ceremony. He will have two alternatives. First, he can tell the europeans that the britannic nation has emerged from a *mauvaise époque* in which the *Lumpenproletariat*, rendered torpid by *la noia* of the *ancien regime*, with its *Unrealpolitik* of *il faut cultiver notre jardin*, possessed no viable *Weltanschauung*, has, *nel mezzo del cammin* of the socialist *renaissance*, rediscovered, through *Sturm und Drang* and the *entrepressement* of the *Zeitgeist*, its *élan vital* and is, *con brio e con amore e molto accelerando*, becoming *au fait* with the *nouvelle vague politique*, *fatigué* as it is with the *faux-naïveté* of *passé chauvinistes* and the *verloren hoops* to whom *laissez-faire* was the *dernier cri*.

Second, he can, with the help of philologists like Mr Patrick Gordon Walker, burst out with a new *lingua franca* (british copyright) called, perhaps, Marcommunish – a name which would ease in, eventually, other socialist countries, if the senior partners agreed. Thus: 'Vu savvy, wijnu in Grobritannia av, post de frichtful en terrible tempo de tory reglierung, wirklich en actualmento shlekt en cattivo en mal reglierung, moltifeel bocoop de gross ding en shoze en cosay registrato. Nu, nun, actually, wijnu begin en commence en initiate un novo tempo...' It's amazing how, whatever the gibberish, the authentic tone of Mr Wilson comes through. I've always felt he was somehow above language.

The Book is Not for Reading

'BEWARE OF wishing for anything in youth, because you will get it in middle age.' Goethe said that and it's not worth both parts of *Faust*. Last year I became music critic of one journal and theatre critic of another. I think, if I'd tried hard enough, I could also have been appointed gastronomic critic for one of the glossy man-about-town fripperies. What a dream for a young man – free entrée to all the theatres, concert halls and restaurants of London. But the fulfilment has to come when the appetite is blunted, the stomach queasy and the ear or brain quickly bored.

Ignorance and poverty are the best condiments for the great feast of the world, but the inexperienced and poor are never invited to it. Books are part of the feast, and when I was young I slavered for them. I can get books now but, inevitably, I don't want them anymore, I seem to have finished with reading.

That's not strictly true, since after the long day's writing, I can't get to sleep without the drug of print. But the prescription has varied little in 10 years. I read miniature scores of orchestral works I know well, Boswell, espionage, Joyce, and what has been called the drowsy, mellifluous twaddle of the worst Elizabethan prose. Sometimes, for real soporific, I reread something of my own. And, whatever I read, I experience the guilt of knowing I should be reading something else – something to improve my mind, fill in old gaps, render me up-to-date.

The up-to-date part worries me least, because, if anybody at a party asks me if I've read So-and-so, I can always counter with: No, but I've read Such-and-such; have you? Such-and-such is somebody I make up on the spot, plot and characters and all. It is sometimes less wearisome to fabricate imaginary contemporaries than to read real ones.

But the guilt about the gap-filling and mind-improving cannot be shrugged off. And it cannot be palliated with the knowledge that I've read certain books that other people haven't. I've read *Don Quixote* right through in English and I know by heart the opening sentence in the original: '*En un lugar de la Mancha, de cuyo nombre no quiero acordarme...*' I've read the Papus treatise on the Tarot cards, which T.S. Eliot never did, at least before he wrote *The Waste Land*. I've read most of Ben Jonson and the first volume of *The Anatomy of Melancholy*. I've read Hemingway's *Fiesta* in German. I've read three Sherlock Holmes stories in the Indonesian language. I've read (with a crib and with difficulty) the Persian verses of Omar Khayyam. But I've not read Jane Austen.

I wish I had read Jane Austen. I wish I'd done the job in my youth (as I did the job of reading Virgil) and thus got it over. My wife is a Janeite, like William Burroughs, and perhaps I feel that, man and wife being one flesh, there is no point in duplication. But that won't really do since marriage is supposed to be a business of shared pleasures. Sometimes my wife quizzes me on the names of Jane Austen's characters, and I can get a lot of them right now (the Bennet sisters are Elizabeth, Jane, Mary, Lydia and Kitty). I have also seen the film of *Pride and Prejudice*, with Greer Garson and Laurence Olivier, scripted by Aldous Huxley, and I have a very clear idea of what Mr Collins looks like. But I know only the surface of Jane Austen, the vital statistics my wife has drilled me in, the odd-remembered line from a radio adaptation, a general impression of high-waisted dresses and genteel parsonage flirtation. This is shameful and hopeless, and I can do nothing about it. There is a very good edition of the novels in our house-library, but the time for my opening any of them is gone.

Why? Is it not 'never too late'? Yes, it is. There was a period in my life when I could well have had my sensibility modified by what I understand to be the gentle elegance, sometimes gently barbed, of Jane Austen. But now, having formed my sensibility a different way, I recognise that I can gain no pleasure from serious reading (I would evidently have to take Jane Austen seriously) that lacks a strong male thrust, an almost pedantic allusiveness, and a brutal intellectual content.

I think I would take it further and doubt whether I could ever approach any woman writer – a woman writer, that is, who exploited her femininity – with any real hope of joyful enlightenment. The Chinese Taoists posit (if Comrade Mao still permits) a universe in which the yin (a female principle) battles endlessly with the yang (or male principle). There is even a Chinese disease, sometimes fatal, in which the male sufferer believes that he is being set upon by the yin, so that the emblems of his sex shrink fearfully into his belly. I think I suffer from this disease. I'm frightened of submitting to a woman author (all reading is an act of submission). Where I can record exceptions I can adduce plausible enough explanations. Harriet Beecher Stowe? Outraged motherhood, protective rather than devouring. Ivy Compton-Burnett? A big sexless nemesis force. George Eliot? The male impersonation is wholly successful.

But (how cussed can one get?) I find in my reading gaps a fair number of writers who are very notably yang. In other words, the fear of having my head shorn is only half the story. I have not read Sir Walter Scott, the man who opposed the big bow-wow to the Austen delicacy. It is possible that his yang is so thoroughgoing that it becomes a parody of itself, something made by a yin personality. All that chivalry, treachery, romantic contrivance reminds one of the day-dream stuff of the Japanese *Tale of Genji*, which was written by a woman. I could not tackle any Scott now, though for my sins, about seven years ago, I had to teach an abridged edition of *Ivanhoe* to a mixed class of Malays, Chinese, Tamils and reformed headhunters. I also saw the film of *Ivanhoe*, with Ava Gardner, and thought that it must be superior to the novel.

But as with Jane Austen, I wish I had romped through Scott in my youth, as I romped through H.G. Wells's sociological novels (never again) and that ghastly *Forsyte Saga*. One ought to have had the experience of childish absorption in a teller of rattling good yarns (Fenimore Cooper, John Buchan, Henty) before maturity set in like rigor mortis. And, to go right back to the nursery stage, one ought to have had bloody Christopher Robin and that Pooh thing and *The Wind in the Willows*. I bought the latter book quite recently and was in fact disturbed by a rat and a mole sharing a picnic-basket full of chicken and ham. And I was worried about a toad riding in an automobile. I also couldn't cope with illustrations that cut nothing down to size, so that a real horse was being pulled by a couple of real rodents. Middle-age is not the period for suspending the particular kind of disbelief that has no part in primal innocence.

I feel certain conclusions coming on and, before I have really concluded, I had better voice them. First, the adult relation to books is one of absorbing rather than being absorbed. In youth, a book is a door: you enter, you surrender everything, you are gladly lost. In middle-age, you want to hold on to your own identity, to consume, to use, to carve a book like a joint and ingest it to feed that identity. But, by the usual human paradox, that identity couldn't have come into existence at all unless it had been moulded, early in life, by others. So youth is the time for submission to books that can't be enjoyed except by submission. And yet, by the usual human irony, youth believes that certain reading tasks can be put off till later in life: 'Some day I shall read Josephus, the whole of Gibbon, all Freud.' That, anyway, is the undergraduate's vow.

But the time for surrender to a big author always comes when the will to surrender is gone. To start reading Dickens or Shakespeare for the first time in middle-age would be like Gauguin discovering he had to be a painter or Saul that he had to be Paul. To turn into a saint (whom I take to be one who surrenders his own personality to a greater) should be a transformation reserved to youth, before marriage, children, a house, furniture, set ways come along and the only foreseeable change is a sea-change.

Second, it is very common only to wish to read a book when you don't possess it. For years I wanted to read *The Cloud of Unknowing*, but I never came across a copy. Yet I eagerly read a good deal about that mystical work and took in, obliquely, much of its content. In Kota Bharu, north-eastern Malaya, I went into a Chinese mahjong den, saw a book-case in the corner, examined it, and found that it contained two books only, one of which was *The Cloud of Unknowing*. A mystery never to be solved. I stole that book and took it back to England. Needless to say, I have never opened it. And I know I never shall. The possession of a book becomes a substitute for reading it.

When I had to get my William Faulkner out of the public library, I read him avidly. Now I have a set of him on my shelves, and the desire to reread him grows weaker all the time. If I didn't have Edmund Spenser's works I'd cry with frustration at not having read *The Fairie Queene*. Well the Fairie Queene is waiting there for me and, for all I care, she can go on waiting. Only with a real woman is possession an act of enjoyment; with books it's Confederate money, Czarist rubles – a ghost of wealth.

During the war an army sergeant spoke to me earnestly of the value of education. He told me of the time he had been in prison and of how he had beguiled the long stretch by reading the works of Sir Francis Bacon. 'And,' he said, 'If I ever go to prison again I'll get down to reading Thomas Hobbes. Reading's a wonderful thing.' So it is when you've already done it, or when you propose to do it. It's the doing of it that's painful. Reading is rather like writing.

New York Times, 4 December 1966

The Comedy of Ultimate Truths

The late Pope John said that any day was a good day to die. He might, nevertheless, have conceded that some days are better than others, and that no Christian could ask more than to die on Easter morning – suddenly, without fuss, having just celebrated the truth of Christ's, and hence man's, resurrection. That is how Evelyn Waugh died. Those of us who loved the books without knowing the man must set a decent limit to our mourning. We regret that there will be no more books; at the same time, we are grateful for the oeuvre we have – one of the richest in all modern literature.

Evelyn Waugh had intimated to the world, off and on during the last ten years, that he was not merely resigned to the propinquity of death but actively ready to embrace it. The first words of *A Little Learning* are: 'Only when one has lost all curiosity about the future has one reached the age to write an autobiography.' For Gilbert Pinfold it was never later than he thought. Waugh knew that the barbarism of the age could not be redeemed. His great war chronicle, *Sword of Honour*, records the passing not merely of the religion of his youth but of the secular values that once sustained Western civilisation. Waugh had, like his hero Guy Crouchback, fought in what at first looked like a crusade, only to see it develop into a sweaty tug-of-war between teams of indistinguishable louts (that is how Scott-King saw it), its outcome the establishment of a Modern Europe animated by cynicism, hypocrisy, the devices of most unjesuitical equivocation. Unconditional surrender had to be made to the facts of history, but the new anti-values must be passively resisted.

The good man retires from the world, cherishing fragments from an incorrupt past, cultivating style, assuming stoical poses that are not without a certain discreet self-mockery. The final capitulation to barbarism seemed to Waugh to be preparing itself in his own Church: the truth remained the same, but the garments of the truth were becoming flashy and vulgar. In the canon of the gentleman and austere artist, vulgarity was a kind of sin. Avoiding it, Waugh seemed sometimes to err on the side of a kind of Augustan superbity.

He was a self-taught aristocrat whose background was decently bourgeois. Critics who condemned alleged evidences of snobbery in his writings (usually with the underdog whine that Mr Pinfold's ear was sharp to detect) missed something deeper even than the patrician pose that was inseparable from his comic technique: they missed the Shakespearian hunger for order and stability. 'Take but degree away, untune that string, / And, hark, what discord follows.' Waugh's humour is never flippant. *Decline and Fall* would not have maintained its freshness for nearly forty years if it had not been based on one of the big themes of our Western literature – the right of the decent man to find decency in the world.

Comic heroes like Paul Pennyfeather and William Boot are too innocent to engage a decadent civilisation, but there is an order above the human (perhaps the comic and the miraculous are cognate) which brings them through safely: the dangerous worlds they enter are purgatorial, not infernal. Hell is reserved for one novel only, perhaps Waugh's best. Tony Last, in *A Handful of Dust*, acquiesces in the breakdown of order and ends his days up the Amazon, reading Dickens to an illiterate half-caste: his innocence has been appropriate to a younger son, but not to a small aristocrat with large responsibilities; hence his punishment. It is in this novel that, despite the fine comic flashes, we come closest to a vision of spiritual emptiness unredeemable by any god of laughter. Brenda Last competes with Ford Madox Ford's Sylvia Tietjens for the title of worst woman in the world.

Brideshead Revisited fulfils the quest for certainty, though the image of a Catholic aristocracy, with its penumbra of a remote besieged chivalry, a secular hierarchy threatened by the dirty world but proudly falling back on a prepared eschatological position, has seemed over-romantic, even sentimental, to non-Catholic readers. It remains a soldier's dream, a consolation of drab days and a depraved palate, disturbingly sensuous, even slavering with gulosity, as though God were somehow made manifest in the haute cuisine. The Puritan that lurks in every English Catholic was responsible for the later redaction of the book, the pruning of the poetry of self-indulgence. It was the revising itch, the scrupulosity of the artist rather than the moralist, which led Waugh to make changes (perhaps less justifiable) in *Sword of Honour*, which now stands as a single great novel, no longer a trilogy, and the final monument to his many gifts – those of the exact historian (military, social, religious), the superb recorder of swift action, the creator of larger-than-life comic characters, the Augustan stylist. If Waugh is to be remembered as a comic novelist, that implies no relegation to a secondary status, as though it were a meaner achievement to make people laugh than to make them cry. He recognised his kinship with P.G. Wodehouse, but comedy with him was not merely entertainment, summer-holiday stuff: it was a medium for the expression of ultimate truths, some of them very bitter. Apthorpe, like young Lord Tangent, has to die. The appalling 'nonsense' which Cedric Line makes of the embarkation in *Put Out More Flags* is desperately funny, but it also encapsulates the real nonsense of the pre-Churchillian days, when England had still not learned what war was about. And even at its most light-hearted, the comedy finds an exact gravity of locution: Waugh's comic underworld – smugglers, deserters, burglars, nightclub courtesans – are accorded the dignity of language appropriate to personages who have, in their various bizarre ways, arrived at acceptable modes of order. The humour is, in the best sense, aristocratic.

Critics may now go to work on Waugh's place in the hierarchy of British writers (equal to Greene? to Forster?) and list his literary creditors (Firbank? Ford Madox Ford?), but mere authors will continue to despair of their ability to approach that prose perfection, though the mere existence of the challenge must make them better writers. Readers will regret that the autobiography, which promised so brilliantly, can now never take the shelf as an expository masterpiece, and that the crass patterns of modern life – on both sides of the Atlantic – will never again find so detached and elegant and devastating a castigator. But, to use Evelyn Waugh's favourite phrase, we must not repine. We have what we have, which is a great deal, and – as the author would wish, if he could have brought himself to accept that we should be thankful at all – we thank God for it.

Europe's Day of the Dead

MALCOLM LOWRY'S *Under the Volcano* is a novel about the last day in the life of Geoffrey Firmin, British consul of the Mexican town of Quauhnahuac, which is set between the twin volcanoes Popocatepetl and Iztaccihuatl. It is the Day of the Dead, November 1938, and Firmin is drinking himself to death, but some thugs speed the process by murdering him and throwing him down a ravine, sending a dead dog after him for company. Firmin is a compulsive drunkard (which is what Lowry himself became) and is clear-sightedly, almost Faustianly, bent on self-destruction. He has opted out of the world, rejecting both duty and love; when love and help are offered – by the wife who has returned to him and the half-brother who has come from the Spanish Civil War – he has to turn his face against them and elect for the hell of emptiness and the palliation of mescal. It is a book about heaven and hell and the necessity of choice between them. On another level, it is a study of the choice that Europe, in the thirties, had already made. The most superficial level presents the self-enclosed world of the dipsomaniac, and this is the level that too many of the book's earliest readers saw to the exclusion of everything else. It was regarded as doing, rather more wordily and with far too many literary allusions, what had already been done in *The Lost Weekend*.

The blurb of the new edition states that, when it was first published in 1947, 'it was acclaimed by a few critics, but largely ignored.' That was not true of America, where it was both a critical and a financial success, nor of Europe, where it was translated into Dutch, Polish and Portuguese as well as the more obvious languages, but it was certainly true of England. Despite its British hero, it was apparently not considered provincial enough here; the study of evil and human degradation was too profound and detailed, the exploitation of myth and language asked for very strenuous engagement. Jonathan Cape, Lowry's publishers, have, simultaneously with the reissue of *Under the Volcano*, given us a selection of his letters, and with noble candour draw the reviewer's attention to Lowry's immensely long justification of the book as he wrote it when Cape were all for surgical redactions. Never before has an author spoken up for his own work with such eloquence, good humour and frankness: '... I had better say that for my part I feel that the main defect of *Under the Volcano*, from which the others spring, comes from something irremediable. It is that the author's equipment, such as it is, is subjective rather than objective, a better equipment, in short, for a certain kind of poet than a novelist. On the other hand I claim that just as a tailor will try to conceal the deformities of his client so I have tried, aware of this defect, to conceal in the *Volcano* as well as possible the deformities of my own mind, taking heart from the fact that since the conception of the whole thing was essentially poetical, perhaps these deformities don't matter so very much after all, even when they show!'

Lowry had no need to excuse himself. He saw that the novel-form's only hope of survival lay in its being taken over by poets. It is doubtful, though, if many ordinary (let alone publishers') readers would have seen how intensely poetical the conception of *Under the Volcano* is without the author's own exegesis. We're meant to see it as an Inferno. In the prologue, the French film director Laruelle plans a Faust film, reads Marlowe, makes Firmin's epitaph Faustus's own: 'Cut is the branch that might have grown full straight...'

The action begins in the Casino de la Selva – the *selva oscura* of Dante; later Firmin enters a 'gloomy cantina called El Bosque, which also means the wood'; Hugh, his half-brother, *nel mezzo del cammin*, recalls Dante's own lines. Mexico is 'a kind of timeless symbol of the world on which we can place the Garden of Eden, the Tower of Babel and indeed anything else we please. It is paradisal; it is unquestionably infernal.' The ravine down which the consul falls is the one which opens for the world in 1939 (the year of the prologue, which looks back to the Day of the Dead just twelve months before); it is also 'the worse one in the Cabbala, the still unmentionably worse one in the Qliphoth, or simply down the drain, according to taste.'

Symbol-hunting could turn into a postgraduate sport if Lowry had not got in first. Laruelle goes to the local cinema during a thunder-storm and Las Manos de Orlac (the film comes from Germany; the poster shows blood-stained hands) symbolises the guilt of mankind. In a similar storm Geoffrey Firmin releases a panic-stricken horse, which finally kills Yvonne, the wife who has come back to him. The careful planting of symbols and correspondences inevitably recalls *Ulysses*, but I think it would be wrong to call Lowry (as some critics have done) a disciple of Joyce. What it seems to me Lowry wrote is the kind of novel that Conrad Aiken wanted to write but lacked the architectonic skill to make structurally satisfying. Of course, *Blue Voyage*, *Great Circle* and *King Coffin* have such Joycean elements as interior monologue and recondite literary allusion, but they lack the Joycean lust for form. Lowry's first letter in this selection is one he wrote at the age of nineteen to Aiken, and admiration for Aiken's work leads him not to the postures of the disciple but to the conversion of the master into a genuine father-figure. The father, as Stephen Spender indicates in his excellent introduction to the novel, has to be destroyed by the son: this is one of the conditions of his own act of creation. But the superiority of Lowry's book to any of Aiken's lies, among other things, in the fact that, where Aiken produced Prufrock figures, small Hamlets, Lowry created in Geoffrey Firmin a giant character whose sloth or accidie ironically suggests the Promethean rebel, whose total alienation from life etches the desired opposite, whose inability to love defines what love is. Firmin is perhaps the last exemplar of one of the forms of Liberal Man. He is civilised, sensitive, idealistic, and he cannot survive in the world of the ravine, dominated by the hands of Orlac. He stands in a phase of history which is also valid as myth, with the carious Mexico of Graham Greene mirroring the torn Spain of all the intellectuals of the thirties. Firmin is diseased, but the remedy sometimes seems to be in his own hands: he is an exact symbol of Europe.

At the same time, he is a human being who, though he contains within himself a picture gallery of all the tragic heroes, from Oedipus Tyrannus and Philoctetes (the names of two ships in the novel) to Faust and Hamlet, is a fresh tragic creation in his own right, since he is a product of our own period. His situation is hopeless, but he doesn't whine: he even maintains a courtesy proper to his rank. He doesn't lie in bed like Oblomov, waiting for the end of a regime; he drinks steadily and, through the drink, achieves the poet's or saint's clairvoyance. He knows precisely what is going on. The attainment of self-knowledge, however cut off from the ability to act, is seen to be an aspect of the heroic.

Perhaps Firmin's glamour is partly a reflection of Lowry's own. Big though the consul is, he is only one aspect of Lowry: other aspects are to be found in Firmin's half-brother Hugh and in Wilderness, the diarist of *Through the Panama*. Lowry has the glamour of all writers who are both scholars and men of action. He went to sea at the age of eighteen, and Conrad Knickerbocker tells of trips to 'Singapore, Shanghai, Kowloon, Penang… a gun battle in which he was wounded in the leg, glorious young drinking in Yokohama bars, a storm with a dock cargo of snakes, a wild boar, panthers and an elephant.' After Cambridge, life was mostly exile – Paris, New York, Los Angeles, Vancouver, British Columbia and, of course, Mexico.

It was also curiously accident-prone – the loss of the manuscript of his first novel, *Ultramarine* (he rewrote it from notes), the lucky salvaging of *Under the Volcano* from fire, his wife's strange illnesses and the even stranger vicissitudes of her own published fiction. Money was short, the houses and log cabins where they lived got themselves appropriated or razed to the ground. And the struggle to get *Under the Volcano* published (in his biographical chronology we read: '1941. *Under the Volcano* refused by twelve publishers and withdrawn from agent, fourth version begun') was, even when critical success came, matched by the twentieth-century writer's hopeless struggle to make ends meet.

But the impression of Lowry we receive from these letters is of a restless, energetic man, incapable either of Firmin's accidie or his inability to love. He is garrulous, serious, yet given to self-mockery and a rather old-fashioned courtliness. He is one of those writers who, antithetical to Gilbert Pinfold, seems quite willing to write a student's thesis for him (American English departments were on to Lowry's importance pretty early). He knew the worth of *Under the Volcano*, was earnest about it but never pompous. The time is coming for a detailed appraisal of his later book, *Hear Us O Lord from Heaven Thy Dwelling Place*. It seems to me as remarkable, in its different way, as *Under the Volcano*, yet sensible reaction to it looks like being as long delayed. But that Lowry is one of the great major novelists there can no longer be any doubt.

Spectator, 20 January 1967
Review of *Under the Volcano* by Malcolm Lowry
(London: Jonathan Cape, 1966)

Surprise from the Grave

FLANN O'BRIEN'S *At Swim-Two-Birds* is one of the ten great comic books of the century, and it is one of the five outrageous fictional experiments of all time that come completely and triumphantly off. What a fuss the French anti-novelists make about their tedious exercises in *chosisme*; how little fuss has been made about Flann O'Brien's humour, humanity, metaphysics, theology, bawdry, mythopoeia, word-play and six-part counterpoint.

He died quietly last year, hardly yet recognised. It is doubtful whether this first of the posthumous books we're promised – a surprise that's waited 26 years to be sprung from the grave – will bring the irony of belated bestsellerdom, or even a move towards universal acknowledgement of O'Brien's genius. It will take the novel-reading public a fair time to accept *The Third Policeman*.

Much of the material is comic, but the overall effect is very gruesome, even (and this is eventually confirmed as not mere fancy) infernal. The anonymous narrator, who has a wooden leg, conspires with the man named Divney to murder a rich farmer and steal his cashbox. It is left to the narrator to pick up the loot from the dead man's house. As his fingers touch the handle of the box, the whole world suddenly changes. The dead man is alive again, the narrator's soul (called Joe) enters the narrative as a disembodied voice, the cashbox has been magically transferred to a remote police barracks. The narrator goes to get it and becomes involved with two strange policemen: the eponymous third is reserved for very much later.

Sergeant Pluck is obsessed with his teeth and with bicycles; Policeman MacCruiskeen makes Chinese boxes, of which the innermost is microscopic; their speech is Irish solecistic sesquipedalian raised to the ultimate power. They record meticulous readings on an unknown instrument; they condemn the narrator to death and start to build his gallows, grumbling about the price of wood; they take him to an underground treasury where all wishes are granted. Kafka, we think crossed with James Stephens. And very nearly, but not quite, something of Joyce.

O'Brien had little to learn from Joyce except a few technical tricks; he was already endowed with Irish poetic pedantry which it was Joyce's achievement to exploit to the epic limit. O'Brien is more modest. He is content here with the creation of a whole bogus scholarship centred on the writings of an impossible savant called de Selby. This mad philosopher is the narrator's personal obsession. He is invoked on every occasion, often in dense footnotes which rise up the page and flood out the narrative. One is reminded of *Finnegans Wake*, but only just. The materials of that phantasmagoria are real life; everything here is made out of the world of the dead. The narrator, we eventually discover, is dead: his accomplice planted a bomb in the house of the robbed and murdered farmer and blew him up. The horrible logic of de Selby belongs to a quiet and somehow friendly hell where bicycles and an entity called an omnium are among the obsessive furniture. It is circular, and we end as we begin ('Is it about a bicycle?' asks Sergeant Pluck).

I will not disclose who the third policeman is. I will say no more except that this book is frightening in its originality, and that only O'Brien could have written it. To say that it is a piece of mad Irishry is not enough: it is mad Irishry used for a profound and terrible end. Sergeant Pluck says: 'Michael Gilhaney is an example of a man that is nearly banjaxed from the principles of the Atomic Theory. Would it astonish you to hear that he is nearly half a bicycle?' First time round we grin condescendingly, as at a bit of fay whimsy. Second time round we know where we are.

It is consoling to know that Joyce read *At Swim-Two-Birds* – and thought highly of it. It's a pity that he never saw *The Third Policeman*, though it was written the year before he died. I think, even with *Ulysses* and *Finnegans Wake* behind him, he might have been envious. The world of the dead was his logical next step.

Observer, 3 September 1967
Review of *The Third Policeman* by Flann O'Brien
(London: MacGibbon and Kee, 1967)

Last Exit to Brooklyn

IT IS unfortunate that so many newcomers to *Last Exit to Brooklyn* will be approaching it in a muddle of expectation that, thanks to its long ordeal in the courts, has more to do with what has been said about the book than what the book itself says. It would be tedious to recapitulate the sad and shameful case in which two British Members of Parliament, motivated by the desire to protect the public from reality, arraigned *Last Exit* under the Obscene Publications Act and – on 10th December 1966, at Marlborough Street Magistrates' Court, London – had the satisfaction of hearing an order for the forfeiture and destruction of three copies of the book. Mr Leo Gradwell, the magistrate responsible, pronounced that *Last Exit*, 'taken as a whole, would tend to deprave and corrupt, and I cannot think, in spite of the evidence I have heard, that it can be justified by literary merit'. The evidence he refers to was provided by witnesses expert in aesthetics, sociology and pornography; despite their contention – and demonstration – that the book, far from being obscene, was a serious study of certain painful and shocking aspects of Western city life, the vague connotations of phrases like 'deprave and corrupt' prevailed. The gravamen of proof of the book's power to debauch its readers rested with the prosecution, but no such proof was provided; nor, apparently, was it needed: stock responses to highly charged shibboleths like 'filth' were enough.

One had thought that the days when men in responsible public positions could confuse tendentiousness with reason were long over. But let a Member of Parliament cry 'I am horrified that any one of my eight children may be exposed to this kind of filth', or a retired headmaster intone Shakespeareanly 'God preserve the boys and girls of England', and many people are satisfied that they are listening to a good knock-down argument. The fact that the Director of Public Prosecutions initially refused, though invited, to take action over *Last Exit* may convince its new readers that not all our public guardians are repressive or frivolous, although they did under pressure finally bring a Crown case. It is the frivolous mind that responds with pious horror to distasteful subject-matter and ignores the genuinely moral purpose for which the subject-matter is deployed. Look into the repressive mind and you will see fear or obsession or both. The mature and well-balanced mind is, when shocked at revelations of human depravity or social sickness, concerned with making that shock fire a reforming zeal or, at least, stoke compassion. Repression does not come into it; rather, the need is felt to extend sympathy by publicising the bad news, broadcasting the agony.

Hubert Selby Jr, whose first book this is, brought a mature, well-balanced and well-trained mind to the execution of a task that must often have revolted him. He felt it necessary to disclose, not in the disinfected generalities of a textbook but through the flesh-and-blood immediacies of literary art, the horrors of a sector of New York where civilisation seemed to have broken down. The corruption of the best is always the worst: the worst depravities can spring out of the most complex social organisation. Take primitive man and you find patterns of behaviour dictated by ecological need: the anthropologist can study them coolly. Take an urban society that has gone rotten and perhaps only the artist (or the saint) is big enough to embrace it: something more than science is needed for its comprehension. In that district of New York whose '*Lasciate ogni speranza...*' is the road sign which gives this book its title, a collocation of misfits, perverts and predators snarls in a symbiosis that makes Dante's hell seem paradisal. This society is not (which our amateur censors appear to think) Selby's tortuous invention. It actually exists, and Selby's presentation of it is undoubtedly the first step in the direction of remedying it.

To call *Last Exit to Brooklyn* a novel is not strictly accurate. It is a group of stories or fictional studies, some of which have long had independent American magazine publication, but there is a unity of intention as well as scene which makes the term 'novel' – implying a larger and more complex organisation than the mere story altogether applicable. Selby, like John Dos Passos before him, presents his small fictional entities; as we continue reading these appear as segments of a larger whole; the final impression is of a planned symphony (or cacophony) which is as validly a novel as, say, *The Big Money* or *Manhattan Transfer*. The style of the book must also suggest the rapportage technique of Dos Passos. Unkind critics may call this 'typewriter prose'. The fingers seem to pound the keys in a mad effort to record conversation and interior monologue white-hot:

the leisurely scratching of the pen might induce too much 'literary' shaping, with a consequent loss of immediacy. If we are aware of Selby's typewriter, we are also aware that his technique comes off: impatience with punctuation, a sudden block of uppercase letters (as though the shift-key had jammed), the logorrhea of over-rapid fingers – these are right for a literature of the machine age.

The direct, machine-like transcriptions of actuality which make up the book are one of the agents of shock. The youths in the first part of *Last Exit* – 'Another Day Another Dollar' – use the term 'shit' too often for readers (like Mr Leo Gradwell) brought up on traditional fiction, with its periphrases and author's monitoring. But American youths of a particular class do, in fact, over-use 'shit' ('Whassa time?' one youth on Third Avenue was heard to say to another. 'Four-thirty or some shit like that', was the answer.) The unedited presentation of the Brooklyn vernacular leads to an equally naked series of descriptions of variations on the sexual act – 'perversions' dignified by sexologists as *fellatio* and *anal coition*. The sad and ironic thing about the indictment of Selby's book as obscenity lies in the fact that true obscenity uses literary condiments to inflame the palate; Selby, committing himself from the very first page to an unedited recording, totally eschews the devices of titillation. Pornography is not made this way.

The literary value of the book, on the evidence of the careful choice of verbal technique and the exactness of the notation (both of speech and act), cannot be gainsaid. It requires considerable artistic skill to induce in the reader attitudes of compassion and disquiet through the immediate presentation of speech, thought and action.

The Dickensian tradition approves the frequent intervention of the author as moralist, nudging the reader, putting the required words in his mouth. Selby is working in a tradition nearly as venerable but far healthier – the naturalistic one, in which judgment is implied but never made the theme of a sermon. As a piece of twentieth-century naturalistic fiction, *Last Exit* exhibits artistic virtues of a very high order.

But in its choice of subject-matter the book goes further than any fiction one knows (I leave out of account sheer pornography, which is concerned not with reality but with fantasy). Violence, peripheral in most British novels, holds the centre here and has a hard light trained on it. It is an aspect of city life. we are forced to look at unflinching, but nowhere in the detailed descriptions is there a trace of that gratuitous elaboration which betrays fascinated gloating and invites it in the reader. The emotion you will feel is a kind of dispassionate classical anger: you do not wish to intervene, you wish to change the society in which this thing can happen. In the second section, 'The Queen is Dead', which portrays Georgette 'the hip queer', the emphasis is on sexual inversion, but a remarkable balance is maintained between clinical curiosity and disgust at human degradation: to be like Georgette is, after all, to participate in the human condition: he (or she) is not one of the insensate *things* of masturbatory fantasy. All Selby's characters are strongly individualised: they invite a response, and the response is normally one of compassion.

The story of 'Tralala' ends with a horrifying image which sums up not merely the depravity of these policeless streets of Brooklyn but the evil of the whole world: the statistics of the concentration camps cannot do as much to provoke shock and horror and fear in us as this picture of the multiple raping of the unconscious girl and the 'kids who... tore her clothes to small scraps put out a few cigarettes on her nipples pissed on her jerkedoff on her jammed a broomstick up her snatch then bored they left her lying amongst the broken bottles rusty cans and rubble of the lot'. Again, the typewriterese triumphs: the facts could not be more naked.

But Selby's concern is not only with the horrifying fusion of sexuality with violence that is part of the pattern of sick civilisations. 'Strike' is a far more poignant study of industrial unrest than anything in Dos Passos, and it presents, in the character of Harry, a brilliant (though depressing) picture of a later Zero than that of Elmer Rice's *The Adding Machine.* We look round at this great modern city, with its triumphs of technology, and wonder when it will achieve the ennoblement of man. We are a long way past Wellsian optimism.

It is through its concentration on one aspect only of contemporary man – man as violent, mindless, predatory, lustful, degraded; man as less than an animal – that *Last Exit to Brooklyn* fails to earn the accolades bestowed on other controversial (and proscribed) novels of this century. *Lady Chatterley's Lover* and *Ulysses* are more important works than *Last Exit* because they are less kinetic: they discharge their emotions inside the book itself, producing the catharsis of art; they do not leave the reader in a state of disquiet which can only be relieved by action. *Ulysses* exhibits enough of the dregs of human minds but grants a final image of man as redeemable; *Last Exit* presents man either as unregenerate or as capable of being cleansed through imposed social change. It fails to show man as aspirant; it selects one extreme segment of human society, and this selection is more appropriate to a piece of didactic pleading than to a static work of literature.

The value of art is always diminished by the presence of elements that move to action: the pornographic and the didactic are, in a purely aesthetic judgment, equally to be condemned. But the irony of the legal situation as regards *Last Exit* lies in the fact that its prosecutors, recognising that the book was kinetic, mistook the nature of the kinesis. *Last Exit* presents social horrors out of reformist zeal, not out of a desire to titillate or corrupt. Those who found the book capable of debauching its readers were evidently most debauchable and regrettably cut off from a desire to expand their charitable propensities. Those who now approach *Last Exit* with open minds will soon consider that there is plenty of reforming to do well east of Brooklyn, and our professional reformers must be the first to be reformed. How this honest and terrible book could ever be regarded as obscene (that is, designed for depravity and corruption) is one of the small mysteries of the decade.

Published as the introduction to the Calder & Boyars edition
of *Last Exit to Brooklyn*, 1968

A Good Read

OF THE hero of his novel, *One Fat Englishman*, a publisher and hence a man dedicated to the advancement of literature, Kingsley Amis says at one point: 'If there was one thing which Roger never felt like, it was a good read.' Any novelist can get away with anything, provided he sticks it in the mind or mouth of a character, but it requires courage for an English university don to say, as John Gross says in his recent book *The Rise and Fall of the Man of Letters*, that he 'can understand the point of view of the character,' meaning that there isn't, after all, an ungainsayable virtue in stocking your house with the best ever thought and said and sticking in every evening to drink it down.

A good read doesn't, I take it, mean a session with the current *Life* or *Playboy* or *Portnoy's Complaint* or *Goldfinger* or whatever Mr Mailer is going to write about the first men on the moon (although this, perhaps, already trembles on the verge of being a good read. Read on. This article incidentally is *not* a good read). A good read means something written in an age when there was nothing to do with your spare time except have a good read. It means *Middlemarch*, *The Virginians*, *Moby-Dick*, *Under Western Eyes*, Proust's monster, *The Golden Bowl*.

It also means anything produced in a later age (an age in which it was, is, possible to do something in your spare time except have a good read) which *pretends* that there is nothing to do with your spare time except have a good read. This means the overfacing water-ices of Sir Hugh Walpole, *Anthony Adverse*, *Giles Goat-Boy*, Arnold Bennett's *Old Wives' Tale*, *A Glastonbury Romance*. The archetypal good read is *War and Peace*.

Good reads are not much concerned with the watchmaker's art, Fabergé delicacy, the chiselling of sentences or week-long waiting for the *mot juste*. *Salammbô* is no more a good read than *The Waste Land*. The true good read is good for you: it has a lot of uplift. It also has a lot of highly visual cameos and scenic description. The uplift is a substitute for the cinema.

Whatever they say in literature classes, if the cinema, complete with Panavision and stereophonic sound, had been going strong in, say, 1837, there would have been no need for all those good reads which we have inherited from the age of gaslight and the family circle, when a good read followed a good feed. 'Where did I leave off last night, my dears?' – 'At where Mr Poddydodge is hauled up from the well and then goes off in a diligence.' – 'Ah, yes. Here we are. "Notwithstanding the indisputable and verifiable fact that our good friend Mr Septimus Augustus Poddydodge, master of arts and justice of the peace in the county of Suffolk, possessed, in addition to a very considerable unresilience of character, a quite remarkable endowment of avoirdupois, to which his recent prolonged bever had not insensibly made addition…"' – 'Hahaha, papa.'

We don't really want to go through all that again, any more than we want to rebuild Crystal Palace. Is it not better to sit in an air-conditioned cinema, seeing the polychrome titles come up on a very wide screen? Or look at the commercials on television – those subtle dissolves, that skilful animation – knowing that, all in colour too, at least five full-length features will be available to come between us and sleep, or, at about 4 A.M., merge with sleep to generate a new art-form? That we're no longer capable of a good read isn't really decadence; it's rather that those who were capable of nothing else were unlucky enough not to be in the position to be accused of decadence. Blacksmith's muscles were a fine thing when there was a need of blacksmiths. Nowadays they would be a load of useless luggage.

I will go some way with McLuhan, though not all the way. The electronic eye has made some literature supererogatory, but not all. It has rendered needless the kind of literature that has come into its own as film or the television serial. A lot of Dickens was trying to be cinema, but unfortunately cinema hadn't yet been invented. Having seen 24 instalments on BBC TV of *The Idiot*, *Martin Chuzzlewit* and *Portrait of a Lady*, and about 48 instalments of *The Forsyte Saga*, I feel absolved from taking the originals down from the shelf.

Madame Bovary, also serialised, is different. I like the plot and the characters, but I'm much too interested in the words to let the book be totally crushed up by the cameras. If it were proposed that *The Waste Land* be televised (it was made into a radio drama – BBC North Region, 1936), then *The Waste Land*, which is primarily words, would still have to be read. I dreamed a fortnight ago, in the throes of chicken pox, of a film of Ezra Pound's 'Hugh Selwyn Mauberley.' I said 'Nonsense!' in my sleep: I'd better add 'Nonsense!' awake too.

Because it's just about technically possible to make a film script for 'Mauberley' and leave out everything that Pound wrote.

One aspect of the book that is a good read is dilution, an easy-going jogtrot spurning of the condensed and the concentrated in favour of the repetitious, the periphrastic, the watering-to-taste with a faucet-filling of good old moral truths or appeals to good old sentiment. I espy an anomaly coming up: is not such reading appropriate to an age like ours, which likes its entertainment highly coloured and glamorous but is not too happy about verbal-cerebral engagement along the lines of *Finnegans Wake* or the poems of William Empson? And is not the alternative (Joyce and Eliot and Pound and so on) something that I (this present writer) wish to integrate into the electronic age merely because I like it? Is not this bookish man speaking, who would like a good read really but is too lazy to get down to it? Would not a man more honest and less verbally prejudiced admit that literature as a big popular force is done for, and that the future lies with a kind of hyper-McLuhanism, led by a man who has not, like ordinary living McLuhan, already read all the books there are and now feels like it's safe to sit down before the box, which used to be called the idiot's lantern? Reply, reply.

My answer is that books must go on being published, for the simple reason that there are people who want to write books. As the old good reads are now gutted to feed the visual media, I would suggest another kind of gutting, or reinterpretation, appropriate to the more literary literature. As publishers have readers, so readers might have readers too (on the analogy of the Vicar's Warden and the People's Warden in the Church of England). America has many universities and, as fewer and fewer classes are held in them, the calls of the armoury not giving time, so more and more of the faculty might get down to what there is already a certain amount of, though not quite enough – I mean criticism. The new books of *difficult* merit will be read, appraised, and be encountered by the successors of today's serious readers only in the form of critical studies. The critical work will be a substitute for the subject – more than substitute really, since it will contain the subject and more.

There are many of us who know certain authors only through Edmund Wilson's writing about them. He summarises them so well, analyzes them so penetratingly, and lists their qualities so clearly that to go to the original would somehow spoil things. The thrill we get from good criticism is incomparably greater than anything we could obtain from the work itself. 'In his later novels Mr Siblegeru becomes increasingly obsessed with the problem of securing maximal tension between form and subject. The first chapter (or the last, depending on which way the reader looks at it) of *Breaks From Thee Then a Billion* is a devotional sonnet sequence cunningly disguised as prose (the final sonnet, in the manner of Milton's 'Tetrachordon' piece, codas added to the sestet). Knowing Siblegeru's aims, we begin looking for a complicated incest motif, and we soon discover that we are witnessing a morning scene in Jack Bickerstaff's apartment, or rather bed, with his mother, sister and father engaged in certain characteristic *mudras*...' Having read that, it would be disappointing to go to the novel itself. I myself might, still being inclined to literature: but by the time the Criticism becomes the Thing Criticised we shall have wide-screen stereophonic television sets; and good literature, for all I care, can go the way of the good read.

New York Times, 15 June 1969

Bless Thee, Bottom?

MR CYRIL CONNOLLY has said that the most sympathetic review-ers are those who have themselves written books: they know the pain that goes into even the meanest production. The gougers and snappers of the Sundays are usually incapable of giving birth to even a sixty-thousand-word baby. In the field of translation a similar situation holds. British writers who try to make a living from their craft regard anything except the coarser pornography and political propaganda as within their province, and they will take on translation as a legitimate chore. Thus they know, if they are novelists who have been translated, the agonies that go on over the water. Like any other Grub Street man, I have done my share of translating: indeed, I translated before I published any original work of my own. My first big effort was a Malay version of *The Waste Land* – difficult to do, since, in the tropics, April is no more nor less cruel than any other month, and summer cannot surprise one if it is summer all the year round. Translation, as the anthropological linguists keep telling us, is not just a matter of words.

Given a language like French, however, which most Grub Street men used to know, it is mostly words, and the turning of a French novel into English is essentially a matter of Part One of the big Harrap, a little book called *Beyond the Dictionary in French*, and the marshalling of what elegance one can find in oneself. I have done three French novels for money, such as it was, and only one was worth doing – Servin's *Deo Gratias*, which became *The Man Who Robbed Poor Boxes* (though I wanted *Now Thank We All…*) and also a rather funny film. It was about a man who robbed poor boxes. Another novel, whose name I refuse to remember, was so indifferent in the original that I tried to transform as well as translate, and I gained a wry satisfaction from seeing my own felicities ascribed by reviewers to the original author and praised as the sort of thing that English novelists could not do. A lady in America considered this book so important that she sent at least twenty copies to her friends; she has not, I think, enough French for the revelation of the original.

I also translated Berlioz's *L'Enfance du Christ*, a very brilliant and moving oratorio, for a special BBC Two Christmas presentation. Berlioz was his own librettist, and not a bad one either, and my difficulties were rarely those usually found in translating libretti not by men like Da Ponte and Boito – trying to make banalities (which do not seem so banal in a Romance language) sound like reasonable, meaningful, and moderately euphonious English. The trouble with this task was the French feminine ending, which is set to the odd flick of a note in the vocal line, often at the beginning of a bar. Berlioz, setting the word *terre*, holds the *terr-* for a whole slow semibreve, and then bites off the *-e* with a staccato quaver which, with English, demands a stressed monosyllable. All this is extremely difficult. At present I am translating *Cyrano de Bergerac* for a new production, and if anyone can tell me how to render the very last word of the play – *panache* – I shall be more than grateful.

I know, then, all about the difficulties of translation, and I am disposed to be charitable to the men and women who, translating my own books and articles, do not always quite understand my meaning. Sometimes, indeed, they find a meaning where none is intended. In a novel called *The Doctor is Sick*, I have a character who yawns. Instead of saying 'He yawned', I make him utter these vocables: 'War, awe, warthog, Warsaw.' The words were literally rendered in one translation, as were my phoneticisings of a man sneezing in *The Wanting Seed*: 'Arch. How rash you are.' I am ready to forgive, since I know that I myself have been guilty of similar nonsense. I did not, for instance, know what a *passage à tabac* was in a novel about Algeria. I thought it was a place for selling black market cigarettes, or something, but that did not seem to tie up with violence. At the page-proof stage I grew scared and decided to render *passage à tabac* as *passage à tabac* – the sort of expression that any decent well-travelled reader would know as well as *coq au vin*.

I am not well able to judge translations of my work into Japanese or the Scandinavian languages, but I get on well enough with German and the daughters of Latin. In French I seem to become French – so much so that a French version of *Tremor of Intent* was impounded by the Maltese postal authorities, French being *ipso facto* a questionable language. The title was *Un Agent qui vous veut du bien*. A week or so after this impounding, the same book was sent to Malta in Danish. The title – *Martyrenes Blod* – ensured that it was whizzed through to me almost with an archiepiscopal blessing. When I eventually, in

Montreal, managed to get hold of *Un Agent qui vous veut du bien* (the shop-girl said: 'Burgess? Un auteur pas trop lu'), I found that the translator, Michel Deutsch, had done far better in his translation than I had done in the original, especially in passages concerned with love and eating. Compare the following:

> ... he saw the girl. At once, with a kind of groan of habituation, his body made its stock responses – tightening of the larynx, minimal pain in the frenum, a shuddering re-stoking of the arteries, a sense of slight levitation. She was beautiful: corn-hair piled up carelessly, a nose like an idealisation of a broken boxer's, a mouth whose scolding ought at once to be stopped with kisses. She was in a straight gold dress, deep cut; legs, arms, neck were bare, honeyed, superb.

> ... *il vit la jeune. Aussitôt, avec une espèce de plainte née de l'accoutumance, son corps eut la réaction globale habituelle: constriction du larynx, infime lancinement au niveau du filet de la langue, frémissement des artères qui s'engorgment, impression de planer légèrement au-dessus du sol. Une beauté: des cheveux couleur de blé négligemment ramenés en chignon, un nez qui était l'idéalisation d'un nez cassé de boxeur, une bouche dont la moue méritait d'être sur-le-champ effacé sous les baisers. Elle portait une robe droite en tissu doré, généreusement échancrée. Des jambs, des bras, un cou aux tons de miel – une créature superbe.*

The French is a good deal longer, of course, but the girl is a good deal more desirable and elegant. Here, perhaps, there is little to choose between the original and the translation:

> Hillier and Theodorescu ordered ahead alternately. Hillier: fillets of sole Queen Elizabeth, with sauce blonde; Theodorescu: shell-fish tart with sauce Newburg; Hillier: soufflé au foie gras and to be generous with the Madeira; Theodorescu: avocado halves with caviar and a cold chiffon sauce.

> *Chacun à son tour, les deux commensaux passèrant commande d'un plat. Hillier: filets de sole reine Elisabeth sauce blonde; Theodorescu: croustade de fruits de mer sauce Newburg; Hillier: soufflé au foie gras – et qu'on soit généreux avec le Madère; Theodorescu: avocats au caviar sauce mousseline.*

But somehow the French sounds more civilised and plausible, less like a dream of gourmandising, than my original.

On being sent a translation of one of his books, any author will look at once to see how the untranslatable has been dealt with. The untranslatable is often a pun, and a mere explanatory footnote seems a feeble way out of the difficulty. The novel I have just finished is a mass of wordplay and riddles, and it will, in translation, be either half footnotes or the translator's basic re-working, in his own tongue, of the whole linguistic fantasy. Translators are frequently not bold or free enough: they behave as though they are sitting an examination. The untranslatable is also sometimes, as with the book of mine the Germans, if they read it, call *Der Doktor ist Übergeschnappt*, a comic take-off of the very language the book is being done into.

I have a German character called Renate, who uses German word-order when speaking English. She says, for instance (I have to quote from memory): 'At the corner is a little shop where man can swineflesh and calf and ox with Sauerkraut and pumpernickel get.' In German (rather cunningly) this has become: '*Um die Ecke ist eine kleine Laden, dort man kann bekommen SchweineFleisch und Kalb und Ochsen mit Sauerkohl und Schwarzen Brot*', which sounds less like German than an English person trying to speak German. In the same book, the hero's attempt to give a lecture on Cockney rhyming-slang gets over the difficulty of a German rendering by refusing to face it:

> '*Arse – arsch,*' *sagte Edwin laut,* '*gibt ein gutes Beispiel dafür. Arse wird im Reimslang zu 'bottle and glass'. Bottle wird seinerseits mit 'Aristotle' gereimt. Dieses Wort wird gekürzt, so dass das Ersatzwort für 'arse' dann 'Aris' heist, sich also vom Grundwort kaum unterschei- det…*'.

This character, by the way, is facetiously introduced before his lecture as 'Dr Livingstone I Presume'. This is so much part of British mythology that the German cannot cope at all: '*Dr Livingstone I zu begrüssen, in unserer Mitte zu begrüssen.*' But who am I to complain?

Eight years ago I published a short novel called *A Clockwork Orange* – a title, by the way, which comes from old Cockney ('he's as queer as a clockwork orange') and is not, as some have thought, my own surrealist coinage. This book has run into great translation difficulties, whereas linguistically the concept is quite simple: I have created a futuristic teenage slang our of Russian elements, and these elements are easily carried over into another host-language (*peet*, to drink, becomes *piter* or *pitare* or *pieten*, and *horrorshow*, good, becomes *horocho* or *oroscio* or *choroschoh*).

The only translation so far published – though a fair number have actually been made – is the Italian one – *Un Arancia a Orologeria* – and its main fault seems to be an excess of local realism: the whole thing sounds like a story about Milanese thugs, inevitably when a kind of modified Milanese slang is used instead of a futuristic linguistic creation, and the fabular point seems somehow to be missed. Since Stanley Kubrick is at present filming the book – another kind of translation – foreign publishers who previously shied at it are trying once again. I have a feeling that the Japanese, whose language is only too ready to embrace Western loanwords, adapting them to the native phonetic patterns without fuss, are likely to do best with it. The Russians, of course, would have no difficulty at all: they would merely have to replace my Slavonic loanwords with English ones. Thus, 'bolshy great yarblockos' could become '*greti bolshoiy appli*' and 'a tolchock in the kishkas' could be something like '*push v belye*'. But official Russia notices my work only to condemn it: they had the nerve to sneer at my interpretation of Shakespeare's character in *Nothing Like The Sun* on Moscow Radio. On the other hand, a furtive message has informed me that I have a small underground readership in the Soviet Union, and that pleases me more while paying me no less.

I am married to an Italian translator – translatrix, rather – whose problems in getting English cis- or transatlantic, into Italian excite my professional sympathy, though they can elicit little help. She and I hope to pool our literary and linguistic resources in order to attempt a translation of *Finnegans Wake*. Our preliminary work on this is already showing, as it was bound to, that the resultant book – if it ever appears – will be less a translation than a sort of free Italian fantasy on Joyce's themes. The working title is *pHorbiCEtta*, which means 'earwig'. The sacred initials HCE have been working in there, but the initial *f* had to be hellenised first. *Orbi* is also present, and will do for Earwicker's universality as well as his prisoner-of-the-vatican postures. But the translation is bound to move away more and more from the Liffey to the Tiber, and Joyce will end as truly Giacomo. The book will be a ghost of what Joyce might have written had he conceived *Finnegans Wake* in Italian.

There are, in this venture, lessons for me as one of the translated. The development of a novelist like myself has to lie in a greater concentration on the resources of my own language and, as I move on, I have to resign myself to being progressively more difficult to translate. Rendering into another language, if undertaken at all, will be transformation rather than translation – Bourgeois or Borghese rather than Burgess. This is in order, if anybody wants it, but it has nothing to do with my own aims. Evelyn Waugh was always presenting translatability as a test of good writing, but such a test would only be valid for the plainest prose. All literature, including the novel, moves in the direction of poetry, and it is always the most poetic poetry – Hopkins, Mallarmé, Rilke – that is the hardest to translate. Campbell, Leigh Hunt and Yevtushenko are easy to do, but hardly worth doing. Writers are not only guardians of the language in the sense of watchdogs; they also gladly open the door to visitors. Dr Johnson, a Grub Street man who was always right, said that we learn Latin in order to read Virgil. I would rather be one of those writers for whom foreigners learn English than a producer of easily translatable plastic. Mickey Spillane is undoubtedly read, completely rendered by Gastvicz Grontjwarlt, in Upper Slobbovia.

Times Literary Supplement, 18 September 1970

Like Mr Priestley, Enjoying It

YOU ARE writing a novel. In this novel your hero and heroine are enjoying a drink or a quarrel or an amatory session, or any two or all three of these, and a man comes to the door with a telegram. What do you do about this man? Do you write: 'Alfred went to the door and found a man waiting with a telegram. He took the telegram, closed the door and tore the missive open. "Good God," he said. "What is it, dear?" she called from the bathroom.' If you do, you may, re-reading the passage in print, become worried about that man – so faceless, so anonymous, what an undemocratic approach to a useful and hardworking human being. But then, unable to make amends, you may reflect that the telegram-bearer has no other function in your fiction than to bear one telegram, so why waste words on him, giving him a face, a set of physical gestures, a minimally revealed treasury of idiosyncrasies? Economy is the thing. 'The maid brought in the tea' is surely enough? Calverley, apostrophising tobacco, achieves the literary limit in impersonality when he says 'Sweet when they've cleared away/Lunch'. Why confuse the issue – which is the sweetness of tobacco – by bringing in faces, skirts, limps, warts, even gender and number?

But some imaginative writers will not have this – Dickens, for instance, and J. B. Priestley. 'At the door was a man with a telegram. His face, perhaps under the influence of his presumed specialisation, was pared to essentials – eyebrows, like commas, were not there; the mouth was a mere pencilled O; but the eyes seemed to reflect the perturbation of a thousand past telegram-receivers.' Something like that, only, of course, better. You never meet the man again, and he has been presented as a mere grotesque conceit, but you feel that the author *cares*: if there were opportunity, he would tell you more about this man. Dickens, one knows, would be very ready to describe his last Tuesday's breakfast.

Of modern novelists, I prize this caring quality in Mr Priestley more than anyone. I have been re-reading his two-volume *The Image*

Men, which is full of toothsome thumbnail cameos (sorry: that, in this context, sounds like a *Good Companions* minor character picking his teeth in the cinema: the film is silent, so you can hear the noise) – like the kickshawses that strewed the table at the Elizabethan banquet. 'Beryl was a girl in her early twenties with not much of a nose, a loose mouth, a receding chin, all suggesting, together with her conversation, a kind of young female village idiot; and yet, so strangely are we put together, she had large and really quite beautiful eyes, burnt sienna flecked with copper. Tuby always felt she must have borrowed them from somebody.' Beryl is only, if that modifier be permissible, a receptionist-typist, with no part in the plot, but she has at least been noticed and she doesn't have to be noticed again. The following fixes a transient character called Rolf Tenzie (though he may be said to be fixed already – very Dickensian – in his name): 'his voice, rather high but resonant, seemed to Elfreda to come out of a sort of blur, rather as if a clever middle-aged actor were playing a charming young man in a colour film not quite in focus.' A waiter 'had black side-whiskers and might have been a Sicilian except that he spoke with a Scots accent.' Brigadier Rampside of the Ministry of Defence 'was a man about fifty, pink and spruce but with rather angry bloodshot eyes, as if he were furious with himself for drinking too much at lunchtime.' And so, always entertainingly, on.

It is possible to imagine a novelist in the Dickensian tradition keeping a notebook to record little descriptive ideas, long before the novel is written: 'straggly bear – face like a page with too little text and too much footnote?... nose like cuttlefish bone stuck in a budgerigar's cage... five strips of hair like stave-lines, frown like a treble clef... might have been an acceptable face if it were upside down...' I don't think Mr Priestley does that, but if he did – well, Brahms kept a notebook full of suitable sonata-form second subjects. It's not only a question of characters, of course, but of anything that can go into a *récit* (I don't think any novelist makes preparatory notes for dialogue): 'The aircraft left a long jet-line in the clear sky; the semibreve sun rose a semitone to meet it... a blackbird's song stuck a pin in the great silence... he came towards them, sadly prescient of his social unacceptability, ringing the ice in his glass like a leper's bell (Graham Greene?)... a sandy path stitched with grass.' This business of descriptive passages beloved of that special half-page in the *Reader's Digest* but primarily waiting for a novel to be put in is, I should think, not uncommon.

In this same *The Image Men*, Mr Priestley has a major female character who looks like the Duke of Wellington. This, I feel sure, is so
that she may beget humorous images like 'And she laid a hand on
Tuby's shoulder that made him feel he was about to be press-ganged
into the Peninsular War.' In other words, I don't think that this
female character swam into Mr Priestley's ken already armed with
a Wellington nose. If you impose on your faceless character certain
historical lineaments then you have a limitless account to draw on, so
long as the comic disbursements are small and infrequent. Thus, you
give a landlady a very unremarkable face with (cf. Beryl supra) the
eyes of Napoleon Bonaparte. She will then be able to look on your
hero, her lodger, like a badly cooked helping of chicken Marengo,
like Barras disclosed as a royalist, or with the patience appropriate to
a long-winded report from stuttering Berthier, or as on a wet afternoon on St Helena. I think, on the whole, that creating a character,
especially a minor picturesque one, is a matter of arbitrary manufac-
ture: there's rarely any question of the novelist painting what he sees
before him and trying to get the details right.

And, to go further, I think that descriptions in works of fiction
are, so to speak, parallel to the real substance: they're a decorative way
of saying: 'these things and statements and events really exist; they
take up positions in space-time, and to prove it I'll hang draperies
on them – see how the contours press through that piece of jazz-
patterned calico.' But if there are no descriptions, this rarely seems to
invalidate the reality, so eager is the reader to *believe*. Pretty women
merely need to be pretty (the colour of eyes and hair is an acceptable
gratuity but no more). 'He was a handsome greying man in a smart
suit, about forty-five' – that will do even for a major character. How
many people can describe Emma Bovary? In *Ulysses*, does Stephen
Dedalus wear spectacles? Food and drink are, since they touch nerves
more sensitive than the optic ones, more important than the pattern
of wallpaper or the hero's best suit, and it is generally agreed that only
second-rate novelists write passages like 'He went into a pub and got
stinking drunk' or 'After a hearty breakfast we resumed our journey.'
Paradoxically Dickens can get away with this kind of ellipsis occasionally, since we know exactly what he means by a hearty breakfast.

In my last published novel, aware that it was necessary to describe
the lobby of a small hotel but having no real idea what that lobby looked
like, I took a page of Wilkinson's Malay-English dictionary (one of
the great works of lexicography, incidentally) and filled the space with

objects described on it. I began the descriptive passage with a girl on
the telephone asking for a number which was the number of that page
and, to provide a further key for anyone interested, specifying the
subscriber – Mr R. J. Wilkinson. I have, on Creative Writing courses
in America, stressed this aleatory value of the dictionary to the fagged
student faced with a chunk of *récit*-making. Page 929 of the *American
Heritage Dictionary* gives you, among other items, *ortolan*, *Orvieto*,
Orwell, *oscillogram*, *osculum* and *Osiris*. You can surely draw the fur-
nishings of a living-room out of these (cushions with the texture of an
ortolan's wings, one's bottom making an osculatory smacking noise
as it disengages from a plastic chair, a new pot of Osiris face cream)
with, for good measure, *Down and Out in Paris and London* playing at
the Osculatorium down the street.

It seems to be dialogue – exterior and interior, when it becomes
monologue, the characterisation achieved through the temporal
flow of speech while empty-stomached space has any kind of scrap
thrown at it – an air-luggage tag with KIN on it (airport code for
Kingston, Jamaica), the prospectus of a kindergarten, a liqueur called
Kindlepoint, a stuffed kingbird, a sleeping King Charles spaniel, a
torn kimono. "'*Sein oder nicht sein*," spat out Hamlet to the damp
corridor outside the palace library. He looked again, grinning wryly,
at the volume of Schelling in his hand. No help there. "*Ja, dass ist
die Frage*." Nobler in the mind to suffer – A toad hopped into the
shadows, uttering one bass note. The slings and arrows of outrageous
fortune? Or to take arms against a sea of troubles. Not, of course,
that you could take arms. The wind blew in keenly from the open
window, a dank wind from the black sea. Troubles, what troubles?
Oh, toothache, the sudden migraine in the night, the melting mouths
and stern eyes of the place-seekers, the mess of endless lawsuits, the
girl whose wagging bottom was both a taunt and a dismissal. You
could, he thought, turn *Hamlet* into a seven-hundred-page novel, no
sea of troubles in that task.'

Having made Mr Priestley's *The Image Men* a starting-point, it
would be only decent to return to it and say what pleasure it has given
me on a couple of headachy days in rainy Rome, far from London
pubs, steak and kidney pie, Cheddar cheese and wrapped bread (not
to mention BBC Two and the sound of London English). When we
talk of the novel's being a solace, we rarely, if we are honest, think
of the novels that the textbooks admire – Robbe-Grillet's *Jealousy*
and Nathalie Sarraute's *Planetarium* and Christine Brooke-Rose's

Out. It's not experimentation we ask for (leave that to the novelist's laboratory) but we don't demand a clear-cut plot either. We want the easy flow of picaresque, meals in inns, people getting into bed with each other (not too explicitly described, since we all have a fair idea what it's like), cabbage that seems to have been prepared by a deep-sea-diver, a woman coming to the door who looks as though she has spent the night in the dustbin, a man who turns his esses into sh ('There'zh shome new shizhzhorzh on the shideboard,' he said). My small son recently, seeing me all knotted up at the typewriter, asked me why I didn't write *for fun?* He's right, of course – a nice flow of dialogue carrying the weight of the story, and doing what the hell you like when the characters aren't actually speaking. Like Mr Priestley, enjoying it.

Previously untitled, unpublished, and undated

The Waste Land

WHEN I was a schoolboy in Manchester, England, I had contemporary literature forced on me not by a sponsor but by a detractor. This
was James Douglas, editor of the *Sunday Express*, who said, I seem to
remember, that he would rather slit his children's throats than have
them read *The Well of Loneliness*. One Sunday he devoted a two-page
spread to an attack of the most slavering savagery on Aldous Huxley:
the great banner headline was THE MAN WHO HATES GOD. The *Daily
Express* into which Douglas's Sabbatarian fury would sometimes spill
over, though somewhat diluted, once organised a poetry competition
for the young. Douglas was ready with good advice under an archetypal portrait of THE POET – an exophthalmic goitrous quill-chewer,
evidently both syphilitic and phthisical. He told young aspirants to
follow masters like Leigh Hunt and Longfellow, who knew how to
rhyme, and to avoid charlatans like Pound and Eliot.

Pound, he said, could not rise above lines like 'Sing goddam damn
damn,' while Eliot, who had written an illiterate gallimaufry called
The Waste Land, went in for such doggerel as 'O the moon shone
bright on Mrs. Porter and on her daughter.' Naturally I was intrigued,
and I borrowed *The Waste Land* from the public library.

I was only fifteen, and I understood very little of the poem, but
I recognised that it was important. I seemed to hear a door, a long
way down one of my mind's corridors, trying to creak open but not
quite making it. But I took in with relish the horns and motors and
the throbbing taxi, the fishing by the dull canal, the carbuncular small
house agent's clerk. I knew this world, since I was the son of a Manchester shopkeeper, whereas I was vague on skylarks. I had even seen
a Bradford millionaire, though not in a silk hat.

I copied the whole poem out, without the notes which I could see
even then were a bit of a put-on. Then I got down to learning it by
heart. This result was that, at fifteen, I could quote Dante and Baudelaire in the original, as well as a few objurgations from the *Upanishads*.
The Waste Land was, and still is, quite apart from its poetic merits,

a kind of big railway terminus, from which you can take a train to various literatures and theologies. In the refreshment room you see Mr Eliot himself, taking tea and refusing a slice of peach tart. He is not going anywhere; he has arrived.

By the time I got to Manchester University, I understood *The Waste Land* pretty well. Without boasting, I can say that I knew the poem better than any of my English lecturers: they did not have it by heart, and I did. In my first year I organised a sort of arty reading of it, with the lines split up among characters called the Hyacinth Girl, the Drowned Phoenician Sailor, Tiresias, Belladonna, and so on. The music was a mixture of ragtime, Wagner, and plain chant, and I myself composed a setting of the Thames Daughters' song, made out of Wagner's own *weilala* wailing in *Das Rheingold*. To accompany the opening 'April is the cruellest month,' I wanted that marvellous chill bassoon solo at the beginning of Stravinsky's *Le Sacre du Printemps*, but I was howled down and we had to have a young music student playing Delius on the piano. Recently, I discovered that Eliot had had that very Stravinsky bassoon in his ears while composing his opening lines. I wish he'd announced that fact in some publication or other in 1937, the year of my production. I hate being right too late.

1937 was fifteen years after the first appearance of *The Waste Land* – a long time by the reckoning of a student. Still, the poem did not seem to belong to an ancient epoch, as the early Chaplin films did, as well as the old ragtime records we swing-followers despised. Eliot was still in early middle age and producing new things – the plays, the first of the *Four Quartets*. The *Collected Poems* had come out a mere year before. James Joyce, whose *Ulysses* had also first seen the light as a bound banned book in 1922, was working on his new unintelligible opus, which I remember my history lecturer, A.J.P. Taylor, sneering at in a lecture. Eliot and Joyce were very much *now* writers, and *The Waste Land* was avant-garde enough to set many of the older professors puffing – quite apart from philistines like James Douglas (who was that year, I think, howling away at obscenity in somebody as teashop-dainty as Mary Webb). And it seems to me now that *The Waste Land* is as fresh and surprising as it was in my youth.

Look at it as a film scenario, which in many ways it resembles, and you can see that it goes much farther – with its jump cuts and flashes backward and forward and montages and intense economy – than anything by Truffaut or Godard or Fellini or Antonioni. We open in April, with a poet in the middle of the road of life seeing, in a mixture of fear and regret and elation, the lilacs pushing out of the earth. How much better it was in winter, when the snow muffled everything, and there was no need to engage the forces of life. The poet is a man we have met before – in Eliot's own 'The Love Song of J. Alfred Prufrock' – but he is less of the clown now and more of a Prince Hamlet. He is inhibited, scared of sex; the spring is an assault on his drab Bostonian security.

The scene changes from spring to summer – a remembered summer in Munich, on the Starnbergersee, when a sudden shower of rain sent the poet and his companion scurrying for shelter. April, sex, rain, water – all are to be feared. Water means fertility, revivification of what prefers to be waste and dry. And now the companion talks, evidently a woman: '*Bin gar keine Russin, stamm aus Litauen, echt deutsch.*' She is, she says, not a Russian; she comes from Lithuania, she is entirely German. She is one of the bastard products of a dry, cracked, decaying Europe. She too is frightened. She remembers a particular fear she felt while staying with the archduke, her cousin, when he took her out on a sled – the descent from the safe high sterility of the mountains, where 'you feel free', to those depths at water level where fecund dirty life is carried on. Her life? She reads much of the night, and goes south in the winter. She will appear again in the poem – a beautiful but sterile woman, waiting for death, the Lady of the Rocks.

And now the poet hears the voice of a preacher, echoing Ecclesiastes: 'What are the roots that clutch, what branches grow out of this stony rubbish?' Dried-up Europe, a world that has survived a great war but does not now wish to live, knows only 'a heap of broken images, where the sun beats'. There is not water, but there is shadow. If the listener will step for a while into this shadow – not the shadow of a tree but of a red rock – he will see a whole procession of human life: 'fear in a handful of dust.'

That image of drought is at once replaced by a memory of water – but water in pretence, make-believe. We are at the opera, and *Tristan und Isolde* is being performed. High on a ship's mast a sailor sings: 'The wind blows us briskly homeward. Where are you wandering, my Irish child?' The story of a great sterile love affair is beginning, one that can end only in death. And yet such hopeless empty passions are magnificent, to be feared by Prufrock as much as the childish sexual encounter among the spring-wet flowers. Nothing is simple, everything is equivocal. The poet remembers a failure of early love, with a girl they called 'the hyacinth girl' – hyacinths are symbols of fertility – 'when we came back, late, from the Hyacinth garden, your arms full, and your hair wet, I could not speak, and my eyes failed'. We have now rushed to the end of the opera, when love is to be fulfilled in death. '*Od' und leer das Meer*' – the sea is not life-giving but bitter and empty.

We now have to meet Madame Sostrosis, famous clairvoyante. An age that has rejected fertility has naturally rejected religion, which has its roots in ancient vegetation magic, and has to make do with such feeble substitutes as cartomancy. Madame Sosostris (her name seems to come from Flaubert's *Temptation of Saint Anthony*) tells fortunes with the old tarot pack. This, with its strange pictures of the Hanged Man and the Day of Judgment and the Tower Struck by Lightning, is of very venerable origin, being tied up with the Grail legend and the myths of death and purification and rebirth that underlie it. Now the cards have been debased to serve a superstitious end, a forbidden prying into the future. Madame Sosostris is herself a debased seer – she has a bad cold and cannot speak very clearly – but she sees certain truths: the crowd of people walking around in a ring, making their own hell; the beautiful woman who is reduced to ruling over barren rocks and managing empty social situations. She does not find the Hanged Man among the cards she deals, for the Hanged Man is Christ or the sacrificed seer-king who will restore water to the parched land. She is very direct in telling her client to 'fear death by water.'

Then we see another kind of hell – not people walking around in a ring, but a crowd flowing over London Bridge, 'so many, I had not thought death had undone so many.' The words come from Dante, and describe the damned. This is the world that Eliot had just left in order to write *The Waste Land*, a decayed world, once magnificent, full of warehouses and money counting: Eliot had been an employee of Lloyd's Bank. The Thames, once bright and thronged with life, is now so much dirty water; the bell of Saint Mary Woolnoth, a Wren church, speaks of a past magnificence but its final stroke ends with a 'dead sound'.

The poet sees one he knew – as Dante so often does in his journey through hell – and hails him. His name is Stetson, a name that sounds dull and ordinary and seems to ask that things stay as they are ('stet'), without hope, without redemption. The poet reminds him of the corpse Stetson planted in his garden and, almost hysterically, tells him to keep dogs away – symbols of busy animality, dream-token of sex – lest they dig it up. Resurrection is not wanted. Then the poet turns, in the words of Baudelaire, to the reader himself: 'hypocrite lecteur! – mon semblable, – mon frère!' The reader is Stetson, we are all guilty.

We are able, in the next part of the poem, to linger for a time in a fixed and static locale, with the camera slowly drinking in the details. We are with a new allomorph of the Lady of the Rocks, the beautiful woman dying slowly in magnificent aridity. Here she is surrounded by luxury sumptuously rendered, by all the glories of a past conspicuously not arid, and her very chair is described as if it were Cleopatra's barge (yet does not that recall another passion that ended in death?). In her boudoir is a representation of the rape of Philomela, but the tragic song of her sister, changed into a nightingale, is reduced to a vulgar throating: '"Jug Jug" to dirty ears.' Her cosmetics and perfumes are synthetic, rejecting the natural juices of life. She is conducting a love affair that has become as routine as 'the hot water at ten. And if it rains, a closed car at four.' Her nerves are shot to pieces; her lover reminds her that they are both 'in rat's alley where the dead men lost their bones.' They are awaiting the knock on the door that is death's summons.

A door opens on to another scene – this time far from sumptuous. In a London pub, just before closing time, a woman is telling a friend about a more basic rejection of life – that of a third woman, not present, who refuses to have babies and has made a wreck of herself with abortive medicines. Her husband, Albert, is coming back from the war, a sort of phallic hero who 'wants a good time', but he will find a wife whose teeth are rotten and whose sexual urges have decayed. Here is the Lady of the Rocks again, but now no Belladonna. The landlord shouts HURRY UP PLEASE ITS TIME, and we are aware that life is running out for all of us. The customers say good night to each other, and then an alien voice intrudes: 'Good night, ladies, good night, sweet ladies'. It is Ophelia, and these are the last words she speaks before going off to a watery grave. She at least died by water.

The next section of the poem introduces us to the Fisher King, Amfortas, with the unhealable wound, wandering the shores of the Thames, the dirty water that was once pure poetic silver, hailed by Spenser – 'Sweet Thames, run softly till I end my song' – in a poem he wrote to celebrate a Christian marriage. The sodality of the pubs mocks the magnificent Wren churches. The suffering of the observer, who drinks the London squalor as a self-inflicted penance, is intensified by his changing into Tiresias, the seer who was both man and woman and who is now doomed to feel the agony proper to both the sexes, set as they are in a loveless sterile hell. Tiresias watches the mean seduction of a typist by a carbuncular clerk. The language is full of the rhythms of a more heroic age; the typist's reflections on her 'departed lover' are followed by a parody of a song from Goldsmith's *The Vicar of Wakefield*:

> When a lovely woman stoops to folly and
> Paces about her room again, alone,
> She smooths her hair with automatic hand,
> And puts a record on the gramophone.

This ironic confrontation of graceless present with gracious past (though the dichotomy is never as simple as that) reaches its limit in the song of the three Thames Daughters, who, having watched Elizabeth and Leicester in a gilded barge, turn into true denizens of a degraded shore, tracing the river from Richmond and Kew, past Moorgate, to Margate Sands, recounting a table of debased and hopeless lives:

> The broken finger-nails of dirty hands.
> My people humble who expect
> Nothing.

At the end of this section, which though set around water is called 'The Fire Sermon', we catch the very faint sounds of voices from another world. Saint Augustine turns London into Carthage – 'where a cauldron of unholy loves sang all about mine ears' – and we remember that all cities fall. London has already been termed an 'unreal city'. An echo of Buddha – 'burning burning burning burning' – suggests that our aridity must be made positive, must become an aspect of fire and not a mere absence of water. We are to see this hell as a sort of purgatory.

In a brief section called 'Death by Water', Eliot translates, from the French, one of his own earlier poems. Phlebas the Phoenician is drowned, having forgotten the 'profit and loss' of the commerce that carried him over the seas. Earlier, another Levantine – 'Mr. Eugenides, the Smyrna merchant' – appeared in London, 'unshaven, with a pocket full of currants', a debased representative of an Eastern wave that once brought more than mere goods to the West. Trade, we now see, is a substitute for free giving. Mr Eugenides pays a prostitute (acted by Tiresias) for 'a weekend at the Metropole': Madame Sosostris takes her fee; London is all buying and selling; even the Wren churches are monuments to trade. Phlebas, who may have sold currants – dried-up grapes, incapable of yielding wine – is now finding that 'a current under sea picked his bones in whispers.'

The final section – 'What the Thunder Said' – is a nightmare that ends with a full statement of the hope prefigured at the end of 'The Fire Sermon'. We seem to witness Christ's crucifixion, then suffer, on a kind of road to Emmaus, the sense, unconfirmed by counting, that another person, 'gliding wrapt in a brown mantle, hooded', is with us. We long desperately for water, for even the sound of water, for even the water-dripping song of the hermit thrush, but we are forced to trudge a cracked dry road in endless thirst. Cities, all unreal, collapse and re-form in the violet air; the bells of London clang from towers that are upside down. Then a cock crows. It is the noise of rebirth, but also the noise of betrayal. But Christ's betrayer was a rock – now dry – on which a faith was built. It is not, however, to Christ or His Church that we turn, but farther east. We hear the thunder, harbinger of rain, and learn to interpret its 'DA'. The Buddha shows us that the thunder is trying to say 'Datta, Dayadhvam, Damyata' – 'Give, sympathise, control' – and the poet at once refers these injunctions to that personal 'Bostonian' level at which love cannot escape from its prison of reserve, where nerve fails and opportunities are lost forever.

> The awful daring of a moment's surrender
> Which an age of prudence can never retract
> By this, and this only, we have existed
> Which is not to be found in our obituaries
> Or in memories draped by the beneficent spider
> Or under seals broken by the lean solicitor
> In our empty rooms

The poem ends with a mass of quotations – Dante, Thomas Kyd, the *Pervigilium Veneris*, nursery rhyme – but does not attempt to sharpen a moral, turning a highly complex structure into a simple homily. 'Shall I at least set my lands in order?' asks the Fisher King. Arnaut Daniel leaps into the 'refining fire'. London Bridge is 'falling down falling down falling down', but is the prospect of ruin – against which 'these fragments' or scraps of knowledge are to be shored – to be taken seri-ously? The last word, thrice repeated is 'Shantih', the formal ending to an Upanishad, carrying the force of a dismissive blessing and best translated as 'the peace which passeth understanding'. *The Waste Land* has didactic elements, like all Eliot's work, especially the later, overtly Anglo-Catholic, writings, but it is not itself a sermon. It is a dramatic poem with many voices, and it would be as unwise to fasten any of its many moral statements on the author himself as it would be to identify Hamlet or Othello or Macbeth with William Shakespeare.

To summarise the poem – as I have briefly and, inevitably, inaccu-rately tried to do here – is to demonstrate that, like a play or a novel, it has a structure separable from language: there is a solidity that conveys the feeling of a three-dimensional artefact. But it is the language, of course, that finally counts. What first struck all the readers of my gen-eration was the way in which avant-garde daring was combined with classic authority. It was something to be recognised also in Joyce's *Ulysses*. The new seemed to be made out of the traditional and these two innovators disclosed a far profounder awareness of the impor-tance of tradition than many of the old guard, its guardians. Eliot's free verse was a very personal development of Jacobean blank verse – sauced a little with Laforgue – and its authority was such as to make Webster, Tourneur, and Middleton sound like very modern authors.

At the same time, Eliot did not shrink from filling his verse with most untraditional properties, at the risk of the accusation of ugliness or even the odd snicker in the wrong place. 'While I was fishing in the dull canal on a winter evening round behind the gashouse' – if this suggests the comic lugubrious, then Eliot's complex seriousness is well able to accommodate it. It is, in fact, able to accommodate most things, from the pills that Lil took 'to bring it off' to 'the agony in stony places' and the 'reverberation of thunder of spring over distant mountains'. English poetry had not known such a breadth of tone since Andrew Marvell. Robert Browning had tried to write poetry in which corns and bunions and tobacco went along with more traditional properties, but he failed in two ways: he never managed to absorb the contemporary speech rhythms in which trivialities are mentioned, and he never elevated trivialities to seriousness.

Eliot could take a ragtime song or a snatch of soldier's obscenity and fit it into a context of tragedy. 'O O O O that Shakespeherian Rag' seems to sum up whole eras of decay when we hear it in the boudoir of that lady dying of boredom. 'O the moon shone bright on Mrs. Porter and on her daughter, they wash their feet in soda water' ('Not White Rock,' Eliot said once); this is followed by a reference to the sacramental washing of the feet in the Parsifal legend, while the boy choristers sing: '*Et O ces voix d'enfants, chantant dans la coupole!*' It is Eliot's own juxtapository device for showing fragments of a decayed culture, but at the same time, Mrs Porter is somehow elevated to the level of a folk myth to be valued because it contains a sediment of ancient ritual.

The technique was to be exploited to the limit by Joyce in *Finnegans Wake* (the hero of which, by the way, seems to be named Mr Porter – a carrier of liquor and of sin). The whole history of man is presented through a technique in which childish, though polyglot, puns jostle with street songs and street slang. The very title derives from a New York Irish ballad, but it is made to bear the weight of ancient myth and perennial faith. Isolde's death song has its opening words – *Mild und leise* – transformed into the nickname of a doubtful Dublin character, Mildew Lisa. The punning and the parody are funny but serious; the concentration of multiple, and sometimes opposed, meanings into a single word is in the service of a literary complexity carried very lightly. And it all, ultimately, comes from *The Waste Land*, complete with resurrection theme, images of a decayed civilisation, and a harkening to calls from the East.

If *Finnegans Wake* is the most massive example of the fertility of that brief crammed poem of Eliot, we can find very few poems and novels of less ambitious aim that, coming after *The Waste Land*, have been able to escape its influence. It was, I discovered myself when I first began to write seriously, hard to get the Eliotian voices out of my ears and my prose. It was so delightful to conjoin mock-pomposity with deliberate vulgarity, to throw in recondite literary allusions for ironic effects, to make statements conveying an authority somehow both professorial and parsonic, and yet, at the same time, tinged with self-mockery.

Apart from writers, the Eliotian phrase worked its way into the most unexpected contexts, so that television weathermen could comment on April being the cruellest month or say that, today, summer surprised us. When, at a cocktail party, a man was described as 'one of the low,' everybody added to himself: 'on whom assurance sits as a silk hat on a Bradford millionaire.' Whether or not the content of Eliot is acceptable, the quality of his phrase-making is so insidious that it cannot easily be rejected. Like Yeats, he is one of the great writers of single memorable lines. In creating these, the poet serves the language, modifying it in the direction of a greater subtlety, and his achievement affects the street and the market place as well as the academic common room.

I don't think the young of today are capable of deriving the authentic poetic shiver from reading Eliot that my generation knew in the thirties. In those days it seemed unlikely that Eliot would ever become an academic text. He was untouched by the professors, a kind of literature of the counter establishment. Nowadays I am sometimes called upon to give a lesson on *The Waste Land* in one American university or another, and I find that the students have a heavily annotated text, obviating the possibility for their finding out anything for themselves. The epigraph from Petronius, in which the Sybil says she wants to die, is duly translated, and the battle of Mylae, at which Stetson fought, is rightly glossed as being an element in an ancient commercial struggle. I gain the impression that many students find Eliot a bit of a bore, with too much Latin in him, and that they regard his erudition as old-hat and reactionary.

The charge of fascism has even been brought against Eliot, as also against Yeats, Lawrence, Pound, and Wyndham Lewis. Eliot didn't, on the evidence of his poetry, care much for the Jews, and though there is no overt anti-Semitism in *The Waste Land* (as there is in 'Gerontion' and 'Burbank with a Baedeker, Bleistein with a Cigar'), there is a suggestion that the mongrelising of Europe is the work of the wanderers – 'hooded hordes swarming' – and the exiles who have made a kind of culture out of their money. There is a sort of subdued desire for a pure Aryanism, best realised in the civilisation of India.

Eliot's brand of Indianism, incidentally, makes no appeal to the young, who prefer the Buddhism of Eliot's contemporary Hermann Hesse to the active philosophy of the *Upanishads*. Both Hesse, whom Eliot had read, and the poet who was eventually to find a satisfactory faith in Anglo-Catholicism, saw that Europe was collapsing and that the only hope lay in the East. But Hesse was all for the opting-out of a pacific neutrality, best realised in a Swiss canton, while Eliot proposes techniques of purgation and prayer and even, in *The Rock*, the Social Credit that Pound also espoused. Ultimately, of course, this sort of thing matters little. What remains is the powers of language, the purification of the dialect of the tribe, the big magic of words that we do not always understand.

The twentieth century has seen bigger and more ambitious poems than *The Waste Land* – such as the *Cantos* of Pound, the *Anathemata* of David Jones, the *Anabase* of St-John Perse – but no poem has been a more miraculous mediator between the hermetic and demotic. It is, curiously when one considers the weight of polyglot learning it carries, essentially a popular poem, outgoing rather than ingrown, closer to Shakespeare than to Donne. It was Pound who said that music decays when it moves too far away from the dance, and poetry decays when it neglects to sing. *The Waste Land* sticks in one's mind like a diverse recital performed by a voice of immense variety but essentially a single organ: it sings and goes on singing.

Horizon, 16 August 1971

My Life and Times

I HAVE spent a sedative summer reading most of Henry Miller. Sedative? Yes, inevitably, since it's the fate of all revolutionary writers to encompass their own supersession. How shocking *Tropic of Cancer* was when I got hold of a smuggled copy in the late thirties; how merely charming it is now, redolent of a Paris in which the coffee and Gauloises were alike more aromatic than they've been since the war, a genuine *vie de bohème*, the physical act of love as fresh as if the French had just invented it. Miller unbuttoned the fly and tore open the placket with a fiercer gust than Lawrence (who was still mother's boy) or Joyce (who let language get in the way). Today's naked generation has learned nearly everything from him – everything, that is to say, except his bookishness, his capacity for recapturing innocence, his sense of wonder, his sense of words.

I remember, when first reading Burroughs's *The Naked Lunch*, feeling that one particular element in the junkie nightmare represented – for me, at least – the limit in the erotically shocking. A man copulates with another man's skull, but first he has to drill a hole in it. Shocking, but (perhaps appropriately) merely cerebrally shocking. Amusing even, the sort of example of the shocking one might give in a lecture. A lot of the shocks administered by today's youthful news sheets are of this order: we're now permitted to shock, so let's get on with it; what shall we shock with today? This is the consequence of Miller's opening the door. Needless to say, it was not what he intended.

For all that the *Tropics* and *The Rosy Crucifixion* try to do in the erotic arena is to convey the simple gross pleasures of straightforward heterosexual coition. This had never really been done before in direct language. Rabelais makes a joke of it, Boccaccio uses elegant metaphor. Those wearisome Victorian chronicles of prowess possess detail but lack gusto. And, to be honest, if no literary man had tried it before on the Millerian scale and with the Millerian intensity, it was because there was the gnaw of the scruple. Is one telling the truth about copulation if one merely describes its mechanics? Miller has never had any doubt that one is, and unfortunately he shares this view with the pornographers. But Miller himself has never written pornography.

For pornography depersonalises, creating an abstract paradise Steven Marcus called Pornotopia, in which the only emotion is lust and the only event orgasm and the only inhabitants animated phalluses and vulvae. In Miller's books there are real people, with guns in their handbags, a need for money, a habit of writing poetry on the wall while the act proceeds, an appetite for big meals afterward and very frequently a temporary resistance to love. Is 'love' the right word? In French, yes; with Miller, whose origins are German, there are sometimes temptations to submit to Goethean transports which get in the way of pure *amour*. Miller himself is always present, naked but a thinking man who reads and writes books, capable of prodigious engorgements but never viewing himself as a synecdoche – part for the whole. Heavily erotic, yes, but pornographic, never.

Many women dislike his books, especially the militant Donna Giovannas, like vengeful Brigid Brophy, who goes so far in her essay on Miller as to cast doubt on his basic sexual endowment. They are right, I think, because, though Miller respects ladies like Anaïs Nin, he cannot help making women the sexual instrument come before women the human entity. He is very ingenuous in saying that he has never thought of women as just *that*: he always looked for something else as well. His autobiographical books – which means all his books – deliver a little too much contempt for women – the classic postcoital *tristitia*, which the boorish or the puritanical transfer to the object of spent desire, a vestigial Victorian horror that women should actually like sex quite as much as men, if not more. Still, at 80 he goes on loving women; and the number of his wives, though not up to patriarchal standards, compares well with an average film star's. His present wife is Japanese; and he is very fond of her, as of her Japanese friends, some of whom live with her, them, him.

To call Miller a glorifier of the phallus and a chronicler of phallic events is not enough. There is more to his long autobiography than sex. *Black Spring* is, I think, one of the finest evocations of low urban life in all American literature. 'I am a patriot,' says Miller, 'of the Fourteenth Ward, Brooklyn, where I was raised. The rest of the United States doesn't exist for me, except as idea, or history, or literature.' The patriotism is expressed in an almost myopically close rendering of a world of 'cancer, dropsy, cirrhosis of the liver, insanity, thievery, mendacity, buggery, incest, paralysis, tapeworms, abortions, triplets, idiots, drunkards, ne'er-do-wells, fanatics, sailors, tailors, watchmakers, scarlet fever, whooping cough, meningitis, running ears, chorea, stutterers, jailbirds, dreamers, storytellers, bartenders – and finally there was Uncle George and Tante Melia.' Though he disavows either a literary aim or a learned technique, Miller belongs to the logorrheal tradition of Rabelais and Sterne (as does Burroughs). He becomes a wordy bore only when he finds it necessary to prophesy; that great American disease we can call vatism is in him as it is in Dahlberg and even Mailer. When Miller starts talking about Love, not *amour*, I feel like giving him a few francs to go to a brothel.

But, of course, there is no need to do this. We come sooner rather than later to lechery as juicy as roast pork and *Kartoffelklöße*. If we require elevation from Miller, then we can best get it in his Hellenic phase. He is curiously German in having found an almost hyperbolic fulfilment in Greece – 'Real home, real climate,' he notes – and the best testimony to its moderating, cleansing, unclotting influence is to be found in his *The Colossus of Maroussi*. But the war sent him back to America and the destiny of sage of Big Sur. Now he appears to be one of America's glories – fulfilled, with 50 books behind him, his 80th birthday last Sunday, Boxing Day, two of his works filmed (stupidly confused with skinflicks), and the *Playboy* tribute to this picture book, Miller talking his life instead of writing it (he has written it already).

There are already cynics and admirers who are saying that the book should be called *My Life and Hard-on Times*. The erotic motif is imposed on some of the photographs – cheaply and irrelevantly. The old man is shown apparently trying to eat the bosom of the Israeli actress Ziva Rodann. He plays ping-pong with a callipygous nude girl. He sits at a table and looks up in a kind of puzzled but gratified wonder as a pair of fine impertinent breasts moon down on him. But there are photographs of Miller serious, with hat and spectacles on, and Lawrence Durrell horsing about with a false moustache, and wives and friends and Paris. There are also reproductions of Miller's paintings (one of the best things in all his writing is his account, in *Black Spring*, of learning how to draw), which are endearingly bright and *fin de siècle*. Finally, there is Miller talking about himself and giving us all hope. A cigarette-smoking, gin-drinking octogenarian, he is a fine advertisement for the longevital virtues of regular sex.

But the book is a mere plaything or playboy thing, in no wise a fitting summation, a glossy toy that might lull the reader into not taking Miller as seriously as he ought. Miller has spent a long industrious life grinding slow and exceeding fine, also coarse. He is a world literary figure, and it is proper to ask where – apart from the long-banned candour – his achievement lies. With whom shall we compare him – Lawrence? Joyce? Beckett? He is not as important as any of these because he has not created a world that is recognizably his own. He has not really created at all. He lacks architectonic skill, a making or shaping drive. He has had only one real subject – himself – and he has not been prepared, or endowed with the ability, to convert himself into a great fictional myth. Called a novelist by some, he has the novelist's ear and eye but not the novelist's power to create great separable artefacts. He has done what any man with his endowments and deficiencies is forced to do – produce autobiography that begs at the door of fiction.

Durrell thinks that Miller's lifework is the best confessional writing since Rousseau. He is probably right; but frank self-exposure was only one small part of Rousseau's achievement – there were *The Social Contract*, *Emile* and *The New Héloïse* as well. Moreover, the things that Miller confesses are somewhat limited. He is honest, but no subtle thinker; we conceive no joy in engaging a personality so lacking in complexity. The sensibility is somewhat coarse; and there is an ingenuousness which, though often charming, charms less the more often we meet it. I have been rereading Gibbon's *Autobiography* as a foil to Miller, and the intellectual excitement of the experience has inevitably shrivelled up the phallic and visceral appeal of the *Tropics* and those productions with the schoolboy names *Sexus*, *Plexus* and *Nexus*. There is humour as well as physical honesty, but there is not one ounce of wit.

George Orwell paid fine tribute to Miller, asking his readers of the thirties to note in *Tropic of Cancer* what, even at that late date, could still be done with the English language. Orwell saw in Miller what many of us saw then – a liberating force, a cleanser of the dialect of the tribe. But how much more cleansing and liberating was Orwell himself who, in *Down and Out in Paris and London*, converted into art the sufferings and low life he shared with Miller, and then, before dying in his early forties, produced genuine prophecy. Industry and longevity are no substitute for genius.

New York Times, 2 January 1972
Review of *My Life and Times* by Henry Miller
(New York: Gemini Press, 1971)

On Lengthy Matters

How FAR should bigness be seen as an aspect of greatness? Does quantity really conduce to quality? In the field of the American novel there are few doubts as to the answers. Eighty thousand words may be good enough for England, and forty thousand for France, but American novelists blithely put in for a million. I read fearfully of what Norman Mailer is doing: the ultimate Jewish family saga from Egyptian bondage to exodus by spaceship. I have looked at Gaddis's *JR*; I tried to read Pynchon's *Gravity's Rainbow*, hampered by a freak of binding which gave me pp. 1–200 twice but missed out on pp. 200–400. I remember Marguerite Young's *Miss Mackintosh My Darling*, reputedly the longest novel ever written. As a mere 80,000-worder I feel properly humbled, on my country's behalf as well as my own. In England we have long lost the knack of fictional longitude.

Economics has nearly everything to do with it. I gather that Mailer got a $1,000,000 advance – not excessive when you consider the extraordinary nutrition and stimulation that work must demand. For the rest, everybody seems to be on campus with a professorial sinecure, honour-bound to spend 10 years or so on a bulky master-piece. In Europe things are different. Universities and novelists have nothing to do with each other Our position is basically that of Dr Samuel Johnson, forced to write the novella *Rasselas* in a week in order to pay for his mother's funeral.

One way for British writers to produce the Great British Novel is to do what Charles Snow and Anthony Powell have done – bring it out in annual instalments. This is really an extension of the Dickensian serial: you earn while you are building, and at the same time you are told whether you are building well or ill. But every self-respecting American high-rise writer must recognise that this is cheating: no *roman fleuve* can ever be *Of Time and the River*. Even Proust failed to be a Michener. The Great American Novel has to hurtle on to the market and knock the stuffing out of you in a single blow. The teeny periodic punches of *Strangers and Brothers* and *A Dance to the Music of Time* are not the same thing at all.

This situation adds to the gloom that British novelists are bound to be feeling anyway. After all, even if we were all given the chance to fill in the matrix of a *Centennial* or a *Raintree County* with a pounding British saga of passion, betrayal and nation-building, we'd end up with something decadent, mocking and bland (the most opprobrious term in an American reviewer's lexis). Since the Victorian giants – who were all Fieldingesque picaros anyway – we've only had one blockbusting theme, and that was the rise of the British empire. It's a theme that's been merely nibbled at, Kipling – who could have written an Anglo-Indian *War and Peace* – being the most shameful nibbler of them all. We're stuck with our muffled curses at the Welfare State and our exhausted records of adultery in Hampstead. We can be delicately witty, but we can't roar.

And yet and yet. Whatever happened to *Gone With the Wind*? It became a movie, meaning an 80,000-word novel. Where can I find a copy of *Raintree County*? Are not both *The Recognitions* and *JR* excessively long for their subjects? Could not even *V* have done its marvellous mythopoeic job in a quarter of the space? Are not both Russia (meaning nowadays – and let's be honest – unreadable Solzhenitsyn) and America over-bemused by some fallacy about filling up geographical space with appropriately big books? Is it heretical to whisper that the really great American novels have all been pretty short?

Meaning *Miss Lonelyhearts* and *The Sun Also Rises* and *The Great Gatsby* and *The Scarlet Letter* and *Washington Square* and *The Catcher in the Rye* and all the works of John Hawkes and Wilfrid Sheed (who's really British, but let that pass). And many many others. Even on the level of the studiable, the shorter works have it. The kids won't read Thomas Wolfe, even in Chapel Hill the Brautigan-Vonnegut cult has as much to do with brevity as with trendy content.

The fact is, as we all know, that the long novel is easier to write than the short, just as an opera is easier to write than a string quartet. Considerations of form, which have much to do with economy of material, don't enter the making of a big book: neither the writer nor the reader can carry in his head the entire configuration of *War and Peace*, while he can hold the shape of *Pride and Prejudice* in his hand and examine it closely like something of Fabergé. *Ulysses* is saved from shapelessness by its imposed Homeric parallel, but even *Ulysses* is too long (consider what it would be like if all its chapters were as brief as the first one). The only long novel that is not too long is *Don Quixote*, and even that can only be read at the age of 15 and never again.

Having said all this, I have to announce that I embarked on a very long novel about two years ago. It has to be subsidised by television and film chores, by university visits, by journalism, and all these means have inevitable become ends. There is no substitute for patronage. I have 30-odd pages already written, nesting in a sun-bleached folder. When asked what I am writing these days I can say: 'A very long novel.' I can go on saying it. It is as good an excuse for not getting down to some real work as I have been able to contrive in a long long time. It is also a supreme example of British fictional defeatism in the face of American fictional accomplishment.

New York Times, 14 December 1975

Last of the Literary Dandies

VLADIMIR NABOKOV died at the age of 78 – a very reasonable age, one would think, for a writer to die at, his best works long behind him and the retrospective honours coming in. But Nabokov's career as the finest novelist of the post-Joyce era began only when he was 60, with the publication of *Lolita*.

This book gave him the wrong sort of reputation, but only with the wrong audience, which converted anger at the lack of lubricity into moral indignation. Those who thought it pornographic knew only the title. If the book was ever shocking, it was stylistically so. People brought up on a sparer literary diet were appalled at the blend of pedantry and dandyism, the aristocratic chic which seemed unfitting in an age of plain prose and social commitment. The novels that followed – particularly *Pale Fire* and *Ada* – were animated by the same verbal passion, to an extent considered very indecent by lovers of a plain yarn. Indeed, it seemed that the only characters in *Pale Fire* were words, with a plot based on a typographical error.

His admirers, who felt they had a right to expect further outrageous rapes of traditional narrative form in the name of a passion for language, will not only grieve but feel frustrated. He and Raymond Queneau were the last of the literary dandies.

Literature in English has, in our century, owed most to foreigners, which includes Irishmen. The special task of the English-writing Slav has been to remind us of the gorgeousness of our language – gorgeousness repressed by puritans and pragmatists – and it is probably right to bracket Nabokov and Conrad. But whereas it was Conrad's vocation to become an English writer, Nabokov became the author of *Lolita* only by accident. If it had not been for the Russian revolution, he would have been an internationally acclaimed glory of his own language. He never pretended that English was anything other than a second best to Russian. It was forced upon him by exile and awareness of producing a rarefied literature for *émigrés* only. The extent of his devotion to Russian literature is to be seen in his four-volume edition of Pushkin's *Eugene Onegin*.

Nabokov's father was one of the great Russian democrats, leader of the faction that tried to act as a reasonable buffer between the Tsar and the Bolshevists. Both sent him to prison; in exile he was apparently assassinated. Nabokov's autobiography *Speak, Memory*, which typically he wanted to call *Speak, Mnemosyne*, tells a shameful story of treachery and dispossession, but with not one grain of self-pity, rather with aristocratic hauteur, and a stoicism that defies the reader to suppose for one moment that he ever minded the loss of an inheritance of a huge estate and two million dollars.

Nabokov's writings blessed the untidy richness of the world, but he had an instinct for scientific order. He was a great lepidopterist, expert at pinning flight and colour into categories. He was a magnificent chess player, publishing some of his invented problems along with his poems, as if they had much the same aesthetic value. The hero of *The Defence* (a worked-over version of a novel written 30 years earlier in Russian) is a chess player of the master class who can find only two approaches to life – that of the jigsaw, fitting shapeless scraps of experience together into a preordained pattern, and that of chess, the perverse self-absorption in closed-in skills. The way out of banality, Nabokov seems to say, is the way into perversity or madness: one or other of these categories encloses most of his heroes.

He was also a great player of word-games which, so say the unkind, are all his novels are. In his hotel suite at Montreux, whither he took his American passport into a final exile, he played much Russian Scrabble with his wife Vera. He created the first Russian crossword. These ludic obsessions are all to be found in his novels. In one of his poems he wonders if there is an ultimate reality corresponding to the fact that *repaid* is *diaper* spelt backwards.

To him words were literal magic. He was a philologist more than a linguist: the reality of language lay on the page, not in the ear or mouth. The villain of *Lolita*, Quilty, seems to be made out of the sentence: '*Qu'il t'y mène*'. But, on the first page of that novel, Humbert Humbert savours the very name of his beloved, bewitched to find that the two 'l's are two different allophones.

Nabokov got a good degree at Cambridge – through, he says, the carelessness of turning in good papers – but he distinguished himself there chiefly as a fine tennis player and a reliable goalkeeper. It seems only by chance that America claimed him. He taught at Cornell, but left academe behind when *Lolita* began to assure him of an income. Though he left America, he shows in his work a fascination with its culture, geography and language unequalled by most native-born Americans. His ear caught American speech exactly, but his mouth could never get round it. His spoken English remained heavily *émigré*, but was always human and charming.

He could be very intolerant, pig-headedly so, finding no virtue in Freud, the Viennese quack, who busied himself with the psyche. The soul was an overrated property, he thought, rather like money, and so he dismissed Dostoyevsky. As for post-Tsarist Russian literature, that, he maintained, did not exist: so much for Pasternak and Solzhenitsyn. Of his kindness, his students may speak, as also those of us young writers whom he believed to be on the right, word-obsessed track.

He did not invent the word nymphet, but he gave it a new meaning, not one well understood. Any nubile teenager is now a 'proper little Lolita', where he meant something far more subtle and magical. His approach to his art was of a Flaubertian or Joycean dedication. He received no international honours, nor did he need them. He did us all honour by electing to use, and transform, our language.

Observer, 10 July 1977

Five-Finger Exercises

LET US take, for a start, the nose-thumb gesture, in which the thumb touches the tip of the nose and the fingers fan out. The tandem version of this has the thumb of the other hand touching the little finger of the first, and, for good measure, there can be a waggling of digits, a protruding tongue, and a leer of derision.

The gesture is known all over Europe, and there is no ambiguity about it (unlike, say, the thumbs-up signal, which it is unsafe for a British hitchhiker to use on certain southern high roads). It is pretty old, too: Rabelais mentions it; Peter Brueghel shows a prancing jester doing the double spread, and it seems to be an animated version of the fool's coxcomb.

It has many names in English – cock a snook, pull a snook, take a double sight, make Queen Anne's fan, pull bacon. As a child I knew it as making fat bacon. In Portugal you *tocar trompete*, or play the trumpet. German children go '*Atsch! Atsch!*' as they make *die lange Nase*. In Italy the gesture is known as *marameo*, which ties it in with a cat's mewing.

In England it seems to be dying out. I last saw it publicly performed in the 1960s by Quintin Hogg at a political meeting, the one-handed version accompanied by a little prance. British children have replaced it with the obscene V sign.

There are two ways of pronging a pair of fingers into the air – one with the palm presented, the other with it hidden. The latter is an undoubted insult, and Churchill, introducing (at the urging of the Belgian lawyer Victor de Lavelaye) the victory sign in 1941, did not at first realise the obscene significance of the back-of-the-hand version. Somebody had to tell that remarkably innocent man of the world that he must not go around signalling up yours (one up the fundament, one up the vulva) to friends and allies, so he turned his hand round.

Mrs Thatcher, in a photograph reproduced in this book, up-yourses very happily in a moment of minor triumph. I do not know what she did with her hand in her recent victory. Properly, the obscene finger prong should be in rhythmical motion and accompanied by a fierce whistle with lips spread. Then it is known as the Old Roman sign.

A lot of work has gone into this manual, which deals with the cultural distribution of 20 selected gestures. There are maps dappled with rings of comparative frequency. Thus, if you kiss your fingertips to signify praise, appreciation, adoration (as in John Bulwer's *Chirologia* – or hand-speech – of 1644, which has the superscription *O, Adoro* over a rapt finger-kissing cavalier), you will be better appreciated in France, Spain, and Germany than in Italy, Sardinia, Sicily or Great Britain. Use the gesture as a salutation, and the deep European South will know what you mean. So will Stockholm and Lisbon. Scotland will be totally bewildered.

It is in Naples that we find the richest proliferation of hand signals. The Neapolitans are a subtle people, fearful of giving too precise a meaning to words. In court a witness will ask in deadly seriousness whether the magistrate requires the regular truth or the true truth, or some other truth on a scale between lying and total veracity. In this wretched vivacious city you will get a variety of manual signals which are more definite than speech, from the ear-touch (meaning effeminacy) to the nose-tap (be on your guard), taking in the cheek-stroke (delicious) on the way.

Modern Britain does not go in for gestures much at all, except for vulgar ones which grow increasingly vulgar, but the evidence of Elizabethan literature seems to show that we were once as manually voluble as the Italians. Evidently the yea-and-nay tradition of Calvinistic dissent outlawed the nuance of the gesture.

Finding etymologies for some of these hand signals is apparently as chancy as looking for the origin of an expression like OK (on which Dr Morris and his colleagues expend a paragraph that, as was to be expected, gets us nowhere). Take the horn sign, the equivalent of the word of fear unpleasing to a married ear. It is over two and a half thousand years old as a device for warding off evil, though the investigative team that Dr Morris led discovered that the cuckold meaning has almost totally driven out the protective effect.

By extension, to make the horns has become a means of expressing generalised deadly insult, but the imputation of cuckoldry is the father and mother of all insults. Why the horns? Still around in Latin Europe, alive in Shakespeare, they make sense as an attribute of the devil warding off the devil, in the final ambivalence of Mediterranean religion, but we have to work hard to make them reasonably signify inability to protect husbandly rights. Do they mean a gelded bull or bullock? Alien penises poking their way in?

Oral language is slippery and highly mutable. There have been serious attempts to recommend a universal language of gesture which could replace speech and restore (or is it destroy) the tower of Babel. This book shows that manual gestures can form as closed a system as linguistic ones. Dr Morris and I were once near-neighbours in Malta, where horns are solely a talisman against evil and where an upward wag of the head means (as it does in Sicily) a negative. I invited some young Maltese to tea and learned belatedly that they were gesturing no to more cake when I thought they were signalling yes. Why were they allowing their plates to be piled up and yet not eating anything? As for the thumbs up, meaning good, fine, OK, it may be used with confidence over most of Europe. But go to Greece, Corfu or southern Sardinia and it becomes a deadly sexual insult.

This book is clearly only a beginning: there is much to be done in the mapping of all the varieties of non-linguistic communication that any person who has travelled, or has merely lived long, has been fascinated to observe.

As a novelist whose craft involves the invention of long patches of dialogue, I am aware of what my characters are doing with their bodies as well as their tongues. Yet I despair of ever being able to set any of it down: the instantaneous flick of a shoulder or bunching up of a mouth requires too much description. One is forced to use words in an area whose virtue is that it is able to dispense with them.

But words, some say, are a kind of upstart successor to visual gesture – invisible but audible signs of the night, to be replaced at dawn by the more satisfying semantemes of the eye. This book shows how dumb the world would be without fingers.

Observer, 13 May 1979
Review of *Gestures: Their Origins and Distribution* by
Desmond Morris *et al* (London: Jonathan Cape, 1979)

Creeping Towards Salvation

SHIKASTA IS the first of a projected series of novels called *Canopus in Argos: Archives*. The collective title, like the component ones (the others are *The Marriage Between Zones Three, Four, and Five* and *The Sirian Experiments*), proclaims that Doris Lessing is working in a genre called space or cosmic fiction, related to Sci-fi and fut-fic and the rest but distinguished from them by a prophetic and highly moral quality. In other words, not an escape into fantasy but an attempt to look at the human condition from an imagined cosmic angle. In her foreword Lessing recounts an experience in the United States. She was lecturing on the salutary changes coming into the novel through the influence of cosmic fiction:

> ... space fiction, with science fiction, makes up the most original branch of literature now; it is inventive and witty; it has already enlivened all kinds of writing; ... literary academics and pundits are much to blame for patronising or ignoring it... I do think there is something very wrong with an attitude that puts a 'serious' novel on one shelf and, let's say, *Last and First Men* on another.

Her professional chairperson at once struck in with 'If I had you in my class you'd never get away with that!'. I have to confess that this is much my own attitude. If space or science fiction is good, then it must be good as Jane Austen or Henry James is good – through the artful delineation of human character in credible situations, through the generation of a pattern out of the chaos of actuality. Lessing's point about Olaf Stapledon's book is well taken, but Stapledon belongs to literature as does Wells, and it is only the specialist SF departments of libraries and bookstores that relegate him to shelves full of BEMs glooming through bad prose. The separation of SF from literature in general has helped to condone a loosening of artistic standards in the SF field. Writers of regular fiction would never get away with some of the psychological implausibilities, unreal dialogue, and ill-managed *récit* that are positively welcomed by addicts of the SF genre as signals of a new kind of literature. But Wells, Stapledon, Aldiss and Ballard can be evaluated as Green, Snow and Mrs Lessing herself are evaluated and not be found wanting.

There is something ontologically disturbing about fiction that deals with human affairs from a fanciful cosmic viewpoint. Space probes are demonstrating that there is probably no intelligence 'out there' yet Doris Lessing now joins those who purvey the somewhat old-fashioned hypothesis of galactic empires, huge extraterrestrial powers that look down on planet Earth (or Shikasta) with shame and pity, an endless Manichaean war between the Great Ones and Shammat (or the Devil). The agonies of human life are, God knows, real enough, but to posit cosmic aetiologies and galactic cures is an evasion of reality as well as a mockery of terrestrial suffering. In Vonnegut's *Slaughterhouse Five* the horror of the Dresden bombings was diminished by the superficial SF frame. It is to Lessing's credit that she so frequently moves from the cosmic view to the human, functioning as the 'traditional' novelist we know and admire, even making her Johor (emissary to Shikasta) assume human qualities and the name George Sherban.

The book pretends to be a compilation of documents 'selected to offer a very general picture of Shikasta for the use of first-year students of Canopean Colonial Rule'. The documents cover the whole history of the earth from the first stirrings of life to the last, or Third World War, in which humanity nearly destroys itself, but not quite. Those nodes in history where, inexplicably, man's urge for extinction is countered by glimpses of the Good or thwarted by an advance in knowledge, are seen to be contrived by the Great Ones out there, Beneficent and discreet saviours. Try as the author may in works of this kind (one thinks also of Kubrick's *Space Odyssey*), he or she cannot evade the traffic of the divine and the human, there always has to be the flavour of a 'sacred book'. 'The sacred literatures of all races and nations', says Mrs Lessing, 'have many things in common. Almost as if they can be regarded as the products of a single mind. It is possible we make a mistake then we dismiss them as quaint fossils from a dead past.' More than possible.

And so, as we were taught a long time ago but now have to be retaught in SF terms, good and evil exist and are at perpetual war with each other, but the war must some time in the remote aeons be resolved. There will be no victorious archangelic trumpets, but there will be a muffled minimal creeping through, on the part of perhaps one per cent of the survivors of the next catastrophe, to salvation:

> Poor people of the past, poor poor people, so many of them, for long thousands of years, not knowing anything, fumbling and stumbling and longing for something different but not knowing what had happened to them or what they longed for.
> I can't stop thinking of them, our ancestors, the poor animal-men, always murdering and destroying because they couldn't help it.
> And this will go on for us, as if we were being slowly lifted and filled and washed by a soft singing wind that clears our sad muddled minds and holds us safe and heals us and feeds us with lessons we never imagined.
> And here we all are together, here we are…

The virtue of Doris Lessing's novel lies in its rage and its hope and, of course, its humanity. The cosmic fancies become a mere decoration, not, as with true SF, the innutritious essence. Tafta, Supreme Lord of Shikasta, may send a dispatch to Supreme Supervisory Lord Zarlem on Shammat about the victory of evil, but the truth is the physical one of polluted seas, crammed prison camps all over Europe, the Third World happy to see its former oppressors starving, the trees dying, the Youth Armies on the march. And Lessing's compassion blazes through in images of human and animal suffering – the dignity of a dying cat, a man and his cow dying together from drought and sharing the final drop of water. And then there are the casebooks which attempt the objectivity of students' texts – INDIVIDUAL THREE (Workers' Leader) and so on – but are indistinct with the author's own agony and incomprehension.

Incomprehension? Doris Lessing does not understand any better than the rest of us why the eternal human mess should exist. But it is in order for a novelist to try to resolve his or her bewilderment by taking a Stapledonian view of history and looking for a pattern. The pain of bewilderment can be eased by invoking a contrived cosmic plan, or even an invented theology – through, as she seems to admit, all theologies are fundamentally the same: they all have to find an explanation of evil. As for the human future which nags us as though it were already the past, it is an altogether worthy thing for a novelist to attempt to predict it. This is one of the novelist's jobs, since it

cannot be safely left to professional futurologists. By viewing the
world from space, it becomes possible to see human time, as it were,
spatially, and Doris Lessing's vision of the next and final catastrophe
gains credibility from her technique of cosmic detachment. But she is
not too detached: her characters are as much alive as they are in her
more orthodox fiction, and her Johor assumes, with a kind of relief,
his human lineaments. I have no doubt that the whole trilogy will be
worthy of standing on the same shelf as *Last and First Men* and *Sirius*
and *The Starmaker*. And this will not be because of its SF trappings.

Times Literary Supplement, 23 November 1979
Review of *Shikasta* by Doris Lessing
(London: Jonathan Cape, 1979)

A Very Blasphemous Fallacy

I WAS thinking of Ernest Hemingway's last years when I was moving slowly over the frozen grass towards the cinema cameras, which had been set up in Ketchum Cemetery near his tomb. We were making a television film on Hemingway, and it was not to honour his literary achievement, not primarily. It was to titillate the television audience with an image of a man who succeeded as a writer (which means he became rich) but ultimately failed as a human being. The great unrich, untalented, unsuccessful public loves to hear of the failure of great men. It justifies their doing nothing with their lives except watching the fall of great men on television.

Hemingway had been a very handsome human being, gigantic, strong, a fine boxer and huntsman, a drinker, a bull-fight *aficionado* a writer of genius. Suddenly, in middle age, he became petulant, a worrier about money and excess air baggage. He developed persecution mania: those two men in the bar were from the FBI, watching him; don't let Bill drive the car, he's trying to kill me; I'm not making enough money this year (despite the annual hundred thousand dollars in royalties, the stock, the property). But even the decade or so before Hemingway's suicide, while he was sailing, swimming, shooting, following *corridas* all over Spain, there was an odour of approaching nemesis. He was living more and more on his past and, as writers will, effortlessly inventing some of it, or at least giving some of it a more satisfactory shape. Perhaps the gods of true enactment are always at war with the muses of fiction and, when they inhere in the one being, that being has to fall apart. It was in keeping with his *persona* for Hemingway to say that he slept with Mata Hari and enjoyed it, though she was a bit heavy in the thigh. Cold historical dates show that she was shot as a spy while Hemingway was still a young reporter on the Kansas City Star. The long streams of reminiscence over wine, running far into the night, had to be taken on a plane where the imagined and the actual became acceptable as the same thing. No reason why not? Pontius Pilate asked one of the great questions of all time, though his choice of occasion was infelicitous. Take Hemingway as one of his own fictional creations, as he himself began to do, and we shall all be happy with Hemingway. But life is life and fiction is fiction, and it is sometimes dangerous for them to touch. One of the troubles with America is that it expects reality to behave like fiction. Hemingway was a victim of that failure to categorise. His readers thought that the author should be at least as virile as his own creations. Hemingway obliged them with the Hemingway myth. This myth helped to kill him.

The Hemingway myth made great play with the Spanish term *cojones*. Hemingway told the world that he had *cojones*. He did not, being fundamentally prudish, exhibit these *cojones* in public, but he was always ready to show the hair on his chest. When one of his critics, Max Eastman, wrote a scathing review of his *Death in the Afternoon*, Hemingway responded by asking Eastman to show the hair on his chest. Eastman had little; Hemingway had much. This proved satisfactorily to Hemingway that he, Hemingway, was a good writer and Eastman a lousy critic. Hair on the chest meant that you had *cojones*. Hemingway's logic was always obscure.

Cojones meant the ability to catch big fish and shoot tigers. It ought to have meant the ability to make love satisfactorily. Of Hemingway's amorous life we know little, but we can guess that he lacked the skills, and even the appetites of Casanova. At school he chased balls – on the football field, in the water-polo pool – and did not chase girls. He was meant for outdoor, not indoor, games. This is always the way. The greatest sexual potency is to be found among timid poets, not big-chested football-players. But Hemingway, turning himself into a Hemingway hero, ought to have been a great lover. He was not. There is an interesting passage in his posthumous novel, *Islands in the Stream*, where the ageing weary hero dreams of making love with a gun. The gun was, as so often, a substitute for a phallus.

This is one of the possible reasons for Hemingway's end – disgust with a failing body that, at its best, had only given him the secondary pleasures of sport and drink, not the primary pleasure of sexual vigour or tenderness. But there are other reasons, and here we have to invoke that great explicatrix, Unreason. Unreason tells us that a man is put into the world to perform a function. An artist is born to do something for art that no artist has ever done before. Hemingway did the unique thing he was called on to do, and he did it early. In his first novel, *Fiesta*, he presented a mode of writing that had not been seen before. It was a prose style that belonged to the twentieth century and did not look back nostalgically – as did the styles of so many novelists – to an Age of Reason or an Age of Feeling. Hemingway's style was exactly fitted to expressing the life of the nerves and the muscles: it by-passed the brain and the heart. When he had shown that such a style was possible, a whole generation of writers was quick to learn it. But Hemingway himself had learnt it with pain and difficulty, slowly and in poverty. When he had given this style to the world, and with it the tough Hemingway hero – all trigger-finger and no cerebrum – his function in the world was finished. His life could consist only in repeating or imitating himself. He did this, but he also yielded to the great American public's desire that he shout enact in life what his characters enacted in print. He did his best, but he reckoned without nature's sad logic – the existence of time and decay, the fragility of the kidneys and livers, the terrible truth that living is never as satisfactory as creating. When an artist ceases to create, he is a tree that must be felled to make way for younger trees.

If Hemingway had been a European writer, he would have been content to let his characters do his strenuous living for him. But he was an American, and Americans have a dim sense of the boundary between what can be done and what cannot be done. Hemingway the creator submitted to the fallacy that the creator must be greater than his creations. It is, of course, a very blasphemous fallacy.

I had all this in my mind as I walked over the frozen grass of Ketchum, Idaho, to the camera and the microphone. But all I could say was: 'The worst failure is always success. When you reach the plateau of achievement, you have arrived. You cannot move any more. You are paralysed. Paralysis is death. Hemingway was dead while he was still alive. That suicide was a mere act of confirmation.' That's what the great public wants to hear. How can you explain to the great public that one of the most important things in the world is to invent a new way of saying things? But nobody cares about style, language, the power of the word. They prefer to hear about failure really being success, about a great writer killing himself at the early age (my age) of 62.

Previously unpublished and untitled; dated 1979

Glittering Prizes

I AM going through a phase of being awarded prizes. The other week I received, from the hands of the Prime Minister herself, one of the British Press Awards. As the occasion was the big Fleet Street event of the year, and marked by an eloquent and lengthy philosophical statement from Mrs Thatcher, I innocently assumed that the daily press would devote retrospective space to it. But only those newspapers which had prizemen on their own staff reported it, and they referred exclusively to those prizemen.

So much for the great myths of journalistic impartiality. The *Daily Mail* report gave the impression that Mrs Thatcher had a tête-à-tête luncheon at the Savoy with a *Daily Mail* photographer and a *Daily Mail* specialist writer. I came back to Monaco to find that I had been awarded the International Prize by the Press Association of Rome on the strength of an article written some months ago for the *Guardian*. Last year I was given a little golden man or *uomo d'oro* as a selection for the Premio Bancarella. Some years back I was told that if I turned up at a particular time in a particular Italian town I would receive a prize as the Film Scenarist of the Year. I was not able to turn up and so did not get it. The Italians, a festive people despite heavy inflation, rampant terrorism and an inability to be governed, love giving prizes.

I love being given prizes, like everyone else, but, like another writer with a far better claim to the homage of Fleet Street, I have long been resigned to 'pushing on my work through difficulties, of which it is useless to complain... without one act of assistance, one word of encouragement, or one smile of favour.' This is the writer's usual situation, and to be given a prize is like having strobe lights switched on in a place of habitual, though comfortable, darkness.

It seemed to me quite in order that I should receive at Sardi's a couple of awards from the New York critics on behalf of the director Stanley Kubrick, who had made a film out of one of my books. The role of vicarious recipient has been congenial; now it seems to be changing.

I would never be so presumptuous as to imagine that the bigger awards are now being eased into propulsion towards this increasingly fatigable hack. Though I have so far here begun nearly every paragraph with 'I,' I have always maintained a kind of humility. Anyone who has contrived to make a living out of writing for the past quarter-century would be wise to consider that he has already been rewarded enough.

But there are British novelists like myself (I had better remind the prize-muses of my primary vocation) who dream of winning the Booker Prize and, to that end, compose novels about living on a Thames houseboat or about Primrose Hill *lasagne* and fornication. There are even British novelists who have covertly learnt by heart a speech in Swedish. This is easiest for writers from the Northern Provinces, where bairns have the belly wartch.

I (there I go again) had a drink the other day with a man very influential with the Nobel committee: he told me that the prize for literature had become too political and would probably soon be abandoned. This ought to be good news for British writers, who have to be reminded annually that the nation which produced Shakespeare now stands no chance in comparison with its upstart daughters or the small oppressed enclaves. The Nobel may be for Chicago or Lower Slobbovia, but it is no longer for the sons of Bingley or Berkhamsted.

There remain for us the small prizes – the handsome paperweight and the modest cheque. (Not always so modest in Italy: this afternoon my representative receives on my behalf from the President himself a cheque for two million lire.) This is as it ought to be – enough to pay an outstanding gas bill and get moderately drunk, a reminder on the tortured desk that somebody has liked our work.

Writers need these reminders far more than plumbers and musicians. Musicians are publicly applauded and plumbers are fawned at. Every writer, especially in Britain, seems to throw his work into a terrible silence. He has, now and again, to know that somebody reads him.

I did not have a chance to whisper to the Prime Minister that writers are not averse to accepting state honours, despite the example of J.B. Priestley and a few others to whom literature and money are their own reward. Evelyn Waugh wanted a knighthood: it was not much to ask for, and it would have cost the state nothing. The stage and the concert hall are over-rewarded; publishers have been ennobled; soon there will be literary agents with the DBE. What writers want, to be truthful, is contingent honour for their wives. Mrs Waugh deserved to be Lady Waugh, all authors' wives deserve something for their suffering. Ask Lady Burgess.

Observer, 25 May 1980

A Talent to Remember

OLIVIA MANNING's major achievement in fiction has generally been held to be her *Balkan Trilogy*, which recounts the story of Guy Pringle, an itinerant adult educator, and his submissive wife, Harriet, against the background of World War II. In the sequence that came after, and which she just lived to complete, the adventures of these two were continued in an Egyptian and Lebanese setting.

The *Balkan Trilogy* and the *Levant Trilogy* were intended to form a hexateuch called *Fortunes of War*. If this is published as a single volume it may well appear to be the finest fictional record of the war produced by a British writer. Her gallery of personages is huge, her scene painting superb, her pathos controlled, her humour quiet and civilised. Guy Pringle certainly is one of the major characters of modern fiction.

Olivia Manning's power of imaginative penetration is best seen in *The Battle Lost and Won*, the second volume of the second trilogy, where she presents the battle of El Alamein from the viewpoint of a combatant – a bold and altogether successful feat. She was never, like so many women novelists, limited to the experiences of her own sex. She recognised, unlike so many of the fictional proponents of feminism, the need for a creative point of view which transcended what her personal life could give her, and this is an aspect of her importance as a novelist and short-story writer.

Stylistically she seems undistinguished, but the unassertive quality of her prose was a deliberately contrived transparency. Where in Lawrence Durrell's *Alexandria Quartet* we meet virtuoso description of the exotic which leaves us remembering the words more than the things, in Olivia Manning's hexateuch we are given impressions of sight, taste and smell with the minimum verbal display. We are somehow convinced that her Balkans and her Egypt must, in topographical and historical fact, have been how she presents them. The solidity of her characters is likewise achieved with very few words.

She worked long and hard at the craft of fiction. Apart from the two trilogies, single novels like *Artist Among the Missing* and *The Rain Forest* show a fine capacity for saying much in a small space, for describing sparely and yet leaving behind a considerable resonance. Some of her short stories are among the finest of our time. There is always evidence not merely of a well-tuned sensorium but of a quiet but incisive intelligence.

Her achievement was little known outside Great Britain. The first volume of the *Balkan Trilogy* was published to critical acclaim in the United States – where, indeed, she is taught in the more discerning departments of contemporary fiction – but she never attained the popularity which might induce American publishers to persevere with her *oeuvre*. With the completion of her *Fortunes of War* the entire literary world will be compelled to take notice of a highly individual talent.

Observer, 27 July 1980

Jong in Triumph

THE WAR between men and women, prefigured in the apocalyptical sketches of James Thurber, has, in addition to such dispatches as the painful *Hite Report*, its literary and critical fronts. One thing I was told rather dogmatically is that women's fiction is for women, and men better get away, man. Men like myself, who want love, not war, are briefly listened to when they praise Charlotte Bronte's Mr Rochester and Jane Austen's Mr Woodhouse as exemplary creations. But to suggest that novelists are really hermaphrodites, that the whole of human life is their province, is to court howls and hits. And to say, as I frequently do, that I admire Erica Jong, both as a poet and a novelist, is taken as an arrogant claim to an impossible empathy. It is like saying that I know the joys and agonies of the American female from the inside.

Erica Jong is too fine a writer to care much about the accidental categories of the activists, categories that are the product of crippled imaginations. If Ms Jong wrote a novel with a male protagonist-narrator, I would pick it up with respect and in the expectation of entertainment and even enlightenment. If she said, in effect, 'Men are like this,' I would know her to be right: I trust her insight and imagination. So far, in *Fear of Flying* and *How to Save Your Own Life*, to say nothing of her poems, she has presented the pains and occasional elations of the Modern American Female. With the confidence in the exterior validity of introspection that marks the true poet (Keats for instance), she has extrapolated from her own life and her own fear an archetype that has had immense appeal, not only with the Modern American Female but also with the Modern European Woman.

In her new novel, Erica Jong has refused to capitalise on an outlook and an ambience that a less scrupulous writer could have exploited forever. She has gone to the British eighteenth century and contrived an authentic picaresque novel with a female protagonist. Her title *Fanny*, as well as the afterword, acknowledges a measure of indebtedness to John Cleland's erotic masterpiece *Fanny Hill*, but the book is neither a pastiche nor a parody. It is, despite its allegiance to an antique genre, a genuinely original creation.

This brings me to an aspect of Ms Jong's work rarely considered by her admirers or her detractors: its stylistic distinction. Style, indeed, must be regarded not as an aspect of a book but its totality. The intention, or pretension, to produce literature – as opposed to the book of a possible film – depends on verbal competence more than knowledge of 'life', whatever that is. Ms Jong's first two books are highly literate: they show mastery of language; they depend for their effects on verbal exactitude and the disposition of rhythm. Subject matter apart, they are models of what orthodox, as opposed to experimental, fiction ought to be in this final phase of the century.

Erica Jong's concern with language has led her to a genuine experiment: the composition of a full-length novel in a mode of English no longer in use, though still capable of expressing a modern sensibility. She has gone further than Joyce, who merely, in the 'Oxen of the Sun' chapter of *Ulysses*, played brief passages in ancient styles. Her eighteenth-century English is not a matter of restoring the second person singular, using tags like 'prithee', or slavishly following old orthography ('musick', 'logick', capital initials for nouns). It is a matter of vocabulary, and also of rhythm:

> If these Pages oft' tell of Debauchery and Vice, 'tis not in any Wise because their Author wishes to condone Wickedness, but rather because Trust, Stark Naked Truth, demands that she write with all possible Candour, so that the Inheritor of this Testament shall learn how to avoid Wickedness or indeed transform it into Goodness. All possible Care hath been taken to give no deliberate Offence to Modesty or Chastity; yet the Author avows that Truth is a sterner Goddess than Modesty, and where there hath been made necessary a Choyce betwixt the Former and the Latter, Truth hath, quite rightly, triumph'd.

So Fanny Hackabout-Jones begins the history of her adventures as a Testament for her only Daughter, Belinda. The disingenuous tone has the right period ring. We know we are in for hair-raising sexual revelations, all in the service of an alleg'd Verity. The pitch is that of *Moll Flanders*, a prototype somewhat too early, and the revelations, when they come, go beyond anything the stationery licensors of Queen Anne or the Georges would have permitted. There is, of course, seduction, but there is also rape, maritime sodomy, obstetrical revelations, and well-researched attacks on such barbarities as swaddling-bands and filthy midwifery. There is, however, no whiff of affronted historical hindsight: Fanny is not a woman of our age riding a time-machine; the impersonation is pretty exact. It is so exact, indeed, that, in the manner of the age of Enlightenment, acerbities take on a curious sweetness:

> Was not my *authentic* History as stirring as Fanny Hill's, or Pamela's, or e'en that of Tom Jones? Orphan, Whore, Adventuress, Kept Woman, Slaver, Amanuensis, Witch, e'en a pardon'd Pyrate! By the Goddes, 'twas my *own* Life History that made a better History than any *fancied* History. And by the Goddes, 'twas the time to tell it all!

The reader will know what to expect from the narrative without any further detailing it. There is no joy in summary when there is so much joy in the language through which the events are presented. Take it that this is the situation of woman in a male-dominated society even more piggish than our own. Woman is a lust-object, even to rarefied poets like Alexander Pope (whose thalamic performance is as inept as one might expect). Her virginity once lost, she must take her shame to a brothel and become a professional lust-object. She may find sodality among witches, who are inevitably caught, ravished and killed by gross males, or among rogues who, turning against society, turn also against its sexual ethics and see woman as a wrong'd Creature. She has no trade except prostitution; she can be fulfilled, as Fanny is, through motherhood is she survives the obstetrics of the time. With luck, as here, she can end as the matriarch of a great estate. She can also become the writer of her own wrongs, and then she is committed, by the nature of the narrative idiom that is the air she breathes, to a glorification of life rather than a self-pitying jeremiad.

Hence this account of the trials of a high-spirited woman, who in our own age would be running an advertising agency or sitting on the High Court bench and taking pills and analysis in her spare time, is heartening and always enjoyable even when the crimson glans or the bloody axe is ready to strike. And the imaginative, and always convincing, reconstruction of eighteenth-century England shows, through that same positive prose, the lineaments of a civilisation better than ours. It was not an age for a women's liberation movement, with all its philosophical distortions, but one in which able women could prevail if they tried hard enough. Ms Jong's Fanny may suffer, but she is at home in the age.

A few critics will condemn what she has done because the writing of eighteenth-century literature is the task of eighteenth-century men and possibly women, and there is nothing to add to what, by its nature, has already been completed. There are answers to that. The romantic movement began with a pastiche of the past – the Rowley and Macpherson fabrications – but also with 'The Rime of the Ancient Mariner', which used the vocabulary and metric of the old ballads. Most of our best-selling novelists write, because they know no better, in a calcified Victorian style. But Bernard Malamud, with *The Fixer*, wrote a 19th-century Russian novel that literature needed; and Erica Jong may be said to have filled a gap in the great tradition of the picaresque novel. *Fanny: Being The True History of the Adventures of Fanny Hackabout-Jones* had to be written, and Erica Jong was the right hermaphrodite to write or indite it. I am delighted to belong to her sex.

Saturday Review, August 1980
Review of *Fanny: Being The True History of the Adventures of Fanny Hackabout-Jones* by Erica Jong
(London: Granada, 1980)

Partridge in a Word Tree

I FIRST became acquainted with Eric Partridge in the 1960s, when he was already old but still very vigorous. I had been commissioned by Penguin Books to produce a dictionary of contemporary slang, but I did not want to do it. My agent had, however, accepted the advance, which I later had to return, though not she her ten per cent. I toiled at the letter B, always the biggest section of an English dictionary, and saw the problems. 'Contemporary' means from now on till the end of time. I envisaged a life spent in updating the dictionary. When I had finished B 'bovver boots' came in and had to be admitted. Meeting Eric Partridge by chance at his club when I was lunching with somebody else, I had the chance to discuss the whole lexicographical agony with him.

First, though, knowing of my project, he cordially invited me to cannibalise him to the limit: dictionary-making was a matter of eating others and always had been. Then he admitted that his craft was one of perpetual revision, that no dictionary was a finished book but merely a photograph of the language at a point in time, always ready to be replaced with a new picture. His life was mostly given up to dealing with correspondents, most of whom were helpful. I became one of those correspondents myself when I decided that I was not a dictionary man, one of the thousands who sent him new words, idioms and etymologies. One of the pleasures of new editions of his slang dictionary was in meeting expressions of warmth, gratitude, friendship within the text itself.

Eric was a human lexicographer, like Samuel Johnson. He was a philologist rather than a linguist. He knew what Chomsky was doing and what had happened to phonology in Prague, but he eschewed the strict scientific approach. Linguistics is scared of semantics and prefers to concentrate on structures, leaving the study of the meaning of words to anthropologists – or, perhaps with misgivings, to Johnsonian word-lovers like Eric Partridge. Eric's etymologies were often, as he admitted, shaky, but he preferred a shaky etymology to none at all. I remember discussing with him the origin of the word *camp*. As it happened, I had written an article in the *Spectator* using the word, and a retired general had asked precisely what it meant and where it came from. I wrote a letter of some length in explication but got no thanks. My view was that *camp* had nothing to do with *kempt*. I thought of camp concert parties with men dressed up as girls and making exaggerated feminine gestures; I thought of those camps set up in nineteenth-century America for the construction of the railroads, when a temporary homosexual culture developed with secondary features of effeminate display. The latest general dictionary (Collins, 1979) defines *camp* and its derivatives admirably but says 'etymology unknown'. I maintain, as Eric always did, that it is better to guess than to be silent. This is amateurish, but it is human.

No academic linguist could be expected to be interested in frivolities like the 'comic alphabets' on which Eric wrote a whole book. I had, like him, heard Clapham and Dwyer on the radio in the 1930s reciting the whole liturgy: 'A for orses, B for mutton, C forth highlanders, D for payment,' and so on, penultimating with the brilliant 'Y for secretary'. I forget Z). What fascinated Eric in the direction of his book was the anonymous human brilliance of this fantasy, and it was the creativity of the humble users of language which, of course, inspired him to that lifelong devotion to slang and catch phrases which produced the great dictionaries. The catch phrase book, which, alas, he did not live to be able to complete revising and enriching, got a great number of his admirers digging in their memories. I wanted him to put in (from ITMA) 'NWAWWASBE' – never wash a window with a soft boiled egg – and great gestures of phatic communion like 'Roll on death and let's have a go at the angels' and 'Put another pea in the pot and hang the expense' and 'Never mind, lads, it'll soon be Christmas'. Many people did not appreciate these catch phrases. I wrote a novel in which a character says, 'Ah well, as one door shuts another door closes' and this was silently corrected to a statement that made sense. Naturally, I unsilently uncorrected it.

Eric had learnt these ludic tropes and others like them in the army. It was in the army that I learned to appreciate the great humorous stoicism of ordinary men and the way in which they expressed it in language. He, like myself, was fascinated by the slow folk development from trope to trope in the direction of greater sardonic truth. In 1939 soldiers were saying: 'The army can do anything to you including fuck you.' This, in 1941, had become 'The army can fuck you but it can't make you have a kid.' At the end of the war the army could give you a kid but it couldn't make you love it. I don't know what the latest embellishment is.

A New Zealander, an Australian, hence a great mistruster of what Joyce called 'those big words that make us all unhappy', Eric was brought up in a kind of dispossessed demotic tradition which prized the speech of the people as the repository of a dour philosophy of life. The downtrodden, who are the great creators of slang, hurl pithiness and colour at poverty and oppression. Language is not, like everything else, in the hands of the haughty and educated: it is the people's property, and sometimes all they have.

I would have wished that Eric, who spoke the finest classless English of his generation, could have paid some attention to the pronunciation of demotic speech, though of course he had enough to do in other linguistic fields. I have always had my tinpot theories about, for instance, the relation of Cockney pronunciation to the whole corpus of English phonology, but I have never dared – as he might have done – to present possibly false but probably acceptable speculations. Why, for instance, are *v* and *w* interchangeable in the speech of Sam Weller? I like to believe that traditional London speech had a bilabial fricative, as in the Spanish *vaso*, which served for both the voiced labio-dental and the voiced labial semivowel. Dickens, hearing the sound, knew it was not quite right but could not tell how it really differed from standard phonemic use: hence he effected a literal transposition. Sam Weller's rendering of *widow* was neither *vidder* nor *wider* but /βidə/. As Eric made the study of meanings and (in his *Origins*) etymology great philosophical joy, so he might have ventured imaginative flights about the Great Vowel Shift and related, with humanity and humour, the pronunciation of Shakespeare's English to that of modern Dublin or Boston. After all, it was language as a living experience that concerned him.

For Dublin's Swift, or rather his modern readers, he performed a great service. The *Polite Conversations* were perfectly annotated, and those dialogues in which nothing is really said were shown to be a kind of ultimate repository of socio-linguistic truth, demonstrating that conversation is never about anything but it is perhaps the only thing that matters. For Shakespeare he performed a service which more orthodox scholars winced at. In *Shakespeare's Bawdy*, it was alleged, he dug out more dirt from Shakespeare than was really there. The 'Will' sonnet, for instance, was shown to be a virtuoso concert about the male and female pudenda. I do not think Eric went very far wrong, and if he did it was on the right side. (In his imagined presence one need never be ashamed of bulls.) Slang was, as he showed, mainly subversive. Literature was closer to slang than to governmental directives, and that had to be subversive too. The people's way of being subversive had always lain in the, figurative, lowering of trousers and the raising of skirts. 'Apples be ripe and nuts be brown. Petticoats up and breeches down.' Slang and literature alike tend to greater obscenity than decent people like to imagine. Eric celebrated indecency.

Because he dealt in a field traditionally trivial, as well as subversive, Eric never received the public honours that were his due. He served the Queen (and Kings before her) as well by glorying in the posterior of her, and their, English as staider men did by debasing it (I am thinking of politicians and newspaper proprietors, not jockeys). He never visited America to tell Americans about the riches of their own language. Reading room, study, club sufficed him, and the pleasure of having friends who, like him, loved English. I once toasted him with 'May you live for ever and I live to bury you.' Sadly, the second clause has just about been fulfilled. So, not sadly at all and not fancifully either, is, or will be, or is being, the first.

From *Eric Partridge In His Own Words*, ed. David Crystal
(London: Macmillan, 1981)

A Movie that Changed my Life

HAS ANY movie ever changed anybody's life? The art or craft of the cinema has had, like any other mode of expression, the chance to modify the ways we think, feel, see, hear, even believe, but it has missed it, muffed it, failed. Books are different; so is music. Spend an evening reading the sixth book of Milton's *Paradise Lost*, or listening to Mahler's *Resurrection* Symphony, and you can feel your attitude to life being changed. This is probably because you are placed in contact with a powerful sensibility, allied to a towering intellect, that is unified and knows what it believes. But movies are not individual works; they are the products of a collective, and, as such, they bristle with compromise. Reputable scriptwriters weep to find their best scenes discarded. Great directors howl with rage at brutal cuts. The film is a commercial form, and it cannot permit genius to rage untrammelled, for the general public does not care much for genius. Originality is dangerous, so is the naked truth. We have had movies that approached greatness – like Orson Welles's *Citizen Kane* – but always had to yield to what the box office would permit.

I speak, of course, of Hollywood, the world centre, as it once was, of commercial cinema. Hollywood produced very efficient artefacts, but it was short on courage – which, anyway, would always be damped by the censors. The situation in Europe has been different, though the American philosophy of film, along with American finance, has finally prevailed. Things were different when Buñuel and Dali concocted *Un Chien Andalou* and Jean Cocteau produced *Le Sang d'un Poète* on a shoestring. And, as long ago as 1926, before Fritz Lang emigrated to the United States, it was possible to approach greatness with the film *Metropolis*.

If any movie got near to changing my life, it was this. It cost a lot of money to make and nearly ruined the German organisation, Ufa, that financed it. But the expense was justified. I still look at it on videocassette – unfortunately in superadded crude tints with the accompaniment of wretched rock music (both of which, thank the

Lord, can be eliminated) – and, in 1975, I had the chance to impro-
vise music for it on the piano at a cinema club showing in Iowa City.
My father had done the same thing professionally (that is, for enough
money to buy a couple of beers) at the film's first showing in Manchester, England. I remember that occasion. It is, as they say, etched
on my brain. I was nine years old, and the publicity of stills and hand-
outs affected me powerfully before viewing it in the sixpenny stalls.
The movie itself was a revelation.

In 1926, my generation drew its childish myths from two sources
– the far past and the far future. The far past was really for the palae-
ontologists – the lost world of the brontosaurus, the tyrannosaurus,
and the pterodactyl. This was explored in boy's magazines, in a novel
by A. Conan Doyle, even in a crude film based on the latter's *The Lost
World*. The fascination was still alive when, in the middle 1930s, *King
Kong* was made. The recent re-make of that masterpiece is a disgrace:
the computerised technology that makes Kong into a credible giant
simian at the same time diminishes him by killing the mythical component. That old black-and-white original was visually crude, trying
to cheat us, but we didn't care. We accepted the limitations of the
art-form as we accept the limitations of opera and Shakespearean
drama. We make adjustments, we use imagination. The De Lauren-
tiis version of *King Kong* killed imagination by being too explicit,
and there were no adjustments to make. Kong had become a kind of
personification of the ecology; there was no room for the ambiguous.

The imaginary future was, as I say, the other side of our mythical
coin. We had been given the future long before, in H.G. Wells's *The
Time Machine* and *When the Sleeper Walks*, and our boy's magazines
presented a cruder version of it, with spaceships, robots, skyscrapers
and even the End of the World. Both the future and the past had in
common this capacity to stimulate the fancy, and this was not easily
stimulated by the 1920s, despite Scott Fitzgerald (I saw the first film
version of *The Great Gatsby*), the Black Bottom, short skirts and fancy
garters. If we British kids had been given the money for a trip to
New York, we would have seen the skyline of the future, but we were
stuck in dull suburbia, feeding on subliterary trash and the trash of
the cinema. But *Metropolis* was not trash.

The novel on which the movie was based was written by Fritz
Lang's wife, Thea Von Harbou. One could buy it in Woolworths
for five cents. I have recently re-read it, though in German: it is a
piece of competent popular literature that refuses to die. It's a pretty

melodramatic story. Let me summarise it. Sometime in the future there is a great city, ruled by one man, a kind of super-capitalist named Joh Fredersen. The community is divided into the workers and the consumers. The consumers live in great luxury, while the workers dwell underground and shuffle to work at the blast of the whistle. These do not seem to require the discipline of a police force: they are inured to the miserable labour of the factory – probably their constraints are purely economic.

A girl named Maria (played by Brigitte Helm) appears one day in the gorgeous gardens of the Club of the Sons – the sons, that is, of the ruling leisured class. She brings a group of miserable-looking children who gape in wonder at the peacocks and the flowers, and she looks the son of Joh Fredersen in the eye, saying, 'These are your brothers and sisters'. She and her charges are bundled off by major-domos and lesser flunkeys, but young Fredersen has a moment of intense revelation. *Metropolis* is founded on injustice, he realises, and he rushes to his father's office to tell him this. His father is not pleased, and he sets a spy to follow him around to see that he does not get into socialist mischief.

But the young man descends to the grim world of the workers, where he sees vast machines that appear to him to be incarnations of the god Moloch, swallowing human fodder alive. The technology is, by our standards, pretty primitive. It unloads a lot of steam, but the steam is appropriate to this vision of hell.

Young Freder Fredersen is struck particularly by the sight of a young slave crucified, as it were, on a huge ten-hour clock, on whose periphery lights flash in unpredictable places: the sweating worker's task is to touch the lights with two prongs like clock-hands. If he fails, the red rises in a vast thermometer and the whole factory is threatened with an explosion. Freder takes over the young man's task and frees him.

In the medieval quarter of *Metropolis* lives an inventor named Rotwang. He was once a contestant of Joh Fredersen's for the hand of Hel, a beautiful young woman who died giving birth to Freder. The loss and ultimate death of Hel have unbalanced him somewhat – he has even erected a stone monument to her – but his inventive faculty is sharp enough. He has created a robot, all metal body and metallic brain, and this he proudly shows to Joh Fredersen. The two men hate each other but are bound together in a kind of hostile symbiosis: inventive brain and autocratic power are joined in mutual need. But

Joh Fredersen's visit to Rotwang concerns a matter of pure politics. Rotwang's cellar leads to the old catacombs, where Peterson suspects subversive meetings are taking place. The two men descend into a region of old bones and, hidden in the shadows, they observe such a meeting.

The meeting is less political than ethico-religious. Maria is in charge. She tells to the assembled workers the story of the Tower of Babel and how the construction collapsed because there was no mediation between the hands of the builders and the brains of the entrepreneurs. '*Mittler swischen Hirn und Händen muss das Herz sein*' – between the brain and the hands there must be a heart. Young Freder, among the attentive listeners, knows that he must be the mediator, a kind of Christ. In Maria, for whom he feels an immense and complicated love, he sees the eternal mother and the eternal virgin. He declares love to her when the meeting is over; she chastely kisses him.

Joh Fredersen tells Rotwang that the workers must by confirmed in their servitude, with no nonsense about human feeling (which might mean strikes and machine-smashing) and that the robot must be given Maria's face and form and programmed to preach obedience to the Master of *Metropolis*. So Maria is captured and, in an impressive but implausible *Frankenstein* sequence, we see the metal robot take on the appearance of flesh and the face of Maria. She has no heart but she seems to have sexuality. Made to dance before the rich habitués of the club called Yoshiwara, she fires glands and provokes duels to the death in the German manner. Then she tells the workers to smash the machines. This was never in the programme. A robot can, apparently, go mad.

Smashing the machines means flooding the workers' subterranean city. There is panic. Rotwang, now mad himself, sees in the captured Maria the lineaments of the dead Hel. She escapes but he chases her into the cathedral, where lifesize effigies of the Seven Deadly Sins come to life for an instant. Young Freder, now disclosed as a kind of god who has descended into hell to redeem dead souls, finds the levels which control the machines that stop the flooding. The workers decide to burn the creature they think is Maria as a witch. She laughs through the flames, the synthetic flesh burns off, and there, in metallic indifference, stands the robot. Meanwhile Rotwang is chasing Maria over the roof of the cathedral. Freder gets up there too, hurls the inventor to his death, and rescues the virgin-mother who will now, presumably, be his wife. It does not look as though the social inequalities of *Metropolis* are going to change much, despite the fact that Freder joins the hands of the Master and the representative of the workers. He is the heart, and brain and hands have found their mediator. There is no talk of trade unions, better housing, fairer wages. A mythological point has been made, and the film comes to an end.

It is a melodramatic plot, and the implausibilities stick out like sore thumbs. Some of the acting would be booed even on an old-time barnstorming circuit. But realism is not wanted here: Fritz Lang is working in the German tradition of *Expressionismus*. The aim of that movement, whose best German exponent is Ernst Toller and whose lasting theatrical monument is Elmer Rice's *The Adding Machine*, was to thud home a thesis, usually political, with every possible device – symbolism, song, choral chant, stylised movement, décor – and a total abandonment of such traditional dramatic properties as character. If the only personage in *Metropolis* that has any allure is the robot as Maria, that is because sexuality has pushed its impertinent way in, and not even sex has any place in Expressionism.

The film is, for all its faults, one of our few cinematic classics, and this is because it provides ikons. The visual exaggerations are metaphors that stick in the mind. Lang first saw the towers of Metropolis when he approached the New York skyline from the sea, but his own imagined city borrows only the Babel aspect – 'Let us build a tower that will reach the sky'. His pasteboard architecture chills because of its beauty: the Paternoster Tower has, in its structure as well as its name, a biblical resonance, a cathedral-like quality which announces a new religion. The worship of power and money is seen in New York not in an architectural philosophy: the skyscrapers are not bound together in an urban plan, they are each a monument to individual thrust, and, in New York, individualism is rampant. But in Lang's Metropolis individualism is the property of one man only, the Master. We are in a totalitarian state, and the architecture is totalitarian.

Lang's vision is, of course, prophetic, but the prophecy has never been fulfilled. Hitler came to power seven years after the film was completed, but his tyranny took a form different from Joh Fredersen's. Fredersen's power is at least sane in the American manner. It is based on money and is totally American. There is nothing militaristic or racial in it. He has never read the philosopher Hegel, with his forecast of the World Soul manifesting itself in the Aryan race.

There is no anti-Semitism, and the only uniforms are the drab ones of the workers, who probably owe something to the state-slaves of Zamyatin's novel *We*, who are called 'unifs' – they are their uniforms and nothing more. Hitler's Germany was a nightmare which not even Lang could foresee, but his own nightmare is more terrible because it creates myth, which the mechanised Nazis never could. All the Nazis could ultimately give to us in the arts is the material of rather vapid adventure movies – dodging the Gestapo, blowing up the heavy water works at Peenemünde. The racial policy was demented and is fitter for psychological probing than for art. The proletarian slavery that Lang depicts is rational: men will submit to anything in order to earn bread. It is American rationalism, Taylorism if you like, and a world away from the Teutonic dreams of Hitler.

None of this is really the point. Film is a visual medium, and, if the task of literature is to stud the brain with quotations, cinema's job is to cram it with images which transcend story-line and feed the need for myth. There are very few films which have done this. *King Kong* is one of them, and so is *The Incredible Shrinking Man*, whose makers could never have foreseen its mythical impact. We are told by the French post-structuralists that the writer doesn't write: the writer is written, is controlled by the language he uses. And so Lang was controlled by the limitations of black and white, by mocked-up urban landscapes which never pretended to be real, and probably by the strange ambiguous beauty of Brigitte Helm. The film can never be remade, though a musical version of it has enjoyed a limited run in London. Its retinting has maimed its essence, and the addition of aspirational pop-songs about setting people free is an impertinence. The film was never meant to be political propaganda. Lang admits that he was primarily fascinated by machines, above all perhaps by the huge machine which is the film-making complex.

When I say, though with many reservations, that *Metropolis* is a movie that changed my life I perhaps really mean that it changed my childhood. 'In the lost childhood of Judas,' wrote George Russell, 'Christ was betrayed.' Perhaps our adult lives are nothing more than sophisticated replays of our extreme youth. The myths which nourish our childhood are implanted for ever. I can never free myself from *Metropolis*.

Previously unpublished and undated

By-products of the Ink Trade

I MAKE IT fifty American authors so far and thirteen British though there are borderline instances, like Auden, Eliot and P.G. Wodehouse, where adoptive nationality tells us nothing. Literature, as the *Paris Review* (an American publication) sees it, is international (five French, one Italian, one Irishman, one Russian, two South Americans, etc.). It is more; it is a kind of Church Militant, according to Joyce Carol Oates, who finds Lawrence not quite English: 'I take seriously Flaubert's statement that writers must love one another in our art as the mystics love one another in God. By honouring one another's creation we honour something that deeply connects us all, and goes beyond us.'

But everything has to be measured, it seems, in terms of the American achievement, and it is mostly Americans who do the interviewing. This is not so much writers at work as writers not at work, writers being pumped by earnest American academics and made to yield everything of their essences except how they work. In the last series, to the loudly expressed disgust of Mr Auberon Waugh, son of the writer, I was made to give the recipe for Lancashire hotpot. He was disgusted by the dish and by myself for liking it, not by the mode of the interview. What we learn about the work of writing is mostly such trifles as Gore Vidal getting down to it after coffee and a bowel movement, and Kingsley Amis starting off unshaven and in a dressing gown, but getting dressed later, when the pubs are open.

It is, however, the non-writing aspects of these writers' revelations which fascinate. Wodehouse was caught by the Nazis because he was fond of his dogs and Britain has draconian quarantine laws. The late Henry Green revelled in his deafness. INTERVIEWER: 'And how about 'subtle'?' GREEN: 'I don't follow. *Suttee*, as I understand it, is the suicide – now forbidden – of a Hindu wife on her husband's flaming bier. I don't want my wife to do that when my time comes – and with great respect, as I know her, she won't.' Isaac Bashevis Singer thinks very highly of Thomas Hardy. The whole collection is among other things an anthology of opinions on Robert Frost. Archibald MacLeish says: '… He worked very hard at his own reputation even when he had no need to… This was damaging only to him.' James Dickey – well, we need a new paragraph for his views on Frost:

> He says a good thing now and then, but with a strange way of averting his eyes while saying it which may be profound and may be poppycock. If it were thought that anything I wrote was influenced by Robert Frost, I would take that particular work of mine, shred it, and flush it down the toilet, hoping not to clog the pipes.

Dickey also calls Sylvia Plath the Judy Garland of American poetry and finds her and Anne Sexton equally embarrassing. He talks of 'poor' Dylan Thomas. Gore Vidal talks of 'poor' Anthony Burgess. Vidal is witty while Dickey is self-consciously redneck. INTERVIEWER: 'Have you ever thought of acting, as Norman Mailer does?' VIDAL: 'Is *that* what he does? I have always been curious.' He finds Bellow 'interesting – which is more than you can say for so many of the other Jewish Giants, carving their endless Mount Rushmores out of halvah. Calder Willingham I've always liked – that frantic heterosexuality.' Tennessee Williams, he tells us, did not go to lunch with E. M. Forster because – oh, let's have the whole anecdote

> As usual with Tennessee, we missed the first train. The second train would arrive in half an hour. Tennessee refused to wait. 'But we *have* to go,' I said. 'He's sitting on one of the lions in front of his college, waiting for us.' Tennessee was not moved by this poignant tableau. 'I can't,' he said, gulping and clutching his heart – when Tennessee does not spit blood he has heart spasms. 'Besides,' said Tennessee primly, wandering off in the wrong direction for the exit, 'I cannot abide old men with urine stains on their trousers.'

Very funny, but he should not have said 'poor Anthony Burgess'. I am glad now I arranged for him not to get into the current *Encyclopaedia Britannica*. The intensest interviews are with Archibald MacLeish and William Gass. MacLeish talks in thick paragraphs like porridge about the old Paris days, old enough to have known everybody: Scott, Jack Bate, Dos, the Murphys. Ms Dickinson is 'Emily': surely he's not that old. Gass talks of writing out of hate: he's a Distinguished Professor at Washington University and can afford to take his art seriously. More seriously, I mean, than everybody else, though there's nobody here who doesn't talk with awe about his or her vocation, except 91-year-old Plum, who's always liked writing and had a jolly good time with it.

Pablo Neruda, like nearly everyone, says something about Robert Frost, who sticks up like a withered flower in all this talk about Soviet writers being proud of the socialist structure and the people's role in the revolution. 'I have never,' he says, 'seen less disagreement between a state and the writers than in the socialist countries.' May he, in the land of the Shades, have all this out with Vladimir Nabokov.

The most impressive interview is with Jerzy Kosiński. This man suffered from the socialists as much as the Nazis and taught himself to write English with a speed that would have astounded his compatriot Conrad. He can also speak it like a natal Anglophone, which Conrad never could. There's urgency in his interview, as there is in his writing. INTERVIEWER: 'You always expect the worst?' KOSINSKI: 'No: the unexpected. I look forward to it.' INTERVIEWER: 'But all the preparations for the future...' KOSINSKI: 'The future? So far all my plans have turned out to be for yesterday.'

This collection is a heartening read. One gets the feeling that, for all the socialist talk of its being a minority sub-culture, literature is going to be able to survive.

Observer, 16 August 1981
Review of *Writers At Work: The* Paris Review *Interviews,
Fifth Series*, ed. George Plimpton
(Harmondsworth: Penguin, 1981)

Pilgrimage

BY NO stretch of usage can 'virago' be made not to signify a shrew, a scold, an ill-tempered woman, unless we go back to the etymology – a man-like maiden (cognate with 'virile') – and the antique meaning, amazon, that is close to it. It is an unlovely and aggressive name, even for a militant feminist organisation, and it presides awkwardly over the reissue of a great *roman fleuve* which is too important to be associated with chauvinist sows. The novel is a bisexual form. If it is claimed for *Pilgrimage* that the female sensibility is exhibited, and the importance of the female point of view is exploited, to an extent very salutary in a male-dominated world, much the same may be said of every major novel written by an author who happens, by chance, to be a man, from *Pamela* to *Take a Girl Like You*. The masculine novel exists eccentrically with Hemingway, though he had to learn from Gertrude Stein. For the rest, any serious novelist regards as a vocational imperative the probing of the sensibility of the other sex. When, as so often in American colleges, I am told that *Madame Bovary* has to be a failure because it was written by a man, I shudder at the loss of belief, promoted by a sectional interest, in the powers of the creative imagination. Jane Austen's men are imaginative triumphs; and so are Shakespeare's women.

Dorothy Richardson's novel is unusual in its length – thirteen volumes and, in this very fine edition, 2110 pages – and in its unrelenting solipsism. The first volume, *Pointed Roofs*, appeared in 1915 and was greeted unsympathetically because its *mise en scène* is a cultured and pacific Germany. But, when *Jacob's Room* and *Ulysses* came out and the 'experimental' novel startled and excited, Dorothy Richardson was seen to have been a pioneer in the breaking of old epistemological conventions. The continuum of life is contained by the observing sensibility, time is as fluid with her as with Proust, of whom she is the sole British analogue, and scene and action are more fictions of the mind than external realities. A corresponding stylistic fluidity encompassed devices like the interior monologue and

a disdain for traditional punctuation. After *Ulysses*, Dorothy Richardson was talked of a great deal but not much read, or else read
desultorily as *Les Lauriers Sont Coupés* was read – to see how much
ground was broken with picks, before Joyce the master came along
with his electric drills.

To be honest, *Pilgrimage* is sometimes laborious reading. Its
author, on whom German influences were strong, accepted Goethe's
programme for fiction: 'in the novel, reflections and incidents should
be featured; in drama, character and action. The novel must proceed
slowly, and the thought-processes of the principal figures must, by
one device or another, hold up the development of the whole... The
hero of the novel must be acted upon, or, at any rate, not himself be
the principal operator...' And so, with a painful slowness of which
Dorothy Richardson herself was painfully unaware, the sensibility
of her heroine, Miriam Henderson, is set forth in its progress from
early uncertainty to eventual maturity. The pilgrimage is that of an
independent woman like Dorothy Richardson herself, a new Aurora
Leigh or Jane Eyre, forced to earn her living in a man's world, despising the traditional female role Victorian society would impose on her,
rejecting men's standards but not altogether rejecting men.

Miriam's experiences parallel those of her creatrix, but the
standards we must bring to the work are those of pure fiction, not
autobiography. By contemporary, or Jongian standards, the experiences are limited. Though an aspect of the novel's undoubted
greatness is the sharpness of sensuous detail, the erotic plays no part
in it. Nor, for that matter, does the feminist activism which was live
enough in the period covered – the late Victorian and Edwardian –
drag the work out of art and into propaganda. There is an intense
intellectual excitement: ideas flash, books are read and the news is
discussed. But *Pilgrimage* is not a cerebral work, and it is far from
tendentious. When, as in the volume *Deadlock*, male domination
provokes irritability, Miriam keeps her thoughts to herself, does not
shout in Hyde Park:

> Because some women had corns, feminine beauty was a myth;
> because the world could do without Mrs Hemans's poetry, women
> should confine their attention to puddings and babies. The infernal
> complacent cheek of it... On whose authority had men decided
> that science and art were greater than anything else? The world
> could not go on until this question had been answered. Until

then, until it had been clearly explained that men were always and always partly wrong in their ideas, life would be full of poison and secret bitterness.

From the moment in *Pointed Roofs* when Miriam notes how the common chord of C is the same as that of E flat and yet different, we know that we are to be in the company of a sensorium to which sound is of large importance. *Pilgrimage* is, among other things, about sounds, especially the sounds of speech. In no other work, to my knowledge, is there such a profound concern with the class and national aspects of spoken English, which is always reproduced with uncanny exactitude. There is no voice, whatever language it speaks, which does not leap from the page straight to the inner ear. The processes of speech, with their incoherences and illogicalities, provide a kind of model for the proclaimed *stylelessness* of the récit. Dorothy Richardson disdained style as masculine posturing, the setting up of syntactical public monuments.

T.S. Eliot said, at tea with Virginia Woolf, that *Ulysses* represented the death of style. Old styles are ostentatiously killed in *Ulysses*, while Joyce's own voice improvises new kinds of music appropriate to whatever subject sails into the consciousness of the operative, or non-operative, character. The same is true of Dorothy Richardson. In the magnificent *Oberland* the alpine scenery which takes possession of Miriam's senses clots the sentence structures, too massive to be contained in elegance. And yet there is always the sense of a substructure, deeper than conventional grammar, which signifies the assurance, the achieved personality, of the mature Miriam. Original as *Pilgrimage* is, like *Ulysses* it abounds in evidence of the traditional novelistic virtues: awareness of the whole range of human experience, fascination with people, especially when they are speaking, the power of psychological penetration to the deepest level, skill with language, the ability to create a world. If we want the immediate impact on the senses of the Victorian and Edwardian age, we must go to Dorothy Richardson.

She resembles no other writer. Perhaps, falsely, we catch an echo of *Last Post*, the final volume of Ford's *Parade's End*. Or we may think, in the slow scrupulousness of notation, we are near to Henry James. But ultimately this is a work of profound individuality. If we find boredom, that is because we are looking for the wrong thing – the fevered activity of the popular novel, the gross exhibitionism of the fiction of the sexual revolution. And if there is a genuine fault, it lies in the consistency of the solipsism: we cannot get outside Miriam, as we can outside Bloom or Mrs Dalloway. But this is the condition of the enterprise and we must accept it. Whatever the motives of the Virago organisation in presenting the first popular edition of the work, lovers of literature, or either sex, unconcerned with sexism, must be grateful to it for the recovery of a great fictional masterpiece. Or, God help us, mistresspiece.

Guardian, 9 December 1979
Review of *Pilgrimage* by Dorothy Richardson
(London: Virago Press, 1979)

Finks and Winchells

THE LATE David Maurer was Professor Emeritus of Linguistics at the University of Louisville. He was one of the pioneers of the study of American cant and argot, starting his work in the wake of H.L. Mencken's *The American Language*, which asserted the separateness of the English of the United States from the tongue of the mother country. While Mencken, who was not a professional linguist, assumed the existence of a unified kind of American English enlivened by regional variations, Maurer sought to emphasise an essential disunity and the absence of a central norm on the lines of the so-called 'King's English'. He believed that the normative approach to language taught in schools and colleges aped a tradition in the motherland that was already fossilised in the eighteenth century, and a reasonable approach to American English might be in terms of American subcultures and their distinctive specialised forms of the language. Two of his former pupils have selected, from over two hundred books and papers and articles published by Maurer, a number of brief glossaries relating mainly to the criminal or sub-criminal trades. If we seem to know many of the words already, this is because a whole generation of specialist lexicographers has drawn deeply on Maurer, who never himself pursued the harmless drudgery beyond the glossarial stage, though his *Argot of the Criminal Narcotic Addict*, with its seventy-odd double-columned pages, could be classified as genuinely a pocket dictionary.

It is commonly assumed that there is, in proportion to the population, more criminality in America than in Europe. Maurer seems to accept the assumption and take some pride in it, though it is rather a pride in the linguistic wealth of the American criminal than in his antisocial enactments. European criminals, like English puritans, found a refuge in the Land of the Free, and the Mafia – which, sadly, has contributed little to the English lexis – has turned America into a hypertrophied Sicily. But some of the organised crime of America finds no counterpart in Europe. The bootlegger and his customers equally defied the Volstead Act, which itself could be glossed as a sort of criminality, and specifically American crime may be regarded as a response to specifically American puritanism. The moonshiners, tucked away in the Kentucky hills, are technically criminals, but it is easier to accept them as exponents of American individualism. The line is always hard to draw. The point, anyway, is not how specialist argots derive from antisocial trades, but how these argots are generated and sustained by the closed nature of the social groups which use them.

Maurer, we are told, was a man well qualified for this kind of linguistic fieldwork. He was big, tough, broad-shouldered, but never to be mistaken for a cop or a fed. The law used him to instruct its undercover agent in the use of one patois or another, but he found it hard to unteach his pupils the furtive predatory manner of the fuzz or pig (which term, incidentally, is as old as 'China Street pig', used for a Bow Street runner in the late eighteenth century). He himself was always accepted, and the lexical fruits are in this book. He began not with criminals but with North Atlantic fishermen, from whom, working with them at the nets, he garnered not only terms like *gurry* (fish entrails), *dong* (penis), *whore's egg* (a small spiny crustacean relished by Italians) and *put your face on* (spoil someone's good looks) but also peculiarities of verb morphology (*I had seed* but *he have seed*; *I does*/du:z but *he do*). Then he fared inland to engage circuses and carnivals.

A number of the terms he picked up from showpeople in 1931 have now passed into the general American vocabulary, such as *cheaters* (spectacles), *saw-buck* (ten-dollar bill), *century* (a hundred-dollar bill, hence *C-Note*), *dip* (pickpocket), *Johnny-come-lately* (greenhorn), *hustler* (prostitute), while other are already dead, such as *jig-opry* (negro minstrel), *mitt* (palmist), *lucky-boy* (lazy young man who lives off a circus girl), and *main guy* (show boss). His list, like all his lists, serves to show how ephemeral much of the argot of a subculture is. All such glossaries tend to be word-museums.

Maurer's verbal gleanings from the prostitute's trade fill a mere two pages, and he explains why. 'Argots originate in tightly closed cliques, in groups where there is a strong sense of camaraderie and highly developed group solidarity based primarily on community of occupation. Since prostitution, by its very low position in the hierarchy of the crime world and by virtue of its internal organisation, denies the prostitute all claim to true professional status, it is obvious that professional pride is lacking as a motive for argot.' Moreover, there is in prostitutes, as is evident from their fantasies (some of which, like Dr Johnson's friend Ben Flint, they try to eternise in doggerel), a desire for conformity and respectability. Their language is a poor thing, but it has, or had, phrases like *hair pie, public enemy* (a customer's wife), and *Oom Paul* (a customer, not necessarily a Boer, who likes cunnilingus). This must be the only trade which calls on the title of a classic play to designate one of its activities: *She Stoops to Conquer* describes fellatio, which, by the less cultivated, may be called *Way Down South in Dixie*. Maurer persistently confuses sodomy and pederasty. He is not interested in the origins of words and phrases, which makes him no true philologist. Eric Partridge was right to insist on providing etymologies, even when these were tentative or mere guesswork. Maurer gives us no hint, for instance, as to why a hooker who accepts coition up the dirt road is called a *turquoise*.

Before we engage genuine criminals, let us consider the language of the moonshiner, very little of whose terminology can be explicated on a basis of straight translation. It is not enough to define *kerosene liquor* as 'liquor contaminated by kerosene.' We have to know that a teaspoon of kerosene in a one thousand gallon vat of beer will cause all the liquor to taste of itself. When the boiler is fired with kerosene the moonshiner must wash his hands carefully 'after filling the pressure tank, and not allow any of his supply bags to lean against a kerosene drum while hauling them to the still site.' *Horse-blanket whisky* describes a crude liquor made by covering a boiling kettle of beer with a heavy horse-blanket which is periodically wrung of its condensed moisture. 'This technique is not approved of by first-class moonshiners.' To *bulldog* is 'to heat used barrels by setting them against a large oil drum in which a fire is built in order to sweat out the whisky that has soaked into the barrel staves.' Half the glossary is richly technical, the other half has to do with beating the *revenooers*.

The cream of the criminal world are probably the Confidence Men, whose complex skills entail a very precise mastery of conventional language but whose inner argot is colourfully arcane. The victim, as we all know, is the *mark*, but he is also the *apple, egg, fink, savage, winchell, chump* and (why?) *Mr John Bates*. On him is played the *big con* or the *short con*. The biggest of the big con games is the *payoff*, and the term is shorthand for a whole scenario. A wealthy mark is led to believe that he has been taken into a deal by which a big racing syndicate is to be swindled. 'At first he plays with money furnished by the confidence men, then is put on the send for all the cash he can raise, fleeced and blown off.' There is also the *wire*, in which a bogus Western Union official convinces the mark that he can delay the transmission of race results to the bookmakers long enough for the mark to place a bet after the race is run. And so on.

Maurer remembers that, while words are the daughters of men, things – which include criminal activities – are the sons of heaven. Glorying in the plenitude of argot, he at the same time deplores the 'major industry' which sustains it. America and presumably other nations will only learn to deal with organised crime when they understand its nature, which involves knowing its language. This sounds like the usual social justification of an academic obsession: in a materialist society it is often difficult to defend the pure as opposed to the applied study. Liquidate criminality and part of Maurer's occupation, or that of his followers, is gone. When he says '... we have seen within the last two decades the mass invasion of a definitely criminal subculture by teenagers (and sometimes pre-teens) from the dominant culture – an invasion that has played havoc with the criminal's culture pattern as well as his argot' it is as though he were trembling at the situation of an endangered species. Yet who could deny the nobility of his vocation or do other than praise the results of his enquiries among the jug-heavy, forgers, faro bank men, three-shell game operators, pickpockets and junkies? He was a Greene or Dekker with tenure.

Times Literary Supplement, 22 January 1982
Review of *Language of the Underworld* by David W. Maurer
(Lexington: University Press of Kentucky, 1981)

The School of Jesuits

IT ALWAYS used to worry me that there was a notorious social-
ite drug-taker named Peggy Hopkins Joyce, as though Antichrist
had deliberately sent into the world a vicious degraded dual sneer,
onomastic if nothing else, at the two modern writers I revere most.
These two, Gerard Manley Hopkins and James Joyce, have a great
deal in common. Hopkins was a Jesuit priest; Joyce was reared by
the Jesuits. Hopkins became professor of Greek at UCD; Joyce was
a student there. Both were employing the English lexis. Both were
musicians. Fate carefully decreed that they were not to know each
other. Joyce was seven when Hopkins died. Joyce's style had already
evolved into the Babylonish dialect of *Ulysses* by the time, in 1918,
Hopkins's poems were first published. Joyce seems eventually to have
read Hopkins, and there is even a brief passage in *Finnegans Wake*
where he seems to parody him. Nevertheless, in describing him as 'an
English Mallarmé', he seems to disclose no very strong understanding of his essence – an essence so like his own.

One sees a resemblance of verbal technique at a quite superficial
level. Neither writer liked hyphens. The German language, which
is cognate with English, gets on well without hyphens. There is a
certain visual thrill in forms like *Selbstgefälligkeit* or *Vervollständi-
gung*, where the basic elements are jammed together, without benefit
of the instant analysis that hyphenisation provides, into what looks
like a totally new verbal creation. 'Beer-hating' too obviously refers to
people who hate beer; 'beerhating' means the same and looks like a
new word. Hopkins gives us 'fallowbootfellow' and Joyce 'silvamoon-
lake.' Both writers loved the Anglo-Saxon element in English and
enjoyed exaggerating it. They liked to reorganise the shape of the
English sentence into the bizarre and just-about intelligible. 'Nor yet
plod safe shod sound,' writes Hopkins. Joyce writes: 'Signatures of all
things I am here to read, seaspawn and wrack, the nearing tide, that
rusty boot. Snotgreen, bluesilver, rust: coloured signs.' The phrases
seem fresh-minted, they sound new.

It is their common concern with music that brings them towards a similarity of verbal technique. Hopkins was a composer. He did not write great music, but he looked forward, even in the 1860s, to such contemporary innovations as microtones. In his song 'Falling Rain' he provides the notation for a half-flat – a division of the tone which was far too revolutionary for his contemporary Richard Wagner. Joyce, of course, was a fine tenor: he might have done as well as Count John McCormack if he had paid more attention to the development of his voice. There is in *Ulysses* a conversation, in Italian, between Stephen Dedalus and his music-teacher which talks of the '*sacrifizio incruento*' – on the altar of literature – of his budding tenor voice: but the love of song remained with him, and both the great novels are alive with melody.

Both Hopkins and Joyce tried to compose sentences which should have the sonic constitution of a vocal melody. When Hopkins writes 'Earnest, earthless, equal, attuneable, vaulty, voluminous… stupendous,' he is producing a vocal line which has a beat's rest in it. Joyce deliberately organises his vowels and diphthongs so as to make the reciting voice perform a vocal exercise. 'He saw his trunk and limbs ririppled over and sustained, buoyed lightly upward, lemonyellow: his navel, bud of flesh: and saw the dark tangled curls of his bush floating, floating hair of the stream around the limp father of thousands, a languid floating flower.' Needless to say, both writers have to be read aloud. Hopkins wrote to his friend Robert Bridges of the danger of tackling his verse with the eye alone. The effect was of a kind of 'raw nakedness.' Both are supreme writers for the blind and keen-eared. They have no appeal at all for the tone-deaf.

But Hopkins and Joyce alike found in music something which literature could not easily imitate. Literature is monody, the single line, the voice unaccompanied. Music is capable of multiplicity of lines all proceeding together, the Western glory unvouchsafed to the East. We call this counterpoint. Aldous Huxley, long after the publication of both *Ulysses* and the collected Hopkins, wrote a novel called *Point Counter Point*, in which a number of separate plots proceed simultaneously, one having no hierarchical precedence over another. Of course, the reader cannot take these plots simultaneously: he can only, having read the book, have a kind of contrapuntal memory of many things going on at the same time.

Hopkins and Joyce wanted genuine sonic simultaneity, and they could achieve it only by compressing more than one meaning into a single word or phrase. In Hopkins's sonnet 'The Windhover' the word 'buckle' resents a forceful ambiguity which is at the root of the strength of the poem. Perceiving the windhover or kestrel in the sky, Fr Hopkins SJ sees in it the beauty of Christ. His heart responds in both a sense of unworthiness and a vast upsurge of love which requires an outlet in spiritual action. 'Buckle' conveys the opposed impulses, for it can mean both to fasten (as a belt for military action) and to collapse (as a bicycle wheel). But Hopkins was not yet living in an age which could deliberately remake word so as to convey a double meaning. When he writes 'treads through, prick-proof, thick, thousands of thorns, thoughts,' he evidently sees the thorns and thoughts as one thing, but he dare not write 'thornts.' That kind of refashioning had to be left to Joyce in *Finnegans Wake*.

Finnegans Wake is real counterpoint. It represents us all with a technique for saying, or singing, more than one thing at a time. On the very first page we read 'not yet, though all's fair in vanessy, were sosie sesthwers wroth with twone nathanjoe.' The image is multiple – Swift and *Macbeth* and the Old Testament all come together. Joyce had played, without success, at making a verbal fugue in the Ormond bar episode of *Ulysses*; *Finnegans Wake* is all fugue, and very tough fugue too. But also very diverting, like an endless music hall song.

Both Joyce and Hopkins were Jesuits, and one wonders whether this verbal obsession and urge to innovate are a special inheritance of Jesuit training. Before an answer can be given – and I don't propose to give it here – one has to relate various things to Jesuitry, such as baroque and the concern with the forceful communication. What was not perhaps specially Jesuitical in both writers was a concern with God's creation as manifested in uniqueness, oddness even.

Hopkins was much concerned with 'inscape' and 'instress', Joyce with 'epiphanies'. They meant alike the sudden shining forth of some aspect of truth or reality – invariably out of the commonest events or objects. Such a revelation requires language that is itself new, fresh and startling, yet neither bizarre nor hieratic. The gift of creating such language was granted to both.

The Irish Times, 2 February 1982

Last Embers of Modernism

MR GRAHAM GREENE, whom I admire quite as much as Monsieur Jacques Médecin, Maire de Nice, though for different reasons, expressed sorrow in the correspondence columns of the *Observer* that I should rebuke him for omitting *Last Post* from Ford Madox Ford's *Parade's End* in its Bodley Head version. He cited a letter from Ford attesting to his own dissatisfaction with the book, dissatisfaction which, in my view, Mr Greene too eagerly seized upon.

One must not take over-seriously an author's dissatisfaction with his own work, of which he is not, after all, necessarily the best judge. Shakespeare never even published his collected works, which may be taken as a gesture of dissatisfaction with them or certainly an unpardonable insouciance. Should Heminge and Condell have declined editorship? I say nothing of Kafka's dying demand that all his works be destroyed, nor of Mr Greene's suppression of his own admirable early adventure novels. In this critic's view, *Last Post* is the right ending for the Tietjens sequence, and there was a time when Ford thought so too.

C.H. Sisson says of *Last Post* that it is the weakest of the four books, but it contains too much of the essential Ford to be cast aside; and that it would be a pity if the Bodley Head Ford Madox Ford was regarded as a sort of canon. I agree. *The Rash Act* ought to be bought and read by all interested in the novel as an art-form. I know that there are not many of these, but for the few, which ought to include all British novelists, even Booker Prizemen, this is a testament of the modernism which our own carelessness has allowed to die.

The Rash Act was first published in 1933, and Ford told Ezra Pound that the book 'is more like what I wanted to write than anything I have done for years.' Six years later, in the year of his death, he told Caroline Gordon: 'It was my best book – more, that is to say, like what I really wanted to write than anything I have yet done.' Ford's denigration of *Last Post* reminds us to take none of this too seriously. But *The Rash Act* is so patently what fictional modernism is, or was, about that we can do without Ford's adjudication and rationalise our own admiring response.

The problem for all fiction writers is to decide who is telling the story. This may not seem, for the average mere novel reader, much of a problem, and he may scoff at the agony I allege I have been undergoing for the past year in deciding how to narrate a new long novel which is, as regards characters, actions, *mise en scène* and even conclusion, quite clear in my mind. If the story is to be told by one of the characters in it, that limits this narrator to what he can see and understand, which may not be enough for a wide and various canvas. If the narrator becomes God, seeing and knowing all, this means that he himself is only a character in the novel since he cannot be identified with a real personage outside it. Omniscience signifies unreliability. The man who says he knows all is bound to be lying, therefore his story is a fraud. Novels are supposed to be about truth.

Ford's solution in *Parade's End* was to provide a multiplicity of viewpoints and, hence, of styles. In a more flamboyant manner this was also Joyce's solution in *Ulysses*. The first thing that the subjective viewpoint imposes is a concept of time which does not accord with objective chronology. Time does not really exist outside ourselves, and our memories do not function in the manner of history books. Subjective time is spatialised, and we can wander over it freely, moving from August back to January and forward to October. The essence of fictional modernism is the subjective viewpoint – which is in accordance with experience as we know it – and a kind of time which has little to do with clocks.

If *The Rash Act* is a smaller work than *Parade's End*, it is because it is tied to only one viewpoint. We don't have the thrilling shifts from Tietjens to Sylvia Tietjens and Valentine Wannop and back again; we have solely the sensibility of Henry Martin Aluin Smith, Rhodes Scholar and son of a candy tycoon, who, in a bright August in 1931 and in sight of the Mediterranean, has decided to kill himself.

The title of the book comes from *The Times* Law Report of 14 July 1931, in which the rash act of suicide is presented by a coroner as a consequence of, *inter alia*, 'the prevailing dissoluteness and consequent depression that are now worldwide.' In other words, it is the period of the Wall Street crash. This Smith meets by chance another Smith – Hugh Monckton Allard – an Englishman whom he had known briefly during the war. An easy, successful fellow, thinks Henry Martin, and wishes he could change identities with him. Ironically, he does. The Smith who seems to have everything to live for actually kills himself, while the Smith who has nothing dithers, evades, but, to save the other Smith's reputation, pretends to be the true suicide.

This sounds an artificial story, but the minimal plot is the armature which supports the web of subjective impression and reminiscence, the notation of the world, both inside and out, as it really is – shifting, luminous, unreliable. Strictures about unsound syntax and deformed vision don't apply: this is how the human mind perceives the world in all its unsyntactical variety. This is modernism, which died in 1939, along with Ford Madox Ford.

If we want a separable content – another bone, like plot, to throw to the dogs of reason – we shall find it in Ford's changed view of things between the last post of the war and the economic and social breakdown of a period which prefigures out own. The action takes place in the French South which Ford loved, but man no longer sustains the tradition of myth and history which that region once represented. Tietjens was, finally, not on his own. *Last Post* shows him building a new life and accepting a future. Here, in *The Rash Act*, we have the death of morality and responsibility – a forbidding theme, but, in the paradox of art, it is made to serve a tapestry of rich colour and galloping vivacity.

Observer, 11 April 1982
Review of *The Rash Act* by Ford Madox Ford
(Manchester: Carcanet Press, 1982)

Medieval Sherlock

IT IS November 1327. The Franciscan monk from Oxford, accompanied by a Benedictine novice from Melk, arrives at an Italian monastery: 'His height surpassed that of a normal man and he was so thin that he seemed still taller. His eyes were sharp and penetrating; his thin and slightly beaky nose gave his countenance the expression of a man on the lookout...'

When we hear that his name is William of Baskerville we at once suspect that he is a preincarnation of Sherlock Holmes, especially since he is coming to investigate a series of crimes at the abbey. We are convinced when he divines that a number of anxious servants are searching for the abbot's strayed horse – 'fifteen hands, the fastest in your stables, with a dark coat, a full tail, small round hoofs, but a very steady gait; small head, sharp ears, big eyes.' He also guesses that the name of the horse is Brunellus. How, asks his Benedictine companion, can he know all this? Elementary, my dear Adso: 'One of the blackberry bushes... still held some long black horsehairs in its brambles.' And so on. And why, Brunellus? 'What other name could he possibly have? Why, even the great Buridan, who was about to become rector in Paris, when he wants to use a horse in one of his logical examples, always calls it Brunellus.'

So we seem to have then a kind of game or joke, the transplantation of the sleuth of Baker Street to medieval Italy, not so much of a game or joke if you have read (which Dr Eco probably hasn't) Owen Dudley Edward's biography of Conan Doyle, in which he presents convincing evidence that Sherlock Holmes is the product of a Jesuit education. Of course, the Jesuits didn't exist in William of Baskerville's time, but – learned in Aquinas and Aristotle and prepared to use the empirical techniques of Roger Bacon – William would make a very good English Jesuit. Although in orders, he lacks the rotundity, Wildean paradoxicality and compassion of Father Brown, but clearly Dr Eco knows his Chesterton. Theology and criminal detection go, for some reason, well together.

The first crimes are purely theological – mere (*mere?*) heresy – but
then monks start mysteriously to die. It takes Williams a good 490
pages to discover the single motivation behind what are obviously
cold-blooded murders – he is a slower worker than Holmes and his
creator is not writing for the *Strand Magazine*. Moreover, the motivation is of a subtlety that forbids even the most educated guesswork,
and some of the clues are in Latin.

The novel is much too complex and interesting in its non-narrative
substance to make a reviewer shy of disclosing the denouement. This
has to do with a book in the abbey library which the librarian, who
is blind and devout and not an obvious suspect, does not wish his
fellow monks to see – or, if they do see it, they had better not survive.
It is the lost second part of Aristotle's 'Poetics,' in which the Stagyr-
ite presents a rationale of the comic. Now as medieval theology was
to some extent based on Aristotelian philosophy, there is a danger
that Christianity may be corrupted by humour: if Aristotle gives it
his blessing people may laugh at the Devil instead of fighting him.
The librarian, Jorge, is sternly anti-Chestertonian. He is evidently not
meant to be that other blind Jorge who, alas, has once again failed to
win the Nobel Prize for Literature.

The pages of the forbidden book are impregnated with poison.
When the reader licks his thumb to turn over the pages he deals
his own death. William, naturally, wears gloves to read it. Jorge, his
plot discovered, eats the book and dies horribly. Lamps fall and the
library sets on fire. Soon the whole monastery is ablaze. The greatest
store of knowledge in Christendom is destroyed. The Italian periodical *Panorama* has described this story as 'perfidiously analogous
to our times.' The French *Libération* says that it is a 'vibrant plea for
freedom, moderation, and wisdom.' I think they both mean that Eco
is against humourless fanaticism.

As the reader will know, this novel has been a bestseller in every
country where it has appeared. It was strange to see it heading the
New York Times bestseller list, with John le Carré, Morris West,
Norman Mailer and Jackie Collins limping behind. Its auguries (and
its American advance) were no indication of great popularity. Dr Eco
is a semiotician and a Joyce scholar; my own personal acquaintance
with him has always been of an academic kind; nobody expected him
to write a novel, let alone a runaway bestseller.

Everything in the book would seem to militate against a wide
readership. It is erudite, crammed with Latin and curious theology,

bristling with strange words, almost devoid of sexual interest. It presents, in quite remarkable detail, the life of a medieval closed male society which, one would have thought, could have little meaning for today's permissive positivists. But it may well be that the sheer wealth of information has helped to make it popular. People read Arthur Hailey and James Michener to learn about the running of airports and power stations and to pick up, in fictional guise, some account of a national history. Read this book and you will never again have to wonder how an Italian monastery functioned in the fourteenth century.

As a somewhat elongated thriller it is far more teasing – and far far far better written – than anything by the late Dame Agatha Christie. Its nearest parallel in British detective fiction is Dorothy L. Sayers's *Gaudy Night*, which also presented crime in a closed society (a women's college), had Latin quotations and a great parade of learning. But this work seems not to have had a large public in mind. It needs no stylistic erudition on the reader's part, and titillates only intellectually.

I rejoice, and the rest of the literate world will rejoice with me, that bestsellerdom remains unsubmissive to cybernetic prognostics, and that a work of genuine literature can out trash. I heard a man say today on Italian television: '*Al meglio non c'è mai fine.*' This seems to mean, among other things, that you can't put barbed wire round the best. Best and bestseller are not mutually exclusive terms.

I probably do not need to recommend this book to British readers. The impetus of foreign success should ensure a large readership here. Even Ulster rednecks, to say nothing of mild Anglicans who detest Christianity cooking with garlic, will feel comforted by this image of a secure age when there was an answer to everything, when small, walled society could be self-sufficient, and the only pollution was diabolic. Patriots will be pleased to find such a society in need of British pragmatism.

Observer, 16 October 1983
Review of *The Name of the Rose* by Umberto Eco
(London: Secker and Warburg, 1983)

The Lords of Limit

GEOFFREY HILL is a poet before he is an academic. Five volumes of verse and a translation of Ibsen's *Brand* come before this collection of criticism. Delivering his inaugural lecture as professor of English Literature at the University of Leeds in 1977, Hill is properly modest about his poetic achievement – 'That I have had some practice in the making of verse is evidence to be noted, I think; if only as a glint of improper goliardic song in the margin of a proper gospel' – but the whole discourse, entitled 'Poetry as "Menace" and "Atonement"', despite its concentration on the work of others, is grounded in the triumphs and doubts of his own practice. One has the impression of so powerful a desire for self-effacement, as a poet if not, which would be unseemly, as one who professes poetry, that a perhaps excessive multiplicity of citation and allusion serves as a sequined motley which, seeming to hide his nakedness, exposes it all the more.

'Atonement' is used in its radical sense of 'at-one-ment, a setting at one, a bringing into concord, a reconciling, a uniting in harmony.' Eliot speaks Hill's own devotional language when, describing the elation of having achieved that arrangement or words which, being right, seems ordained and inevitable, he speaks of a sense of 'exhaustion, of appeasement, of absolution, and of something very near annihilation.' The humility, then, of one who has attained the vision. Wherein lies the 'menace' of Hill's title? If I read him right, it is in the pride of rhetorical achievement, of verbal mastery, that opposes self-surrender. When Yeats, in 'The Circus Animals' Desertion', submits to lying down in 'the foul rag-and-bone shop of the heart,' the language he uses denies the theme. 'How is it possible… to revoke 'masterful images' in images that are themselves masterful?'

The poet, and the imaginative writer in general, rest in a state of dilemma which may be morally glossed as hypocrisy. There is empirical as well as theological guilt. One makes errors and one sins, but while sins may be forgiven, as Chesterton says, there is no forgiveness for *faux pas*. Or, to put it in the weightier words of Helen Waddell's

Gilles de Vannes, '… There is no canonical repentance for a mistake.' Hill's theological stance is firm enough for him to see the comparative absurdity of the knitting editor's guilt at publishing an error which ensures that 'there are jerseys all over England with one arm longer than the other,' but (how about a published recipe which accidentally gets the quantities wrong? Sophia Loren, I remember, was near suicidal over an error in her *L'amore nella cucina* which turned a *dolce* into an emetic) he does not condemn Simone Weil as an obsessional neurotic for proposing penal servitude for sinners against accuracy in printed texts or radio broadcasts. Grammar itself is a 'social and public institution', and to offend against it may be regarded as a criminal act. Sin, however, is a different matter. Or is it?

The poet's responsibility to agonise over his statements (with, one might think, a scrupulosity that kills creative joy) exists on both a theological and a social level, but properly these should coincide. In law, morality is based on expediency only when society is debased or, in an emergency like war, is compelled to blur its sense of moral absolutes. No society can be wholly secular. In an essay entitled 'The Absolute Reasonableness of Robert Southwell,' Hill takes an English Catholic poet best known, though very inadequately known, for 'The Burning Babe', a poem which looks to many secular readers like mawkish devotionalism but must be seen in a wider and more poignant context than the *Oxford Book of English Verse* can provide. Southwell was a flame of Elizabethan recusancy, whose writings show skill in polemic and also in silence, 'choosing not-to-say' as his tormentor interpreted it, calling him a 'monster' of 'strange taciturnity'. Robert Cecil, seeing Southwell subjected to a 'new kind of torture,' remarked that he remained 'as dumb as a tree-stump; and it had not been possible to make him utter one word.' Here was the ultimate scrupulosity.

But one word that Southwell did utter was 'equitie', a word describing a principle of justice based on something larger than expediency. Southwell found that Topcliffe was 'not open to reason', meaning that he had forfeited a traditional principle of law for the new, hypocritical and destructive device of 'reason of state.' No man submits to martyrdom lightly. If, like Southwell or Campion, he has the duty to state his position in words, he must think about those words carefully and even decide when silence is a word. Thinking of words in prospect of a shameful and agonising death means seeing them less as the counters of the marketplace than an ambiguous complexities, the material of the poet. 'Atonement' and 'menace' now relate to more terrible immediacies than those of a professional address The 'reasonableness' of Southwell encompasses both religious discipline and what Fr Devlin terms 'an element of supernatural wildness.' Hill finds in Southwell a 'complex simplicity' appropriate equally to the poet and the martyr.

It is perhaps in order to see in another poet, one who considered himself to be martyrised by 'reason of state', a failure of scrupulosity unforgiveable in one committed to getting words right. Ezra Pound was an important poet but not a satisfactory one. The strength of his work lies in a brilliance of rhetoric which is often set parallel to meaning. We can read the *Cantos* with excitement, but we take the obsession with *Usura* as a discardable eccentricity. Unfortunately, history forces us to take it as something else, for the obsession got out of literature into the real world of political reality and war. 'The crime with which he is charged,' said one of the experts at the Washington hearing, 'is closely tied up with his profession of writing.' Literature, in an age which has lost its sense of 'absolute reasonableness', is no longer appropriate to sanity or right action. 'Our word is our bond,' Hill says, not only in the title of his essay, and Pound ought not to have misconstrued 'a fine point of semantic.' Shelley did a lot of harm with his boast about poets being unacknowledged legislators. What poets *can* do is to judge after the act. It was perhaps in order for Pound to denounce *Usura* as a historical wrong, but he believed that poets' 'judicial sentences' could have a legislative or executive validity. The 'world's revenge', during his court hearing and its aftermath, was unwittingly to pay him back, confusion for confusion, with legislative or executive acts presuming to be true verdictives.'

Moral concern illuminates Professor Hill's discussions of Jonson's *Sejanus*, Swift's poetry of 'reaction', *Cymbeline*, and the dangerously perplexed world of T.H. Green. He is perhaps at his best in an essay called 'Redeeming the Time', in which, after respectfully differing from Iris Murdoch on her statement, in her essay on Sartre, that the disruptive forces of the nineteenth century were 'dispossessed and weak... incoherent, disunited, and speechless,' he seeks to demonstrate how the very rhythms of Victorian poetry and prose, to say nothing of public rhetoric, illustrate doubt and breakdown. Hopkins's ear he takes to be the organ best attuned to the sense of dissolution in that time. 'Decomposition' is set against 'composition', and in no Gilbertian pub. If 'Harry Ploughman' combines work song, shanty, and liturgical chant – the organic rhythms – 'Tom's Garland' is crabbed, harsh, and near-incoherent in mimesis of its subject, the Victorian unemployed. 'Tom's Garland', thinks Hill, is a failure, 'but it fails to some purpose; it is a test to breaking point of the sustaining power of language.' Hopkins considered the poem to be too highly wrought, over-composed rather than a model of decomposition: I would say that its skill lies in its appearance of failure. But Hill is not often wrong about Hopkins.

The age, says Hill, was decadent, and critics of Hopkins have heard in him the voice of that decadence, particularly Donald Davie's: 'He cultivates his hysteria and pushes his sickness to the limit.' For hysteria read passion and ecstasy; for sickness the dark night of the soul. Such terms have become sectarian. All of Hill's essays imply, if they do not directly state, a useless regret at the fissure that was opening in British life and letters when Southwell saw the burning babe from the scaffold. His perceptions are exquisite and his reading is wide. 'O Lords of Limit, training dark and light...' The epigraph is from Auden. A more pertinent one is from J.L. Austin's *How To Do Things with Words*: 'And for this reason we call the doctrine of *the things that can be and go wrong* on the occasion of such utterances, the doctrine of the *Infelicities*.' Hill is good on the infelicities.

Times Literary Supplement, 4 May 1984
Review of *The Lords of Limit: Essays on Literature and Ideas* by
Geoffrey Hill (Oxford: Oxford University Press, 1984)

Locutions of Sex and Death

THE FOLLOWING comes from the second page of Ms Jackie Collins's novel *Lovers and Gamblers*:

> 'Al', suggested the blonde, shifting so that her well-developed mammaries hung invitingly over his mouth, 'Al, baby, why don't we fuck?'
>
> Al grunted. Stick it into these two? They must be kidding.
>
> 'Just keep at it,' he pushed the redhead back into position.

This is the permissive age, in which things can be spelt out, but the old literary tradition of evasiveness, circumlocution, euphemism, what you will, dies hard. Ms Collins could have said 'large breasts' or 'big tits', according to the preferred register, but one brutal basic term in a sentence is enough. Moreover, if she had written this paragraph totally in Krafft-Ebing's Latin, or in a Latinate English owing much to Krafft-Ebing's example, we would still, with a dictionary if need be, be able to find out what is going on. Euphemism, like patriotism, is not enough. It never really deceives. That is why a book on it, or even a dictionary on it, has a ludic or charade quality about it, diverting but teaching nothing. What studies of euphemism are really about are the things we fear. Or, strictly, the reasons why we fear what we fear and how these fears can be allayed.

Robert Burchfield the lexicographer, the only professional linguist on D.J. Enright's list of 'distinguished contributors' (distinguished for what?) to this symposium, takes the Indo-European root meaning *bear* – *rksos*, surviving in Sanskrit *rksas*, Greek *arktos* and Latin *ursus*. The form is acceptable in regions where there is no fear of bears, but the Russians evade the beast's hug by calling it *medved* or honey-eater, the Lithuanians by terming it *lokys*, the licker, and those of us who speak Germanic tongues by naming it *bera*, *bär*, beer – the brown one. This is pure apotropaic magic, like calling an ugly fish a *bonito* or a weasel a *donnola*. The fear of fire, or the fear of the gods' stealing it back again, seems to be perpetuated in *focus* and *fuoco*, where the container, not the contained, is nominated. We all know these things, and they are mainly of antiquarian interest. We fear different substances nowadays, but still go on playing the game of pretending not to be afraid.

People used to be taught to fear God; the contemporary churchgoer has learnt to fear being thought of as fearing God, and the translators of holy scripture and devisers of liturgies are there to help him. Peter Mullen, Vicar of Tockwith and Bilton with Bickerton in the diocese of York, calls the Alternative Service Book 'a kind of long-running... euphemism for the real Prayer Book'. Holy Baptism is no longer holy – 'the place of holy water in the mystical washing away of sin – but only pretty, a sentimental prelude to the booze-up and the cake, an opportunity for photographs: photographs that will evidence *what*?' In the Nunc Dimittis 'Lord, now lettest thow thy servant depart in peace' has changed into 'Lord, now let your servant go', which, says Revd Mullen, 'evokes the image of a schoolboy in distress of bladder, rather than of spirit'. The Jerusalem Bible translates *Makarioi*, blessed, as 'happy', so as to avoid too firm a commitment to a belief in life after death. The New English Bible's fiery Paul is house-trained and urbane, and a clean-shaven Peter tells his flock not to worry too much about the Day of Judgment: 'My dear friends, do not be bewildered by the fiery ordeal that is coming upon you, as though it were something extraordinary.' A failure of nerve is Mullen's diagnosis, a fear of imputations of credulousness, but also perhaps of a malignant reality (like cancer or the nuclear holocaust), a belief that God exists demonstrated in a kind of denial. Perhaps the traditional approach to our Maker, dysphemistic, relishing the old roarer and guardian of the furnace, denoted a healthy disbelief. It all depends on how much you accept that words relate to things.

We are all scared of death, though few are scared of it for a sound eschatological reason. Committed to their bodies, few people want to lose them, or perhaps the real fear is of that terminal asthma which contains the ghastly rhythms of dissolution. Our pathetic attempts to disinfect the reality with daisy-chain verbiage or learned orotundities is no new thing, but the true euphemistic evasions are to be seen more in the elaboration of the death industry than in mere words. It is all there in *The Loved One*, in the specialist offices of the thanatologist or psychopomp. (Across from where I live is a qualified thanatologue, who rubs his hands wherever he observes my progressive decrepitude – discreetly, however, being French.) Scared of death – meaning medicines, the predatory looks of our relative, the irony of preparing for a long sleep where we used to relish short ones – we ought not to be scared of being killed, but apparently we are. But do not such terms as 'termination with extreme prejudice' (a favourite of the Health Alteration Committee of the CIA) in fact prejudice our fatalism through the sheer transparency of the charade? It is all a game, like finding an acceptable shirk-word for prolonged unemployment (State-Paid Leisure or GARDENING – Grant of Aid in Recompense for Diminution of Employment Necessitated by the Incompetence of the National Government).

It is in the genital area that, despite the new libertarianism, verbal evasion continues most notably to operate. This goes back so far that one wonders if there ever was a neutral vocabulary for the *pudenda* and their ambiguous functions – except perhaps for the word *piss*, which, in a sense, has always been too expressively onomatopoeic to be wholly offensive. It is in the Old Testament, where 'people who piss against the wall' seems to be used (though, naturally, not in the *NEB*) to mean people in general, men in the street: you define humanity in terms of what it most commonly and visibly does. *Shit*, which remains offensive, finds its etymology in an Anglo-Saxon verb specifically meaning to defecate diarrhoeally. It has a harmless cognate in words like *schizophrenia*: the concept of splitting – the sense that the lower body has turned into a floodgate – is essential to its expressiveness.

Of terms for the lower organs themselves, *arse* has existed for a long time; but there seem to be no firm native words for the organs of generation. *Penis* is a Latin loanword and a prissy one. John Florio, in his still useful Italian-English dictionary, gives 'pricke' for *cazzo*, but must have been doubtful about it. When Adam named things he left out of the Edenic glossary what was soon, anyway, to be occluded with fig-leaves. (The Italians, calling the female organ the *fica*, make Eve's leaves wholly fitting.) The male organ has no name, and hence it is not strictly in order to talk of either euphemistic or dysphemistic terms for it. The word *cunt* has a long history of usage, but it has always been felt to be a dysphemism for something else. It does not have the right associations, except in Leopold Bloom's description of the Middle East as 'the dry shrunken cunt of the world': three consonants strangle one vowel, the word seems hard and, yes, dry. But the female organ is muscular, which the male one is not, and there may be a deeper descriptive element in the word than we wish to accept. Meanwhile, the euphemisms and dysphemisms grow, are replaced, savoured, rejected, but there is no circle in which word and image meet.

One of the late Kenneth Tynan's achievements was to use the word *fuck* for the first time on television. He kindly demonstrated its proper usage by composing a sentence: 'A man fucks his wife.' This may be termed the Lawrentian heresy, for a man does not, at least not regularly, do anything of the sort. *Fuck*, like its German cognate *ficken*, denotes sexual penetration but connotes aggression. It has nothing to do with making love or sleeping with, or any of the other euphemisms which centre on copulation, but Ms Collins's 'Why don't we fuck?', anaphrodisiastical as it is, is preferable to 'Why don't we copulate?' But it is *faute de mieux*. A vast hopeless vocabulary tries to penetrate the vacuum, but to no avail; the vacuum is still there.

Dr Enright leaves Joseph Epstein, editor of *The American Scholar*, the chapter on 'Sex and Euphemism'. It is a coy chapter, as it probably has to be, and it is wholly on the side of circumspection:

Suffice to say that in contemporary writing about sex, the stakes rise all the time. We are not talking, and haven't been for some years, about your simple Sunday afternoon off the Grande Jatte fornication. Not only must sex in the contemporary novel grow more regular but it must become more rococo. Thus Mr Updike presents us with an activity known euphemistically as California sunshine…, Mr Roth has a woman in his most recent novel the contents of whose purse include 'a nippleless bra, crotchless panties, a Polaroid camera, vibrating dildo, K-Y jelly, Gucci blindfold, a length of braided velvet rope'. Mr Mailer, relying on fundamentals, concentrates on heterosexual sodomy. Ah, me, the literary life.

Here one sees how easily the amateur philologist can move into the area of referents and forget words. It is the thing itself he is worrying about. Whatever kind of terminology the contemporary novelist employs, he is still being too open about sex. And not only the novelist. Epstein notes that in his journals of the 1920s Edmund Wilson used expressions like 'I addressed myself to her bloomers' but in the 1940s was ready to talk about his 'large pink prong'. There is not really an increase in candour. But there is a decrease in discretion:

Would always run her tongue into my mouth when I kissed her before I had a chance to do it to her – and would do it so much and so fast that I hardly had a chance to get my own in. Would clasp her legs together very hard when I had my hand or my penis in her – seemed to have tremendous control of the muscles inside her vagina. Her frank and uninhibited animal appetite contrasted with her formal and gracious aristocratic manners.

Epstein finds this distasteful – 'sex written without euphemism – and it is quite devoid of tenderness, is in fact chilling, even loathsome'. Agreed, but it has nothing to do with the eschewal of the euphemism: there is not one word there that shocks. What shocks is the reduction of the marital act of love to a set of mechanistic movements. The depiction of love-making (I am not using a euphemism) has the primary task of finding a figurative language for intense emotions which are, so to speak, set in parallel to the excitation of the nerves. The writer is now free to set it all down, let it all hang or stick out, but his freedom is a very dubious one. What is really going on in bed or on the floor is an experience that requires a high poetic talent for its expression, and no amount of verbal emancipation can confer that.

Are Americans more bemused by the magic of words than the British? Simon Hoggart, whom Enright invited to write on the euphemism in politics, does not think that it plays much of a role in the British system:

> Abuse of the language is, of course, as common at Westminster as it is in any other national legislature, but more often it takes the form of hyperbole, evasion, vagueness and plain untruth. The principal reason for this is the adversarial nature of British politics. Every time someone tries to slide a euphemism into the language, his opponents promptly match it with the corresponding dysphemism.

This says something about the comparative locations of British and American authority. Hoggart cites an extract from Hansard, in which Mr Rooker, a Labour MP, asks the Conservative minister Norman Fowler: 'Are the Government still looking to see where in the system they can make the cuts? Will the Rt Hon Gentleman spell it out for us?' the Rt Hon Gentleman replies: 'We are examining a number of areas inside the social security system to see if savings can be made.'

'Cuts' and 'savings' mean the same thing, but the harmonics are different. 'Cuts' suggests the savage slicing of a knife, 'savings' the virtues of thrift and responsibility. The real word, which we do not know, lies somewhere between the opposed benches.

It is clear that euphemism and dysphemism are sides of a single coin which forms part of the currency evasion. Enright, in his admirable introduction, says that a good deal of the book he has edited is given to dysphemism, a fair example of which he provides in a footnote: 'Rather than complain that the coffee is weak, tell your hostess that it's like love in a canoe, i.e. 'fuckin' near water'.' The provenance is Californian. And he rightly points out that the discrediting of the euphemism in our age had led not to a neutrality of diction but to a swing towards the opposite:

> We find ourselves in a strange and (some will say) sadly ironic situation. Literature, 'creative writing' we used to call it, once elevated or ennobled or strengthened. With the help of dysphemism, it has now been turned upside-down: motives are customarily mean, the hero is a pathetic neurotic or well-meaning wreck, love is replaced by fornication, the evil may come to a bad end but the good certainly will. You might well suppose that fiction, as we hopefully call it still, is out to destroy the human race by rubbing its nose in its own filth, while only governments, political ideologues, military experts, business men and sometimes psychologists still consider the race worth saving. Why else would social scientists regard the backward as (even so) 'exceptional', and advertisers continually compliment us on our love of excellence, and the military come up at vast expense with a device called 'The Peacemaker'?

The truth, of course, is that neutrality can be a property of grammar, while semantemes have always been soaked in some emotional fluid or other. In the army, I remember, the dysphemism was the norm, and in my north-western childhood there was no fairness of speech ('Have you got a shithouse that won't work?' asked the plumber, and the housewife replied: 'Aye, but he's out drawing t'dole'). The food of the lower classes joined that of the public schools in being loathsomely appellated (*dead baby in its own blood*, and so on). One of the phenomena of our age ignored in these essays is what is termed food-hype, in which stale eggs are paraded as not merely dawn-new but still echoing with the triumphant cluck of the layer under the freshly risen Illinois (or wherever) sun. The euphemism of the menu takes none of us in, even early in the morning: we prefer fair words to the other kind, even when they lie. We cannot subsist without white lies; black lies are another matter.

A final point. The delusion still persists that the Victorian age invented the euphemism, and that before 1837 both speech and literature rang with a fine frankness; moreover, mealy-mouthedness was a unique property of the puritanised Anglo-Saxons. The truth is that the Victorians merely took to the limit (drumsticks for chicken legs, turkey bosom for turkey breast, and so on) a squeamishness about words that is built into the human character. The Romans put people to silence, and, of the newly silent, said that he *vixit*. The Malays have earthy words for micturition and defecation (*kenching* and *berak*, for instance) but are happier talking about *buang ayer kechil* and *buang ayer besar* – throwing little and big water. Examiners in the language, as I recall, would set little problems of translation with 'At this ceremony the princes throw water at the princesses'. Word-evasion is such a universal characteristic that it hardly seems worthwhile issuing books about it. All they tell us is that human fear continues but the objects of fear change. And that takes us outside the realm of mere words.

Times Literary Supplement, 12 April 1985
Review of *Fair of Speech: The Uses of Euphemism*
ed. D.J. Enright (Oxford: Oxford University Press, 1985)

Why I Write

I WANT to speculate as to why the question 'Why do you write?' should be posed at all. After all, you don't ask a shoemaker why he makes shoes or an aeronautical engineer why he dreams of a faster Concorde. Clearly there is sometime mysterious about the desire to wield words, especially in a world increasingly in the grip of visual images. There is also implied in the question, I think, a kind of wonder that anyone should want to write at all – anything, that is, above the level of an office memo, a piece of newspaper reportage, or a computer programme. To produce a book is a desperate undertaking. To try to make one's living out of the production of books is a kind of lunacy.

You will notice that the authors who make fat livings out of books are not asked why they write them. The question is unnecessary: the reply would be nonverbal – the author being served with a cocktail beside his private swimming pool, at the wheel of his Mercedes-Benz, signing a five-million-dollar contract in bed. The end of the writing of a best-selling novel is the writing of a best-selling novel. The responses of the reader of a best-selling novel have, strictly speaking, nothing to do with literature in its Ezra Pound sense of 'words charged with meaning'. The words of *Lace* or *The Carpetbaggers* or *Princess Daisy* are minimal triggers for the explosion of sex and violence. The reader does most of the work, building his voluptuous dreams of rape or mayhem with the least possible artistic assistance from the author. He would resent ambiguity, complexity, poetry, any verbal construct above the level of the near-cliché. Needless to say, not everyone can produce that kind of book. It requires a special sort of talent, though it is strictly a talent of deprivation – an inability or unwillingness to look beyond the glands, muscles, and the vocabulary of technical processes.

Real writers take seriously what writing is about – wrestling with words. Words are not inert counters like cloak-room tickets. They are living creatures which resent being treated as if they were knives, forks and spoons. You cannot take them out of a drawer, use them, then stow them away again. They are stubborn and they sometimes refuse to mean what the writer wants them to mean. It's not merely a matter of the word itself – there's also the delightful agony of arranging them in patterns, making music out of them. Dr Johnson, a very great wordsman, wrote in the Preface to his *Dictionary* that words were the daughters of men while things were the sons of heaven. True, but we have to try to bring the sons of heaven down to earth, and only words can do this. Moreover, there's an order of reality above things – the sphere of ideas. Ideas cannot exist until they are cast into the form of words. We human beings are intensely verbal creatures. Not many people realise this, but writers live with that awesome knowledge. They are the custodians of a primal human truth.

Being, for the most part, modest and intensely uncertain about both the practice of their craft and their achievements in it, writers don't care to speak out much about the loftiness of their vocation. I personally tend to disparage what I do. You will often find me talking of the need to earn a living and, having failed in everything else, assuming the writer's trade because there seemed to be nothing else available. This is what writers frequently say, though they may not always mean it. It is, so to speak, a defensive attitude. If they worship the Muse, the Muse, with feminine capriciousness, may fly away: best to pretend not to take her too seriously. Authors are also extremely sensitive to criticism, and the attitude of merely getting on with the trade (like your cobbler or aeronautical engineer) is sometimes a means of warding off the attentions of the enemy. The don't-care pose is a kind of armour. But underneath the carapace there is a quivering hypersensitivity which is not much salved by timid visits to the bank.

There is a book still to be compiled with some such titles as *Why Critics Criticise*. Critics are writers of a sort – indeed, I'm a critic myself as well as a sort of novelist (note the fingers-crossed modesty) – but they couldn't exist unless there was a creative meat for them to tear at – or, to be fair, sometimes consume with a qualified relish. When a writer finishes a book, he thinks less of the pleasure or enlightenment he has tried to contrive for his readers than of the reviews he is going to read in the quality newspapers. He knows there are reviewers out to get him and he knows, far better than the reviewer, the faults that are going to be castigated. He submits to being butchered to make a Sunday holiday. He is to be butchered for faults so deeply ingrained in his nature that he can do little about them. And there is one answer to the question 'Why do you write?' which he is rather unwilling to give.

For the answer is 'I write to exhibit myself, to show the world what, underneath the writing skill, is a representative chunk of human nature.' The writer strips himself naked, well aware that he is not, like the professional strip-tease artist, necessarily all that well worth looking at. There is a paunch, and the toenails are growing yellow, there are boil-scars on the left buttock. We find in authorship degrees of compulsive exhibitionism. The poet is most naked. The novelist tries to hide behind characters, but his prose style gives him away. The dramatist is luckiest: there is no point in looking for him even in the wings: he is agonisingly patrolling the street outside the theatre, biting his nails. Shakespeare is not Hamlet. But most other writers are, in mourning for literature, wondering whether to be or not to be. Writers, that is.

The variety of responses to the great question, as manifested in this collection, all conceal the true answer – compulsion. A writer writes because he has to. Writing comes before eating. And that is not just a matter of the priority of vocation over subsistence. If we don't write we don't eat either. We write, among other things, for grub. That is why the London thoroughfare of needy scribblers – no longer on the topographical map but still very much part of the spiritual townscape – is called Grub Street.

Previously unpublished; dated 1985

Still Life

A.S. BYATT is, as she must be, in the new *Companion to English Literature* edited by her sister Margaret Drabble, and there is even a plot summary of her last novel. 'Her most substantial work, *The Virgin in the Garden* (1978), is set largely in the Coronation year of 1953; the second Elizabethan Golden Age is celebrated by a performance at a Yorkshire country house of a new verse drama by public schoolmaster Alexander Wedderburn, in which schoolgirl Frederica Potter plays the role of the Virgin Queen. Rich in complex allegorical allusions to Spenser, Raleigh, Shakespeare and many others, the novel also provides a realistic and vivid portrait of the Potter family, and of provincial life in the 1950s.' This is, as it must be, a mere logarithm of a remarkable piece of art (rich, complex – the epithets are just) which overwhelmed me in the reading and disappointed me in the ending, which seemed arbitrary and left all the characters up in the air, dangling. I should have had the sense to perceive that a sequel was necessary. *Still Life* is the sequel, and there seems to be no reason why there should not be a sequel to the sequel. Quite apart from her duty to her characters – which are far too substantial and too much, event after about seven hundred pages, still in a state of urgent psychological growth to be permitted to bow their way off – A.S. Byatt has a duty to postwar British history. She is still recording the fifties in *Still Life*, and no one has done it more sharply or aromatically. As I lived in the Far East from 1954 until 1959, I missed that particular phase of social evolution in, so to speak, the flesh. There is here all the flesh I need, as well as the taste and the colour.

The colour is important, as the title suggests. Alexander is writing a play about van Gogh, whose wonder at the mystery of colour is partly expressed in his letters by his unwillingness to let colour-epithets obey the laws of French accidence: colour is primal, separable from objects, an entity divorced from gravity and physical extension. The novel itself is flooded with colour, and the question seems to be raised: how far can language, a kind of spectre, cope with the reality of the spectrum? The novelist herself raises questions directly, though not that particular one. She tells us she is writing a novel and indicates its roots in certain images, but the subtlety and complexity of the whole structure forbids our accepting her occasional presence in the naïve terms of traditional auctorial intrusion. There is a terrible moment in the narrative when an accidental death occurs, and one feels: A.S. Byatt is a kind of Borges; she can reverse this event, if she wishes. Then we realise that she cannot. She is not manipulating, as Borges always is: she is presenting personages and events which have a disjunct reality. The writer herself is being written.

Still Life would seem to be an inept title for a novel so full of movement, but altogether appropriate for a work in which the world of colour and form demands to be looked at. Frederica Potter, the exasperating but fascinating virgin of the previous novel, bloodily but voluntarily deflowered in Scarborough towards the end, herself becomes caught by the sun in Provence, a chromatic feature to be examined. But there are modes of examination quite distinct from the aesthetic. There is a wonderful and shocking moment when the bulky curate Daniel, husband of Frederica's elder sister Stephanie, makes love to his wife. The descriptive register shifts from the realistic narrational to the biological: we observe the swimming spermatozoa dying, the surviving Noah reaching its goal. We are tempted to think of Aldous Huxley in *Point Counter Point*, but Huxley's science was in the service of irony; A.S. Byatt's promotes awe. The shifting of levels is always surprising. The terrible accidental death is caused by an unearthed refrigerator. A sparrow has got into the kitchen, a search for it causes the calamity. While a woman lies dead the sparrow flies out through the window, and we are struck by the significance of the epigraph from the Venerable Bede: '...*adveniens unus passerum domum citissime pervolaverit; qui cum per unum ostium ingrediens, mox per aliud exierit...*' We are faced with the ghastly fragility of life.

Babies are born, and the obstetric details are presented without flinching, in the language of epic struggle and victory. We fear for these children, not because of any dark omens inserted into the plot but because of the mystery of life itself, with which reason has no covenant. The mystery of colour may be taken as a correlative of this. The symbols of the novel are woven with great skill, enforcing the notion of an artefact as cunningly contrived as a van Gogh still life, but the book is thoroughly valid as a narrative in the great realist tradition, in which we are concerned with what the characters are going to do next.

Our concentration is, as in *The Virgin in the Garden*, on the flame-haired Frederica, now up at Cambridge, having affairs but wholly absorbed in literature, which is more mysterious than life. Her sister lives her married life with Daniel in his Yorkshire curacy, bearing children, looking after her introverted brother whom their father's loud dogmatism has ruined, starved for the opulence of language in which Frederica wallows. The divisions and hostilities of the previous book are now to some extent resolved, though at a shocking price. Meanwhile art is a reality parallel to life and, through the magic of the narrative method, the parallels seem to meet. There is an appearance of looseness, sprawl, casualness of construction, serving the unpredictability of life, but this is a mere illusion. Never was a novel more tightly organised. The two novels together represent a highly distinguished contribution to British art. We are in the presence of a remarkable intelligence which recognises how essential it is for literature to absorb literature. The allusiveness of *Still Life* is part of its strength, but the primal strength derives from the courage of the clear eye and an almost frightening compassion.

Fiction Magazine, 28 May 1985
Review of *Still Life* by A.S. Byatt
(London: Chatto & Windus, 1985)

The Anachronist Strikes Back

THE CRITICS have been having a stab at me again. Me that is, in my capacity as a novelist. In my capacity of critic I never stab anybody, for I know how life-denying it is to be stabbed. Writing a book is damned difficult work, and you ought to praise any book if you can. But praise is a bland commodity and readers don't like to read it. Hence the almost wholly destructive connotations of the term 'critic'. When somebody says: 'Oh, don't keep bloody criticising all the time', you know that somebody has been stabbing with at least paper-knives. When you're in a critical condition it's assumed you're not going to get better. Criticism is in a critical condition.

The process of feeling (I don't think thought comes much into it) that animates critics of my novels is something like this: (a) this is not really a bad book; (b) I don't like its author; (c) what can I pick on to make it seem to be a bad book? The easiest answer has nothing to do with the characterisation or style; it has to do with the piddling business of factual accuracy. Make a list of, say, historical gaffes and you're in critical business. 'The *Titanic* did *not* go down in 1913' (the whole point of one of your characters' thinking it did says something about that character, but never mind). When I publish a historical novel the critics can really start bloody criticising. All they need is *Pears' Cyclopaedia*.

The great word is anachronism. There are three kinds of anachronism. There's the blatant kind used for an easy laugh by George Bernard Shaw – making Cain in the Garden of Eden quote John Ball, Cleopatra quote Shelley, the Christians sing 'Onward, Christian Soldiers' as they're thrown to the lions. There's the don't-give-a-damn-history-is-bunk-the-past-is-really-the-present kind dear to the unscholarly heart of Shakespeare. Clocks strike in ancient Rome, Brutus and Cassius wear hats, Caesar gets knifed in the doublet. And, while the Bard's hand is in, Ancient Britain is contemporary with Renaissance Italy, with Augustus Caesar as a probable patron of Michelangelo. The third kind is supposed to be unwilled and reprehensible, and I'm supposed to go for it.

My latest incursion into historical fiction is set in the first century of the Christian era. A professor of Latin reviewed the book and didn't like my narrator's quoting a line of Juvenal a few years before the line was written. Fair enough, but how about my using the word 'assassination' in the very first paragraph? That's a far worse anachronism, since an assassin was a hashish-eater sent on his mission of murdering Christians by the Muslim Old Man of the Mountains. Plenty of Christians in the just-pre-Juvenal time, but Mohammed didn't start keeping camels till a few centuries later. Once you're committed to using a modern language for presenting ancient history you're committed to anachronism. But your pedantic critic will permit that: not even a professor of Latin would demand that you write about Romans in Latin. *He* could have a stab at it, of course, but he doesn't have to make his living out of novels.

But even if you could wield the scandalous idiom of Suetonius or Petronius, getting all the details right, you wouldn't easily avoid anachronism. My Argentine namesake Borges wrote a short story about a twentieth-century Spanish writer writing *Don Quixote* the same as Cervantes. No difference at all, except that you know you're reading a modern writer. If I make one of my characters quote Catullus, you can't help knowing that I'm a twentieth-century writer making him do it. That means I know that Catullus has influenced Ben Jonson and Herrick. I've been sophisticated by history. I'm not a Roman innocent.

Talking about Ben Jonson, he has a line in his *Volpone* about Lollia Paulina coming in like starlight, hid in jewels. Now in my novel I actually have Lollia Paulina in the flesh, and I'd be a terrible Roman innocent if I didn't swathe her in Jonsonian jewels stellarly scintillating. Pretending to be ignorant of what you know all too well is not easy. My Latin professor is upset about my making St Luke, who was a Greek doctor, know too much about phagocytes. Well, why shouldn't he have met some madman who had a theory about phagocytes and then dies in a drunken brawl before he'd been able to publish it in the Roman Empire equivalent of *The Lancet*? That's the sort of thing that any good-hearted reader unspoilt by being a professor of Latin (surely phagocytes are Greek?) would naturally take for granted.

What my critical professor apparently didn't notice – it wasn't in his professional sphere, anyway – was that I committed the unforgiveable sin of bringing Sigmund Freud into Neronian Rome. What all historical novelists are supposed to stick up on the wall behind their typewriters is a reminder that neither Freud nor Marx existed before they were born. It's probably out of order for Shakespeare to know about the unconscious (although he did, of course) or Socrates to brood on the theory of surplus value (well, he might just about do that so long as he didn't call it the *Mehrwert*). I have Freud in my novel as a doctor someone has heard about somewhere, perhaps in Vindobona in Pannonia (Vienna in Austria to you), who thinks, though not in so many words, that neuroses have no somatic etiology. I call him Efcharistimenos, which is Greek for Freud. That's the rich full-cream milk of anachronism, and this man has to niggle about phagocytes.

I also have Oscar Wilde in the depraved imperial story. I call him Selvaticus, which is wild enough, and I have him kicked out of Rome by Claudius for blatant sodomy, but not before he's passed on his depraved wisdom to Petronius. Surely somebody's going to pick on that as a ghastly anachron? If you look carefully you'll find the Rolling Stones performing at an imperial banquet and people seeing off St Paul on his mission to Spain singing 'Now is the Hour'. If you want the best anachrons, we have them.

The point is, I think, that the past is made by the present. The pattern we call history is not in history: it's made by us. The historical novelist knows he's shoving the only people he knows – those who read the *Guardian* over breakfast in Hampstead – into fancy dress. If he can avoid making them say 'Gadzooks' on the one hand and 'Okay' on the other he's doing as well as can be expected (though Franco Zeffirelli has sent me a film script about Marcus Aurelius in which the plebs are okaying like mad). The only thing we will not accept is an American novel about Geoffrey Chaucer in which people say 'ass' instead of 'arse'. That's too much of an anachron.

Times Literary Supplement, 2 August 1985

Spirit of Cervantes

W.H. AUDEN, who had not done so himself, denied that anyone had ever read *Don Quixote* through. I have to boast that I have read it five times – in Shelton's, Motteux's, J. M. Cohen's and now Smollett's translations. The fifth (properly third) reading was in the original Castilian, a language I started to learn when stationed in Gibraltar.

There is no substitute for reading a great classic in anything but the original, but *Don Quixote* is one of the two works that seem, though foreign, to be part of our own literary heritage. The other is *Gargantua and Pantagruel*, which is probably better (meaning more Rabelaisian) in Sir Thomas Urquhart's version than in the original that the French no longer read, finding its archaic quality difficult. There is the matter also of the modern Gallic mind taking less kindly to Rabelais – unless diluted in the Asterix cartoons – than to Descartes. Rabelais is ours. *Don Quixote* is very nearly ours.

Thomas Shelton's translation came out as early as 1616, the year of Cervantes's (and Shakespeare's) death. The work was thus known as early as it well could be in England. I have a private fantasy that Shakespeare knew it, or at least of it, by being among the King's Men when the British peace delegation went to Valladolid in the spring of 1605. Cervantes was there, and also, as in a Macy's Thanksgiving procession, the Don himself and Sancho prancing in the bullring. Shakespeare could have been there, acting in a tarted-up production of *The Spanish Tragedy*. The two might have met, conversing in the Arabic Cervantes learned as a slave and Shakespeare as companion to the Earl of Southampton on a trip to Tangier. It is a pleasant idea, and I offer it free to anyone who wishes to fictionalise about it.

Shelton uses the language Shakespeare himself knew, and his translation is vigorous, though not always accurate. Motteux's version is eighteenth century and belongs to the age when the Cervantes influence was strong in the post-Richardsonian novel: it should be good but it is not. It is a little bland, though mostly accurate. The Cohen translation is scholarly but lacks panache, though it is better than Motteux.

It seems to me that the best we have is by Smollett, a Cervantesque novelist himself and possessed of a large dour vigour. We do not usually associate him with Hispanic scholarship, but the fact that he dedicated the work to Don Ricardo Wall, 'Principal Secretary of State to His Most Catholic Majesty, Lieutenant General of the Armies of Spain, Commendary of Penauzende in the Order of St Jago, &c&c,' implies linguistic confidence, though we may wonder how native was the Castilian of a man called Wall.

'*En un lugar de la Mancha, de cuyo nombre no quiero acordarme, vivia un hidalgo…*' So, as I remember, the story begins. Smollett starts:

> In a certain corner of la Mancha the name of which I do not choose to remember, there lately lived one of those country gentlemen, who adorn their halls with a rusty lance and worm-eaten target, and ride forth on the skeleton of a horse, to course with a sort of starved greyhound.

That, I think, will do very well. Smollett gives us footnotes. '*Salpicon…* is no other than cold beef sliced, and eaten with oil, vinegar and pepper.' *Duelos y quebrantos*, which has always given translators trouble, he knows to be literally gripes and grumblings (rendered by Motteux as 'griefs and groans') but Smollett – with that concern with his own and other people's stomachs which characterise his travel book and was justified by his profession of ship's surgeon – knows it means more. It means a dish of cucumbers, greens and pease-porridge. 'Such eatables… generate and expel wind' and so 'pains and breakings' is a fitter translation, though only in the context of a footnote. In the text, 'gripes and grumblings' sounds better.

The professional novelist in Smollett is quick to spot errors and inconsistencies in his master. Signor Quixada's housekeeper complains that the hidalgo has been absent six days on his first quest, but Smollett rightly corrects her: 'The author seems to have committed a small oversight in this paragraph; for the knight had not been gone above two days and one night, which he spent in watching his armour.' When he translates over-freely, he is scrupulous in pointing this out. Sancho says: 'The best and wholesomest thing we can do, will be to jog back again to our own habitation, now while the harvest is going on, to take care of our crops, and leave off sauntering from post to pillar, and falling out of the frying-pan into the fire, as the saying is.' What Sancho really says is 'sauntering from Ceca to Mecca.' The

Moors, as Smollett obligingly tells us, used to make pilgrimages to both places; Ceca was a Muslim shrine in Cordova.

Smollett is remarkably scholarly and conscientious; it is the Scot in him. He is better informed on knight errantry than Don Quixote himself. There is little poetry in the learned Smelfungus, as Sterne unkindly called him, but when he translates Cervantes's verse it is into good Augustan homespun, no worse than Dr Johnson's.

I have always cried at the death of Don Quixote, in whatever translation and even with the cello glissando (the best translation of them all perhaps) with which Richard Strauss ends his symphonic poem. Smollett is tough and little inclined to sentimentality (he was an anti-Richardsonian) but he manages pathos as well as action. He is not as funny as Shelton, but he finds room for Scots irony. The narrative reads wonderfully. You will, in reading this book, be as close to Cervantes as you can get without Spanish.

Carlos Fuentes tells us what a great novelist Cervantes is, which we knew already. Smollett hardly requires his sponsorship. The original copperplates by Hayman, 'engraved by the best ARTISTS', are all here. The translation has been out of print for a hundred years. Look on your shelves to see if you have a 'Don Quixote.' If not, go out and buy Smollett's.

It is a good thing to start another bad year with a reminder that the world is always bad, and that it was the job of knights errants to render it a little less bad. The term Quixote was once pejorative, but now any generous act seems quixotic. The mad comic knight has become a patron saint of sanity.

Observer, 19 January 1986
Review of *The Adventures of Don Quixote de la Mancha* by
Miguel de Cervantes, translated by Tobias Smollett
(London: André Deutsch, 1986)

Defector as Hero

AND, AS all the other reviewers will say about *A Perfect Spy*, a perfect title. When Mountjoy says to Jack Brotherhood that the trail of the wife of the defector has been lost and that it 'sounds a bit of a muddle', Brotherhood thinks: 'No. It is not a muddle. To make a muddle you must first have order. This is inertia, this is normality. What was once a great service has become an immovable hybrid – half bureaucratic, half freebooter, and using the arguments of the one to negate the other.'

The great service is that of British Intelligence. In the James Bond stories this is dedicated to the tracking down and eliminating of great and impossible evils. *Chez* le Carré ends are less important than means, and means are all we hear about. Squareland is not Fleming-land or Greeneland. There are no large threats to the safety of the Free World, and the only morality is that of the public school.

Magnus Pym, a counsellor at the British Embassy in Vienna, goes missing. He is called back to England for the funeral of his father Rick, and then he holes up in a Devonshire boarding house where he writes his memoirs. These take the form of a long letter addressed partly to his son Tom and partly to Jack Brotherhood, the secret service man who drew him into espionage when he was little more than an honourable schoolboy and is now pursuing him. When Pym lay down his pen he evades his captors by shooting himself. This seems a pity. He has disclosed the narrative talent of a le Carré, and his defection to the Czechs has done little harm.

Why do defectors defect? Lederer the American attempts an explanation to Brotherhood: 'If defection is a self-renewal, it requires also a rebirth… Know why so many defectors defect?… It's in and out of the womb all the time. Have you ever noticed that about defectors – the one common factor in all that crazy band? – they're immature. Forgive me, they are literally *motherfuckers*.' We are not supposed to expect wisdom from the CIA, only gobbledygook, tech-nical excellence, and mistrust of the Brits. We can ignore the womb theory, but Lederer is right about the immaturity. What Pym needed was a father.

He had a father, Rick Pym, conman, black marketer, floater of unsound companies, self-styled colonel or baronet according to need, robber of widows and orphans, lover of lovelies and bubbly, whose cheques to pay his son's school fees regularly bounced, wholesale exile but a loving father. He dies in the arms of a couple of raddled whores and a small villainy pursues him literally to the grave. He had sold his head for medical research and £100, and a man comes to claim it. Magnus Pym buys him off with a cheque that does not bounce, then he circuitously takes his more expensive head to Devon and his memoirs.

The big point about Magnus is that he has a capacity for love and an even stronger need to be loved. In Berne as a boy, conducting one of his father's grandiose and doomed enterprises, he is inducted gently into the lowest possible echelons of the Firm, which feeds a need for loyalty. He also makes a friend of a certain Axel, a Czech battered by the Nazis, and develops a different kind of loyalty. When Magnus, first while doing his National Service, later as a fully accredited Intelligence agent, finds the two loyalties in conflict, it is the human factor (to invoke Graham Greene) that prevails. But that is perhaps too simple a way of looking at it.

A more plausible way is hinted at in Pym's words to his son. He sees himself as a 'bridge' between his own disreputable father and a cleaner and freer life which will have no dubiety about loyalties. Rick Pym, rogue as he was, used the language of uplift to disguise villainy, and even stood for Parliament as a Liberal. He was full of Kipling's 'If' when addressing Magnus (the name itself is an inflated sham, deflated by a priest who calls Magnus Parvus). Magnus has carried on his father's conmanship at a higher level, though without harming anyone, and effected a purge of his sinful house. His defection has been conducted with a rogue's smoothness and has carried notional treachery from Central Europe to the great citadel of Washington. And, at the end, he has not really been found out.

Admirers of John the Square will find where what they have learned to expect and to admire – the long bumbling high-level meetings of Brits and the cousins, the authoritative details of Intelligence technique, the bared souls of operatives and their wives, a gallery of people we wish we could like but would run a mile from meeting. When love is really the main theme, it is a pity that there is nobody who is lovable. But the Intelligence services were probably founded to accommodate the unloved. The details about the look and taste and smell of things in Vienna, Berlin and London are as vivid as ever. Mr le Carré's talents cry out to be employed in the creation of a real novel.

A Perfect Spy is a perfect selling title, and we can expect this book to head the bestseller lists all over the world, but especially in the United States. The general belief among American litterateurs is that we, the British, excel in the spy novel, but that all the rest of our fiction is desperately lightweight and parochial. The very bulk of this book – 463 large pages – is an American recommendation, as is the lack of ease with which the reader gets into it. In other words it has the appearance of the difficulty of real literature and, when bought, cannot be read through in a sleepless night: it can go on the shelf and be continued later. Thus American bookbuyers, who like their purchases to have the durability of furniture, will not feel cheated. It is, finally, somewhat disturbing that the greatest postwar contribution of the British to world myth should be the figure of the traitor. The defector is the hero of such popular fiction as Mr Greene's *The Human Factor* and Bryan Forbes's *The Endless Game*, with Mr le Carré's new book somewhere in the middle. He is there in fiction because we have had him in real life. We used to produce missionaries and explorers and learned private investigators; now we produce defectors. The popularity of *A Perfect Spy* will help to keep this historical truth alive. It will also sustain the myth that the only literature the British can produce on a world scale is sub-art about spies.

Observer, 16 March 1986
Review of *A Perfect Spy* by John le Carré
(London: Hodder & Stoughton, 1986)

Where Sex Meets Self-Improvement

I HAVE spent the last month or so taking the bestseller as seriously as it takes itself. Books are commodities bought and sold on the free market, and money is the only available index of their value. Some of the books I have been reading must be very valuable indeed. Their authors and publishers and agents are enriched by them and are driven to a unitary view of value.

The term 'value' as used by the older type of philosopher was recognised as capable of several interpretations, but the metaphysicians outmoded by the logical positivists preferred to divorce it from the marketplace. When my old professor Samuel Alexander produced his book *Beauty and Other Forms of Value*, he defined value as something that had nothing to do with the world of subsistence. The world of subsistence is the world of consumption, and consumption is regulated by the laws of the market. Outside subsistence lie beauty, truth and goodness, and these cannot be bought and sold.

Now, literature, being art, is concerned with the creation of beauty, but as it is a verbal art and words are a vehicle of truth and morality, it must touch the other values as well. It is not properly concerned with value as the markets teach it, but it is a commodity, and it is bought and sold. It is natural for those who sell it to think more of the utilitarian meaning of value than the metaphysical one. A first volume of poetry may scale the heights of beauty, which is a value, but the book itself may have little value. This is the kind of contradiction that I have been trying – in these last weeks of bestseller perusal – to resolve.

The term 'bestseller' itself is an awkward counter to deal in the game of appraisal. It has not too many meanings and hence no real meaning. When it was coined in America in the 1890s, it meant merely the book that sold best. Now the book that has always sold best is the Bible, but it would be regarded as vaguely blasphemous to call it a bestseller. This is because we assume for sound psychological and historical reasons that bestselling novels are frivolous and sensational. They appeal to a mass audience, and a mass audience has no desire for uplift.

What the mass audience does desire, apparently, is escape from the conditions that make it a mass audience – namely the dullness, grind and anxiety imposed by industrial society on the masses that sustain it. The mass literacy that is one of the products of industrialism operates on a mainly utilitarian level. Language must denote rather than connote. It must be tied to simple referents. In other words, it must not be literary.

The bestseller, then, may not be judged in the aesthetic terms that apply to literature, which is concerned with the exploitation of language. The bestseller ought to be subliterary. If its appeal may not be aesthetic, then it must attract through subject matter. Such subject matter ought to excite the imagination by drawing on dreams of escape – escape to exotic locales, to the exercise of lusts and passions that urban industrialism keeps quiescent. The bestseller that specialises in such arousals performs a classic Aristotelian task – it artificially excites primitive emotions, of which combined pity and terror is only one, and it artificially discharges these emotions through the device of a plot.

'Bestseller' thus becomes a term descriptive of genre, not merely a kind of integer in the arithmetic of the market. But clearly this definition breaks down when we consider that some books that have sold sensationally well patently fulfil the conditions of literature. Vladimir Nabokov's *Lolita* was a bestseller, and no more rarefied literary exercise could be imagined. Here evidently the mass audience was attracted by the subject matter – an extension of the conventional bounds of sexuality – and it ignored the technique. Indeed, it failed to understand the true theme of the novel, misread the definition of 'nymphet' and was ready to apply (facetiously) the name Lolita to any girl of precocious puberty. 'Lolita' was a bestseller by mischance. High literature was mistaken for pornography.

But what can we say of Umberto Eco's *Name of the Rose*, which climbed the bestseller charts almost in spite of its publisher? The story of crime and detection in a medieval monastery made no concessions to the hunters of sensation, had no sex in it, though plenty of violent death, and was highly intellectual, to say nothing of theological. Moreover, it was a translation from the Italian, except for those passages that were in Latin. Clearly, a mass audience was looking for something other than titillation. The book offered exotic escape, but one could imagine more alluring boltholes than an ascetic all-male community. What it offered more abundantly was information. Mr Eco instructed the reader exhaustively on the life of medieval monks, but he made the way in easy by contriving a cunning anachronism. His William of Baskerville is a Sherlock Holmes transported to the past, and his Conan Doyle provenance was spelled out in his very name.

The readers of bestsellers seem, then, to require not only titillation but also instruction. This would seem to explain the popularity of James A. Michener's *Texas*, the reading of which was one of my self-imposed duties. *Texas* is just one of a series of huge novels by Mr Michener that present, with unassailable scholarship, the history of a place in fictional form. That form makes the assimilation of information easy, and the sense of being instructed mitigates the possible guilt of the reader as reading a mere novel. 'Only a novel,' said Jane Austen, and the disparagement of the form is still with us.

If we remember James Joyce's literary aesthetic, as propounded by Stephen Dedalus in *A Portrait of the Artist as a Young Man*, we will find a certain piquancy in the anxiety of the bestseller readers to avoid the static aesthetic emotion and seek the uplift of the didactic or the sly stimulation of the pornographic. The aesthetic lies on a continuum whose extremes are the pornographic and the didactic, and it frequently shades into one or the other of those forbidden zones. It is hard for the artist to stay with pure art. But the most acceptable book for a mass audience ignores that static middle, takes the line of the continuum and bends it into a circle, so that the didactic and the pornographic meet. If fictionalised information about the history of a state, the mysterious operations of banks or pharmaceutical firms, the truth about politicians or doctors, can be tempered with a little sexual sensationalism, then the conditions of bestsellerdom have been fulfilled.

I have been reading Arthur Hailey's *Strong Medicine* with some pleasure and, if his information is accurate (which it usually is), with some profit. Here he presents the inner workings of an American pharmaceutical firm in a loose fictional saga. He follows a formula he has made his own. His novel *Hotel* has little literary merit (nor would Mr Hailey, who knows what he is doing, claim such merit), but it is informative enough about the running of hotels to have become an assigned text in colleges where hotel management and catering are taught. His *Airport*, *Moneychangers* and *Wheels* do respectively for airports, banks and the Detroit automobile industry what *Hotel* does for hotels. The novels are readable and even thrilling. What they are not is literature. Yet it would be churlish to demand something more Jamesian or Joycean than Mr Hailey's plain homespun *récit* and occasionally improbable dialogue (improbable because it is primarily a device for imparting exhaustive information, while real-life speech is primarily phatic).

Mr Hailey is readable, but there are many bestsellers that are not, and this is, paradoxically, what makes them bestsellers. Buyers of Mr Hailey's books must be disappointed to find them difficult to put down. Once read, they are discardable, and the buyer feels he has wasted his money. An unreadable book can be put on a shelf and join the household furniture. It is an investment. Many a household has a copy of *Don Quixote* or *War and Peace*, unread or partly read but reserved for a mythical time in the future when it shall be read. The purchaser feels far more comfortable with such a possession than with a vacuum cleaner, which is too utilitarian to represent that margin of the useless that defines opulence; a vacuum cleaner, moreover, will break down and have to be replaced. The unread Tolstoy or Cervantes becomes a family heirloom.

Leslie Fiedler, the Clemens Professor of English at the State University of New York at Buffalo, published a few years ago a book called *What Was Literature?* It says in effect that literature is morphology, a mass of cadavers to be laid on the pathologist's slab. Literature is a name for what the professors find profitable to dissect; it is the raw material of the critical trade. Outside literature lie other genres of imaginative communication – science fiction, the comic strip, above all the best-selling novel. These are what the bulk of the population peruses, but there is no academic discipline – other than sociology – qualified to take them seriously.

Perhaps the time has come for the development of a criteriology that can, by taking the popular sub-literary forms seriously, help to elevate them into literature (which, despite Mr Fiedler, does not merely languish in the chill vaults of the autopsy department). Criticism exists not merely for the reader but for the writer as well. My own personal acquaintance with the practitioners of subliterature leads me to believe that they would welcome the unfacetious attention of the critics. Meanwhile, the book trade is largely sustained by genres that the professional appraisers ignore. This ought to worry us more than it seems to. 'A good book is the precious lifeblood of a master spirit.' All these vague terms require redefinition.

New York Times, 1 June 1986

The Academic Critic and the Living Writer

THE NOTICING, reviewing and criticising of works of literature to some extent merge into each other, and one is aware of a cline in the critical and pseudo-critical profession or pseudo-profession. At the bottom lies the bare notification of the act of publishing – 'Albert Throgmorton's new novel will please his fans' – and at the summit we expect to find the leisurely, scholarly (though not necessarily elegant) consideration of Throgmorton's new work, relating it to his previous work or the work he may yet produce, to the entire genre in which he practises, to the school, real or imagined, of which he may be considered to be a member, to the moral and aesthetic climate of his day and previous days, tentatively or dogmatically placing him in the whole corpus of literature of which he is a corpuscle, judging him in terms of an aesthetic or a moral system, in short taking him seriously. This kind of criticism, which may call itself a review, is sometimes termed academic. It may not necessarily be produced by academics, but it presupposes conditions associated with academia – leisure, a library, regular discourse with well-stocked and cultivated minds. It is not journalistic reviewing in the sense that most people, inevitably pejoratively, take that activity to be. The journalistic reviewer has little time, little space and often little learning. His tasks are imposed, he is expected to entertain as well as fulfil the first obligation of the reviewer – to notify that a book exists and to make a rough judgment on it (a judgment he may, even in a short time, regret).

It is possible for the rapid scribbler of a brief notice to disclose a clarity of insight denied to the academic critic ('Mr Eliot's *The Waste Land* extrapolates a personal sexual crisis on to a decaying civilisation observed during an exceptionally dry summer'), but we expect critical insight to be one of the rewards of long brooding and wide reading. Academic criticism does not smell of the need to earn a quick fee; in this sense it is civilised, and civilised also in that is does not obtrude unseemly spite or bad temper, or the wilful ignorance that goes along with them, on to what should be an objective assessment of a creative writer's work. There should also be a dignified humility appropriate to the practitioner of a comparatively lowly vocation. An academic critic may not like Milton, but he knows that Milton is better than he is. When F.R. Leavis inveighed not merely against C.P. Snow's doctrine of the Two Cultures but again C.P. Snow's own novels, he was not behaving as we think an academic should. There was altogether too much spite and dogmatism in Leavis, as well as palpable ignorance and obscurantism, and yet he is taken to be the very model of the academic critic.

The academic critic can let us down as spectacularly as any fee-grabbing Sunday reviewer. Leavis refused to believe that the art of fiction existed after D.H. Lawrence. William Empson was fond of asserting that 'there is no good writing to be found anywhere now' and said that 'Byron... only at the end of his life escaped from the infantile incest fixation upon his sister which was till then all that he had got to say', though Byron did not meet his half-sister till he was twenty-four. T.S. Eliot foisted on to a whole generation of literature students the fallacy that the Elizabethans got their five-act division from Seneca. Eliot, indeed, perpetrated a number of ill-considered judgments – about certain people not being men enough to be damned (highly Kiplingesque), about Marlowe as primarily a caricaturist, about the dissociation of sensibility as a historical event, and so on. He can be excused because he was practising literary journalism in a not entirely academic way: he had the *Criterion* to bring out. His critical misjudgments can usually be excused also because he was a poet, as perhaps Empson's can. Poetry is characterised by its daring shots in the dark, and the daring is permitted to qualify the sobriety of the critic.

There is a deliberate 'false note' in my first paragraph. I have suggested that academic critics might be prepared to write at length about Albert Throgmorton, but they are rarely willing to accord a living writer the full critical treatment, though they may stoop to the occasional brief review. They have a professional stake in the writers of the past, since literary history does not encompass the present, but they are perhaps right, though probably for the wrong reasons, to be cautious in their approach to the contemporary. It is difficult to assess a living writer. The Sunday reviewer takes a short view of the author he has under consideration, relating him to the taste of a segment of his own age; the true critic has to justify his assessment in terms not only of the past but of the future too. Certain authors have appeared in our time in whom serious critics have scented the quality of permanence – William Golding, for instance, perhaps less because of his aesthetic content than his ludic treatment of original sin, which is a venerable doctrine safe to endorse. No academic critic ever had to live to regret his espousal of Hugh Walpole (despite Henry James's enthusiasm in 1916) or, in our own age, the verse plays of Christopher Fry. While we deplore Leavis's blindness about the post-Laurentian novel, we have to admire with a certain reluctance the closing of the eyes of less eminent academic critics to it. They are protecting their nests, but they are also exhibiting the prudence not permitted to the mere reviewer.

As a living writer, though old as well as old-fashioned, I have to welcome PhD theses and even published books about my work, most of which inevitably emanate from the United States, though Kantian critiques sometimes thud in from West Germany and Crocean dissertations from Turin or Bari. There is a certain mean satisfaction in recognising oneself as recognised, but much more important is the writer's need to be understood and thus understand himself. The writer is written, as the post-structuralists tell us, and his work is the product of forces over which he has little conscious control (though far more than Derrida thinks). The academic thesist may find more in his work than may be there, but no writer is likely to reject the imputation of depth where he had thought himself to be shallow, nor the crediting of him with an erudition he does not possess. If he enjoys the flattery, that is because he needs the unction after his summary, and often hostile, treatment by reviewers.

No novelist likes to spend years on the construction of a fictionalised life of Napoleon in the shape of a Beethoven symphony only to have this work dismissed in the Sunday press as a 'resounding tinkle'. He likes even less disclosure of evidence that the journalistic reviewer has not read his work or has read it cursorily. A novel I wrote on the theme of free will and the nature of evil was dealt with very summarily and denounced as 'a nasty little shocker'. The academic thesis is a salve to deep wounds. Authors, especially novelists, are easily hurt and brood excessively about being misunderstood: the immaturity of response to bad reviews has to be deplored, but a certain emotional infantility seems to be one of the conditions for creating art.

No writer objects to the review which tells him what his work really means, though this runs counter to his own conscious intention, or rebukes him for remediable faults (though few faults in writing are). But such reviews rarely occur, and what the writer is most strongly aware of in journalistic notices is a prepared position, a ready-made judgment unqualified by the act of reading, personal malice, the lack of humility appropriate to a self-publicist. Few reviews amount to genuine criticism, yet it is criticism that the writer needs. The academic critic is his ally in the desperate struggle to make words make sense.

I have, then, to posit a situation the reverse of that once romantically held – Walther against the Meistersinger, Dylan Thomas scared of I.A. Richards. The writer's enemies are among the journalists, his friends, at least potentially, in academia. It is only academia, in the post-Leavis era, which is equipped with the tools for literary appraisal. No working author, unless he is David Lodge or Malcolm Bradbury, professionally concerned as an academic with theories of narratology and post-structuralism but also out in the windy field of the practising novelist, can hope to understand fully the processes which produce his art. He recognises that modern criticism is no longer Quiller-Couch amateurism or the vague Leavisite commitment to 'life', but he has not himself either the time or the temperament to arm himself with the right critical battery. He must leave that to the academics.

I say that the academic is potentially the friend of the writer, but, while the whole of the literary past remains to be explicated, there is no possibility of the forging of a healthful relationship between the living author and the professional critic. For caution has to remain: only the future can decide who is as good as, or not too inferior to, William Golding. But, in dealing with the literature of the past, the academic critic can set for the living author the standards by which he would wish to be judged. The reviewer can do nothing for him.

I imply, of course, academic criticism at its best – meaning at its best informed and full of informed insight. It remains difficult, however, to expunge the pejorative which is attached to the term 'academic'. The academic fugue is form without feeling: one shudders at the notion of the academic, as opposed to campus, novel. There is a load of academic rubbish regularly disgorged by the university presses, lifeless ill-written pseudo-criticism whose only purpose is to gain tenure for the author. There is also the cashing in, to the end of professional promotion, on a fad which develops into an industry whose operatives ensure it will be self-perpetuating. I am thinking particularly of the academic Joyce industry, which should by now have decided to train its techniques on authors less cultic – H.G. Wells, for instance, or Arnold Bennett. When, in the late 1930s, I first read Joyce, it could never have been dreamt that he would become the occasion of endowed chairs and international conferences. He was banned, a literary outsider. He is less thrilling to read now that the professors have domesticated him.

What is being done to Joyce in the universities exemplifies the dangers of academic leisure, the presence of unformed student minds that have not yet learned to answer back, bookishness, colleagual discourse, and sheer professorial ingenuity. There is plenty of wayward trickiness in Joyce, a sufficiency of subtexts, evidence of the language manipulating the author, as well as cabbalistic arithmology, but it took Richard Ellmann, after proving himself to be one of the pioneers of textuality, to remind us that *Ulysses* is a novel about the need for love. It seems to me often that what the professorial industrialists are doing to Joyce they could well be doing to Ian Fleming and Frederick Forsyth, who are also writers written and could, with sufficient probing and the occasional world conference, disclose marvels of crypto-symbolism. The academic critics have been granted by the over-ingenious French an opportunity to deploy criticism for its own sake, an autonomous craft like juggling. Still, the professors are all we have.

I include among the professors those who merely take on the temporary honorific after displaying, outside academia, the skills that academia is there to promote – men like Edmund Wilson, whose *Axel's Castle* opened to my generation the door to modernism and showed the pundits within the ivied walls how learning could be worn lightly and expressive exactitude be congruent with elegance. The critical spark has to be there to begin with, but only the conditions associated with academia can blow it and make it flare. My own literary career, such as it has been, owes much to certain academics, and the term academic criticism has for me, living outside the walls, no whiff of dead scholarship, condescension, or the disparagement of those who, working with the safe dead, refuse to grant life to the living.

Times Literary Supplement, 14 November 1986

The Master of Erudite Silence

SAMUEL BECKETT's birth certificate gives the date of his birth as May 13, 1906, but he insists that he was born on Good Friday, April 13 of that year. That date is too symbolically apposite to be contradicted. The Friday the thirteenth stands for ill luck that man suffers but does not earn, and the Good Friday for God's suffering on behalf of human redemption.

But it has been suggested that the day after, Holy Saturday, is Beckett's true symbolic date. His best-known play, *Waiting for Godot*, which lowbrows used to sneer at but which has now become as popular as any item in the stage repertory, presents two tramps, Vladimir and Estragon, who wait 'with a large measure of despair and a small measure of hope' for an enigmatic redeemer who never arrives. This is not to suggest that this is a Christian play, despite the allusions to the thieves who were crucified with Christ and the tree by which the tramps have been told to wait. But the symbols of Christianity are drenched in suggestive richness, and it is convenient to invoke them when trying to attach a meaning to the play. The tramps wait on the Saturday that comes after Good Friday, but that Saturday obstinately refuses to become Easter Sunday. All they, and we, can do is to wait, even though we can be pretty sure that the waiting will not be rewarded. Life is a wretched grey Saturday, but it has to be lived through.

And who is the Godot who never comes? To say he is the God of the Old Testament, or Christ bringing redemptive *eau*, is too easy. He may be someone more sinister. It is well-known that Beckett, travelling by Air France, heard the announcement '*C'est le capitaine Godot qui vous parle*' and wanted to leave the aircraft. That anecdote seems to make the author as absurd as his characters, but the term absurd has to be invoked when dealing with Beckett. His absurdity is of a special kind. In his book *The Myth of Sisyphus* Albert Camus spoke of that 'divorce between the mind that desires and the world that disappoints' which makes man's situation on earth an absurd one.

Like Sisyphus, we roll the stone up the hill only to see it roll down again. We live in a void of action and are led to despair or rebellion or, in extreme cases, to a kind of religious rehabilitation. If Camus's book makes a full philosophical statement about the absurdity of the human condition and suggests an existential way out of it – the way of choice – it is the task of Beckett merely to show men and women unable to choose, stuck in what he calls the *merde universelle*, absurd but, through their hanging on to the last human endowment, which is language, somehow noble in their absurdity.

Beckett, though an Irishman born in the Dublin district of Stillorgan (the place sounds as appropriate as his elected birth date), is a French writer – one who, according to the late Jean-Paul Sartre, has written the most distinguished French prose of the century. The roots of his thinking are French. If we read his early book on Proust, we will see him praising a quality in that master which was to become his own. Proust refused to wrench the phenomena of the world into a logical order. He rejected a chain of cause and effect, the making of the world intelligible. In other words, things are inexplicable; the scientific mirror lies; we know nothing. Beckett learnt his aesthetic from Proust; in his works – plays and novels alike – he gets down to the stripping off of illusion, showing what is left after the dissolution of shape, colour, habit and logic.

Beckett's turning himself into a French writer had a good deal to do with his distrust of the Irish literary temperament. If we read his novel *Murphy*, written in English, we see a tendency to the lush and romantic which sooner or later had to be expunged:

> The leaves began to lift and scatter, the higher branches to complain, the sky broke and curdled over flecks of skim blue, the pine of smoke toppled into the east and vanished, the pond was suddenly a little panic of grey and white, of water and gulls and snails.

In other words, a mistrust of words, highly dangerous phenomena resounding with false echoes, had to lead to an abandonment of English and at length to silence. Beckett moves towards the vacuum. Other writers, especially Irish ones, have glorified the plenum. In the greatest Irish prose writer of the century, James Joyce, we meet more than a plenum, we meet a plethora.

Beckett's association with Joyce is well known. Both Irish exiles in Paris, they admired the shape of each other's mind. They were a foil to each other, shared talk and silence, drank equally, meaning too much. Joyce's daughter Lucia fell in love with the young handsome Beckett, who failed to reciprocate and brashly stated that his visits were to see her father, not her.

The devotion to Joyce was extreme. Joyce was proud of his small feet, and Beckett tried to make his own feet as small in homage. The over-tight shoes were not merely a homage; they were a mode of self-excruciation wholly in keeping with the Beckettian view of the world as a place of pain. But the association with Joyce and the extravagant devotion have misled some people into thinking that Joyce and Beckett – though both Irish avant-garde writers exiled to Paris – were after the same thing. They were not. Joyce willed language into becoming reality – the Real Presence in the symbolic bread. But Beckett learnt from him to distrust language while, para-doxically, seeming to affirm that language was all humanity had.

Moreover, Beckett was never the same kind of Irishman as Joyce. The family was originally French Huguenot, and Beckett's elected exile in France was no more than a kind of belated repatriation. He went to Portora Royal School in Enniskillen, Northern Ireland, and to Trinity College, Dublin, great Protestant establishments both. If free-thinking Joyce never quite threw off the Catholicism of Clon-gowes and University College, Beckett had none of that accumulation of guilt and Jesuitry to lose. Renegade Irish Catholics like Brendan Behan never quite understood the kind of Irishman Beckett was and still is. They assumed a convivial bibulosity in a man who was natu-rally given to temperance and shocked by excess. Catholic Irishmen grow fat and sedentary. Beckett was always something of an athlete, a tennis-player and cricketer. He is the only Nobel Prizeman to be listed in Wisden. Sunday travellers on Air France have observed him skim lightly over the literary section of his Sunday paper and become absorbed in the sports pages.

Rightly given less to philosophical pessimism than to a realistic disillusionment, Beckett was heard once on the verge of admitting that life might have some good in it. That was on a sunny day at Lord's. But the characters in his plays and novels do not even have the consolation of being able to read the cricket scores. The *Molloy* trilogy, *Malone Dies*, *The Unnameable* present the last gasp of human despair qualified by a dogged determination to survive. The characters have nothing to live for, but they are not suicidal. Malone ends with

'Where I am, I don't know, I'll never know, in the silence you don't know, you must go on, I can't go on, I'll go on.' The curious thing about these monologues of desolation is that they are not depressing. There is even a kind of exhilaration in their rhythms. The human condition, which is always presented as terminal, is absurd. We ought not to be entertained, but we are.

The later works of Beckett move ever closer to impotence and silence. *Fin de Parti*, or *Endgame*, shows Hamm and Clov and others playing out their final phase of irritable senility in dustbins. *Happy Days* shows Winnie buried up to her waist in rubbish but still clinging to the particularities of her handbag. *Come and Go* with its three female characters limited to a 120-word text, prepares for *Breath*, which lasts for 30 seconds. *Not I* is a scrap of monologue given to an illuminated mouth. The mouth then shuts for ever. Dr George Steiner has praised this logical conclusion – the inarticulate vacuum – as Beckett's contribution to the literary situation which has to prevail after Auschwitz. There are not words left to express the horror of the twentieth century. We have to opt for silence. Dr Steiner has said all this very eloquently.

Beckett's own view of his art is a modest one. 'My characters have nothing. I'm working with impotence, ignorance… My little exploration is that whole zone of being that has always been set aside by artists as something unusable – a something by definition incompatible with art.' Of his own life, he says that it is 'dull and without interest. The professors know more about it than I do… Nothing matters but the writing. There has been nothing else worthwhile.' This writing he calls 'a stain upon the silence'. We ought not, in celebrating his eightieth birthday, to embarrass him by mentioning his kindness to his fellows in the damnable craft, his courtesy, his courage under pain, difficulty and danger. There is, he would say, nothing to congratulate him for. Let me then mutter inaudible thanks and then opt for the silence which he has so notably stained.

The Times, 1986

Verbal Subversions

CONSULTING ROGET under the heading Prospective Affections, Evelyn Waugh's Major Ludovic finds: 'Cowardice, pusillanimity, poltroonery, dastardness, abject fear, funk, dunghillcock, coistril, nidget, Bob Acres, Jerry Sneak.' Looking up *coistril* in the dictionary he finds 'a groom, knave, base fellow' and the quotation 'the swarming rabble of our coistrell curates'. This phrase, once found, is too good not to use, but how does one use it? Applying it to a recent military intake, he is at once suspected of madness by his second-in-command. It is just a suspicion. People who use a thesaurus to find the *mot* thoroughly *juste* are probably mad to begin with, but thesauro-mania leads to taking off in a word balloon, the hawser holding the gasbag to hard reality severed.

Jonathon Green's compilation provokes a more dangerous kind of madness than Roget's. Under Disorder he gives us 'Chinese fire drill, dog's dinner, grunge, Horlicks (UK upperclass use), pig's ear, pit, (right) two-and-eight (rhy, sl. = state), scrounge, schmutz, what the cat brought in'. These slang terms never had much of a hold on reality. When Carl Sandburg called slang 'a language that rolls up its sleeves, spits on its hands and goes to work' he was being exemplarily inept. Slang shirks rather than works, encapsulates bloodymindedness, avoids exact denotation, is a kind of vague poetry quickly outdated, the voice of whingeing subversiveness. Nobody knows the etymology of *slang*, but it suggests *sling*, the throwing of a noise or a far-fetched metaphor into the air, like muck off a shovel. It rolls up its sleeves and spits on its hands, casts dirt to justify leaning on its shovel, waits for the tea-break.

Nobody doubts that we need slang dictionaries, chiefly to find out the meaning of what is already demoded. On one of my rare visits to London a year or so ago I saw on a hoarding 'Milk Delivers Bottle'. I did not know the meaning of the term. I had known *bottle* in 'bottle and glass', signifying *arse*, but this was clearly something different. When it had got into the slang glossaries with the Milk Marketing Board's usage that usage was already old-hat. An actor of the Royal Shakespeare Company told me that he was glad to see I was still wanking, which I took, offended, to mean masturbating but he meant being lazy, meaning not being lazy. One cannot keep up with slang, especially the slang of the young, which is designed to be unintelligible to adults and, once decoded, has passed into history, or, since today's young reject history, has turned into vapour or unspeak. Still, one accepts Partridge's great dictionary as a record of the various ephemeral modes in which underdogs, public schoolboys, prostitutes, thieves and obstetricians have affirmed group solidarity or, overwhelmingly, the put-upon have responded to being put upon. It is social more than lexical history, affirming the need to debase or distort the language of the establishment to the end of denying the establishment's values. Slang changes with bewildering swiftness, but it is always recognisable as slang.

Do we need a thesaurus of it? Green has already done good work as a slang lexicographer, holding fast to the delimitation put forward by J.Y.T. Greig in 1938: 'The chief stimuli of slang are sex, money and intoxicating liquor' (to which we must now add drugs). His aim in this compilation is, using the Roget taxonomy, to show us how to slangify more general concepts, though Greig's categories predominate. There are a great number of slang terms for the genitalia, the sexual act, sexual perversion or inversion or permissible variation, for booze and for money. Thus, to drink is to 'bend one's elbow, booze, - it up, chug, chug-a-lug, crack a bottle, - tube (Aus.), di the bill, - the snoot, farm gargle, get a load on, get a snootful, get an edge on, - one's nose painted, - one going, hit the booze, - the bottle, - the jug, - the sauce, hoist one, inhale (a snort), irrigate the tonsils, knock (one) back, lush, - it around, - it up, oil the tonsils, put one/a few back' and so on. The question is, having being introduced to this plethora, what does one do with it? If one is a novelist, one must be grateful for the chance to give the look of authenticity to low-life dialogue, but there is the problem of verifying location, trade, period. Register is a very delicate consideration in the employment of slang, and Green can give us no help there.

A subcategory unknown to Roget is television. Who calls a television set a custard and jelly (rhyming slang for telly) or a Nervo and Knox (box)? We can guess, though I still have to have this confirmed, that the idiot-board (cue board) and the idiot girl (cue-board operator) belong to the studios, as do Acton Hilton (BBC rehearsal studios) and the mug-book (casting directory). But to whom is a religious programme a God-slot and a director a lenser or megger? Since we cannot define everything, let's put the whole lot on to the page or into the air in the form of a Rabelaisian catalogue. 'He kicked him up the blot or brown-eye or cornhole or dirt chute or gazoo or dinger or elephant and castle or heinie or kab ebis or labonza' and so on for a whole page. Or 'He fondled her apples, bazoomas, brace and bits, BSHs, cats and kitties, charlies, cupcakes, gazunkas, norks, pumps or wallopies' for at least a column.

The disposition of derisive or cynical low-life terms into the Roget format does at least show how little slang is capable of dealing with faith, hope and charity. A religious person is a bible-banger, bible-puncher or Holy Joe. A church is a Godbox and Christ has H. as a middle initial. There is little hope anywhere. To be in love is to be stuck on, go for, have a thing for or eyes for or one's nose open for the beloved. Something beautiful is cutesie or a dreamboat or a corker, daisy, dish, eyeful, hot stuff, looker, nifty, peach, pip, spanker, stunner, sweeties. To learn slang thus is to learn a limitation of the nobler faculties. The whole book proposes modes of dehumanisation, though with no sinister intent. If we want to translate the elevated or the merely neutral into the colourful animalistic, here is how to do it. The question is whether we want to do it.

For slang derives directly from a situation; it cannot be frigidly applied from without. You have to be pretty far gone in homosexual public lavatory soliciting to know about having kidney trouble, or, when one has failed to hide one's homosexuality, to speak of wearing a cut-glass veil. We are, most of us, on the outside, watching other people's bunch punch or daisy-chain or gang-bang or group grope or sloppy seconds (a girl moving from one partner to the next). There is altogether too much of the voyeur or the how-quaint slummer in such a compilation. However we use its terms, we shall always be using them in inverted commas.

This is not to denounce slang itself: far from it. It is good to know how much of it there is and to be able to admire its variety. I did not previously know that Australians with too many sexual partners speak of climbing trees to get away from it, or getting more arse than a toilet seat, or having more pricks than a second-hand dartboard or being so busy they have to put a man on to help. Knowing this kind of thing – and Green admits to compiling his thesaurus for those who are curious or logophiliac – is a very marginal accomplishment, like being able to fart 'Annie Laurie' through a keyhole. Either we learn slang in situation contexts, as many of us did in the armed forces, or we look it up, if the dictionary comes out quickly enough, when its use, in speech or journalism, hinders communication.

There are one or two marginal lessons that Green teaches, and one of them is the great truth that standard English has still to provide us with acceptable terms for the organs and processes of generation and excretion. There are so many slang expressions for the penis – steak, trumpet, blow stick, cannon, cherry splitter, dagger, nimrod, joy prong, mouse mutton, IBM (itty bitty meat for a small penis) – that the catalogue looks like a search for a word that ought to exist but does not. The same is true of the female pudendum – fern, ha'-penny, hide, jelly roll, moneymaker, ruby-fruit, you know where (very tame), cuffs and collars (pubic hair the same colour as head hair). The Latinate terms smell of Lysol, but the slang words are so face-tious that they continue to attach a sniggering kind of shame to parts which, though private, need a sober public nomenclature. Similarly there is a whole range of sexual activity which can either be named by translating Krafft-Ebing or handed over to the slangmongers. There is nothing in between. The sexual revolution has succeeded only in making general currency out of a secret mint.

Green's glossary of the so-called drug culture is horrifyingly fas-cinating. He teaches us that olly is speed (Oliver Reed), Tuinal is a Christmas tree, an ab is an abscess caused by injecting, cotton is a cloth through which heroin is sucked into a syringe, and to shoot gravy, fire up, or jack off is to pump a mixture of blood and heroin into one's arm. Much, much more. His thesaurus is an index of what is going on in the world, and the rich underworld vocabularies are an earnest of the continuation of crime, prostitution and various kinds of slaughter. But the great truth is less the forms of slang than the need for it. Humanity is unregenerable and hates the language of con-formity, since conformity has a whiff of the inhuman about it. Green has at least shown us, though without exact definition or historical placing, the range of slang in English. In effect, he makes a general statement: there is a lot of this kind of thing around. But to amass slang in a void is a useless activity. It is better to look meanings up, and Mr Green's admirable *Dictionary of Contemporary Slang*, along with the recently edited Partridge, is the place to do it. A treasury of slang has to be fairy gold.

Times Literary Supplement, 5 December 1986
Review of *The Slang Thesaurus* by Jonathon Green
(London: Elm Tree Books, 1986)

Eye of a Stranger

NAIPAUL IS always brilliant, but the term probably has the wrong connotation here – the only scintillation is of flints in a country road, momentary tears, sad Caribbean sunlight. The tone of the book is reminiscent, elegiac. It is dedicated to the memory of Naipaul's brother Shiva, who died in 1985, and it ends with a memory of the death of a sister equally beloved.

The theme, as it emerges at the end of the book, is 'life and man as the mystery, the true religion of men, the grief and the glory.' The book is called 'a novel in five sections,' but it reads like an autobiographical meditation, not a novel at all.

As I know that a violin sonata cannot properly be called a symphony, I doubt whether a book of this kind ought to be called a novel. But everybody except the Americans is becoming increasingly vague as to what a novel is. The Booker fiction prize was a few years ago given to *Schindler's Ark*, which was a biography. Julian Barnes's excellent *Flaubert's Parrot* was presented in English as a novel, but *Le Perroquet de Flaubert* won its Parisian prize in the *belles lettres* category.

I worry about this melting of categorical barriers. A novel, as Flaubert himself said, is a damnably difficult machine to construct. It has a diversity of characters, a plot, a denouement. It is, above all, an imaginative construct, a triumph or failure of artifice.

There is nothing of artifice about Naipaul's new book. The protagonist-narrator does not give himself a name, though there is an intimation that his first name begins with a V. The tribulations of the writer whose soul is bared are all Vidia's, from Trinidad to Europe and back again. If this is not autobiography, it is because it admits more poetry, more descriptive detail, indeed more soul-baring than we expect in a mere bundle of memoirs. Autobiography is not meant to be art, though it can be high craft. This book, whatever we call it, is art of an exceptional order, but it does not admit the novelist's artifice.

The opening section presents the writer-narrator in a village not far from Stonehenge. He is alienated, a foreigner,

A man from another hemisphere, another background, coming to rest in middle life in a cottage of a half neglected estate, an estate full of reminders of its Edwardian past, with few connections with the present. An oddity among the estates and big houses of the valley, and I, a further oddity in its ground. I felt unanchored and strange.

His imagination anchors itself to Jack, a very ordinary man living in a farm-workers cottage, tending a garden 'surrounded by ruins, reminders of vanished lives,' himself a remnant of the past.

He likes to think of Jack as an earth-rooted solidity, a precious symbol because of the West Indian's own insecure past – 'peasant India, colonial Trinidad' – and the rootless insecurity of his present writer's existence. But, with Jack's death, he sees him not as a symbolic remnant, but as one who had built his own tenuous life in silence and with courage: 'All around him was ruin, and all around, in a deeper way, was change, and a reminder of the brevity of the cycles of growth and creation.'

Just before dying, on Christmas Eve, Jack had risen from his bed and taken his last beer in the village pub, asserting, 'at the very end, the primacy not of what was beyond life, but life itself.' Jack's widow becomes a townswoman, the new weapons are tested on Salisbury Plain, modern diary technology supervenes on the old way, Jack is gone but has to be commemorated. This is the duty of a middle-aged writer from Trinidad.

This first section, and the third and fourth, are a remarkable testimony to Naipaul's capacity for expressing the spirit of place. Wiltshire yields to his eye as does India, Argentina or Africa. Nobody has done better what he does here – describing meadows, villagers, sycamores, 'the whitening hedge against which the rabbits fed.' But there is a strangeness – the sharp eye is not that of the native. The anonymous writer who is really Naipaul is full of 'the rawness of response – every excursion into a new part of the country was for me like a tearing at an old scab.'

In his second section, 'The Journey,' we learn the explanation of the title of his book. He comes across a reproduction of a painting by Chirico, reproduced on the dustcover and ponders the meaning of its name – 'The Enigma of Arrival'. It was to suggest a story with that title, filling out in words what Chirico intimates with a few brushstrokes – 'a sunlit sea journey ending in a dangerous classical city.' The story was not written but the title has found its target. The dreamlike quality of Chirico's picture is matched by the author's own recurring nightmare – an explosion in the head which throws him into a degraded posture before strangers. It is the moment of arrival, and the hope perverted to panic is part of the enigma.

The writer's journeys follow Naipaul's own routes – the expectations and shocks of many arrivals – but there is a double homing: to the Wiltshire village where Jack toiled and died, and to the site of cremation in Trinidad where his sister's body was consumed in Hindu ceremonies. The enigma of arrival is balanced by his final section title – 'The Ceremony of Farewell.' He discovers the purpose of writing this book – 'Death and the way of handling it – that was the motif of the story of Jack.' The sacred Hindu world vanishes, as does the Druid world of Stonehenge, and the memory of dead empires blurred:

> Every generation now was to take us further away from those sanctities. But we remade the world for ourselves; every generation does that, as we found when we came together for the death of this sister and felt the need to honour and remember. It forced us to look on death.

The book moves towards reconciliation, the glory inseparable from the grief. And so Naipaul ends as he began – with Jack.

If Naipaul wishes us to accept his book as a novel we will. The description at least imposes a sense of distance and impersonality and, most of all, a pattern. If it is a novel, it is one lacking in the trivial facetiousness and the fleshly sensationalism of the genre as we meet it these days. It has great dignity, compassion and candour. It is written with the expected beauty of style. It is philosophical and yet it smells of the earth. It does the opposite of what is increasingly being seen as the aim of the novelist (who, said Auden, must be dirty with the dirty). Instead of diminishing life Naipaul ennobles it.

Observer, 15 March 1987
Review of *The Enigma of Arrival* by V.S. Naipaul (New York: Viking, 1987)

Wilde with all Regret

RICHARD ELLMANN wrote the two greatest literary biographies of our century. He died having just committed the typescript of this second of his masterpieces to his publishers, and he can never know the gratification of the universally laudatory response that must greet this product of long and meticulous labour, which is also an expression of his exquisite critical sense, wide and deep learning, and profound humanity.

Why, having written his monumental life of James Joyce, did Ellmann turn to Oscar Wilde? There was, of course, a lifelong concern with Anglo-Irish literature, but he might have been expected to produce a great critical biography of Yeats, who matches in verse Joyce's achievement in prose. Wilde has been considered minor, and his art still tends to be overshadowed by the scandal of his life. Joyce, too, was scandalous, but not in Wilde's way. He lived in sin until testamentary prudence, rather than reconciliation with the Church he had abandoned, prompted him to regularise his ménage with Nora Barnacle; his great novel *Ulysses* was banned.

Wilde knew censorship too, but the proscribing of *Salome* and the murmurs about *The Picture of Dorian Gray* were nothing compared to the outrage aroused by the disclosure of his sodomy. Heterosexual fornication in the manner of his father, the ear and eye specialist, who begot bastards in the careless manner of the Irish Protestant ascendancy, would have done Wilde no harm. But, falling for Robert Ross at Oxford when Wilde was already a family man, and later, disastrously, for Lord Alfred Douglas, he precipitated a downfall which remains the major myth of homosexual martyrology. This continues to get in the way of sober appraisal of his literary achievement.

Of his importance as a writer Ellmann has no doubt:

Oscar Wilde: we have only to hear the great name to anticipate that what will be quoted as his will surprise and delight us. Among the writers identified with the 1890s Wilde is the only one whom everyone still reads. The various labels that have been applied to the age – aestheticism, Decadence, the Beardsley Period – ought not to conceal the fact that our first association with it is Wilde, refulgent, imperial, ready to fall.

These epithets are just. No one glitters as Wilde does but disaster was always just round the corner. He was kind and he was not worldly: paradox for him was a substitute for cunning. He made his own life an art in a manner calculated to infuriate the dull. He dressed too extravagantly, but always in accord with a philosophy of beauty sincerely held. He despised the rabble that included the Victorian establishment.

Physical disaster prepared itself early. As a student at Oxford he contracted the syphilis which was to kill him at 46 – paradoxically, since this was the great disease of womanisers. He could have picked it up later in his homosexual encounters through anal coition, but Wilde was not strictly a bugger: Ross probably introduced him to the oral and intercrural modes of release which he seems regularly to have practised. Wilde's tendency to cover his mouth with his hand when speaking was a consequence of the mercury treatment, which did not cure but turned the teeth black.

And the work? Ellmann is not bemused by the shallow Keatsianism of much of the poetry. He cites

> This English Thames is holier far than Rome,
> Those harebells like a sudden flush of sea
> Breaking across the woodland, with the foam
> Of meadow-sweet and white anemone
> To fleck their blue waves...

and points out that 'the meadow-sweet blooms in June and the anemone in April, while the harebell, unlike the bluebell, does not grow in oceanic profusion'. *The Ballad of Reading Gaol*, usually considered sentimental doggerel, is treated with some respect: it introduces the colloquial and still appeals to readers who would shudder at aestheticism. It has branded an unforgettable phrase onto the language – 'Each man kills the thing he loves'.

As for the unforgettable witticisms thrown off in speech, the one about having nothing to declare except his genius seems apocryphal, but he certainly remarked that only a heart of stone could fail to laugh at the death of little Nell: he said it while tremulously on bail. Of the brilliance of his conversation there is a plethora of evidence: he held Paris salons, which knew all about conversation, totally spellbound. So remarkable a man had to be pricked for slaughter.

The American lecture-tour was a kind of preparation for slaughter of the aestheticism which Wilde promoted. The Americans had laughed at the fleshly poet Bunthorne in *Patience*; D'Oyly Carte enabled them to laugh at Bunthorne's prototype, extolling the house beautiful in velvet breeches and hyacinthine locks. But few laughed. This six-foot-three tough Irishman, who could drink any congregation of scoffing miners under the table, got his points across about the importance of beauty in a brash nation dedicated to piety and money.

One lady, Helen Potter, made an amateur phonetic transcription of Wilde's delivery, which Ellmann reproduces in an appendix. She was impressed, and she was not alone. But the doctrine of beauty proved a dangerous one, since it seemed to deny morality. Between 1895 and 1900 at least 900 sermons were preached against Wilde in the United States alone.

That was after the great trial and Wilde's condemnation to two years of hard labour. Ellmann spares us nothing of the horrors of either. As always, it was the common people who showed both tolerance and compassion, applauding Wilde's sermon on male love in court, regretting that he should have been brought so low when tramping the prison yard or breaking his nails picking oakum. One warder was dismissed for compassion. There was no compassion above.

Worse than the ordeal of jail was the total ostracism afterwards. Few come well out of the wretched story: Shaw, Henry James, Max Beerbohm maintained a discretion unseemly in brother artists. There was no dignity in Wilde's death: 'He had scarcely breathed his last breath when the body exploded with fluids from the ear, nose, mouth, and other orifices.' Unlike Joyce, he died in the Church.

Joyce was a Parnellite, and Wilde was thinking of Parnell when he said: 'There is something vulgar in all success. The greatest men fail, or seem to have failed.' As Ellmann concludes, we inherit Wilde's struggle 'to achieve supreme fictions in art, to associate art with social change, to bring together individual and social impulse, to save what is eccentric and singular from being satirised and standardised, to replace a morality of severity by one of sympathy.' Wilde cleansed of scandal, is a towering figure, 'with parables and paradoxes, so generous, so amusing, and so right.' It is an ending worthy of a great subject and a great book.

Observer, 4 October 1987
Review of *Oscar Wilde* by Richard Ellmann
(London: Hamish Hamilton, 1987)

Mr Gibbon and the Huns

THIS, I think, is a very reasonable passage of English prose: 'In the second century of the Christian Era, the empire of Rome comprehended the fairest part of the earth, and the most civilised portion of mankind. The frontiers of that extensive monarchy were guarded by ancient renown and disciplined valour. The gentle, but powerful, influence of laws and manners had gradually cemented the union of the provinces. Their peaceful inhabitants enjoyed and abused the advantages of wealth and luxury. The image of a free constitution was preserved with decent reverence. The Roman senate appeared to possess the sovereign authority, and devolved on the emperors all the executive powers of government. During a happy period of more than fourscore years, the public administration was conducted by the virtue and abilities of Nerva, Trajan, Hadrian, and the two Antonines.'

And so on for the space of, in my edition, 1,300 closely printed double-columned pages (printed in 1840: what remarkable eyesight those early Victorians had). This is, of course, the opening of Edward Gibbon's *History of the Decline and Fall of the Roman Empire*. It is Augustan English of the kind that makes the Declaration of Independence both moving and authoritative. Note the balance of the phrases, the exactitude of the language, the sly 'abused,' which is like a deliberate flaw in the marble of eulogy. It is the prose style of an age secure in its convictions, the style of a Jefferson but not of an Eisenhower, Nixon or Reagan. It addresses a cultivated readership and it never deviates into the colloquial, which all too easily degenerates into the loose and imprecise. It is not the kind of English we associate with word processors. It is an English of very black ink, sharp quills and fine handmade power.

As for its author, we are as I write poised between two of his anniversaries. He was born in 1737 and he completed his massive history in 1788, eliciting the response from King George III, 'Another damned big black book, Mr Gibbon. Scribble, scribble, scribble – eh, Mr Gibbon?' In 1788 it was actually a number of damned big black books. He had published the first volume in 1776, to applause but some murmurs, for he seemed cynical about the growth of Christianity in the later Roman Empire. The second and third volumes appeared in 1781, to a response of moderate warmth. 'Prolix,' everybody said, and Gibbon agreed, blaming 'superfluous diligence' for his wordiness. With the end of his task, Gibbon felt that ambiguous elation known to all authors who have completed a weighty work – a sense of freedom but also a 'sober melancholy' at taking 'an everlasting leave of an old and agreeable companion'.

A huge history of the decay of one of the greatest empires the world had seen was enough for any man's lifetime. But Gibbon also wrote an autobiography, published posthumously as *Memoirs*, which frankly displays a personality apparently more indolent than illustrious, a typical product of a monied family of the age of Enlightenment. He was born in Putney, a suburb of London, was a sickly child and the victim of a somewhat irregular education. He went to Magdalen College, Oxford, where he spent an 'idle and unprofitable time' in an atmosphere 'narrow, lazy and oppressive'. He became a Roman Catholic at the age of 16, to his father's intense horror, and was sent to Lausanne to be reconverted to Protestantism.

Out of the inner conflict between the claims of the opposite faiths, Gibbon emerged as a rationalist, an anticlerical sceptic. Five years in Switzerland taught him the pleasures of reading – what else was there to do except gaze at the lake and the Alps? – and the madness of love. He fell heavily for Suzanne Curchod, later the wife of the French financier and statesman Jacques Necker and the mother of Napoleon's *bête noire* Mme de Staël. His father, who had broken one attachment for him, now shattered the other by ordering him home. From 1759 he served as a captain in the Hampshire Militia, but he was back on the Continent in 1763. It was in Italy that he first felt his lifework stirring:

'It was at Rome, on the 15th of October, 1764, as I sat musing amidst the ruins of the Capitol, while the barefoot friars were singing vespers in the Temple of Jupiter, that the idea of writing the decline and fall of the city first started to my mind.'

'The first of earthly blessings, independence', Gibbon wrote in those same *Memoirs*, and it was independence that he lacked when his father died after a life of improvidence, leaving no comfortable patrimony as a cushioned seat for the undertaking of the huge work. Gibbon went into Parliament in 1774, and was made a commissioner of trade and plantations. The secure greatness of the British colonial system was already being challenged in America, and the publication of the first volume of a work which, in effect, warned that all empires must someday fall came opportunely in 1776. From 1776 on, the *Decline and Fall* did not permit of a life much worth recording. He was back in Lausanne in 1783 and died in England in 1794, at the early age of 57. His life is no great example to today's young and ambitious. His portrait shows a man run unhealthily to fat, and anecdotes about him tell of his distaste for exercise. His sexual life is nowhere mentioned. Gibbon is no more than the pen that pushed through reams of paper to execute the greatest work of historical research in the entire world canon.

It is a work which, though two centuries old, does not have to be excused on the grounds of primitive methods of research, the lack of brisk card-indexing, the absence of a cybernetic retrieval system and a manly independence of scurrying research assistants. In an age when Dr Samuel Johnson could produce a dictionary single-handed, the notion of collective labour on a work which today would absorb a whole synod of historians had not yet come to birth. The astonishing thing about the *Decline and Fall* is that it has not had to be revised in the light of fresh discoveries. Gibbon used no secondary sources, for these did not exist: he went back to all he had – the primary documents, all duly footnoted. Some of these primary documents detailed the Roman decay with a frankness of particularity not agreeable to an age that preferred blanket generalisation. 'My English text is chaste,' says Gibbon, 'and all licentious passages are left in the decent obscurity of a learned language.'

It is the style that enchants. Writing on Antoninus Pius, Gibbon says: 'His reign is marked by the rare advantage of furnishing very few materials for history; which is, indeed, little more than the register of the crimes, follies, and misfortunes of mankind.' Of religion he writes: 'The various modes of worship, which prevailed in the Roman world, were all considered by the people as equally true; by the philosopher, as equally false'; and the rhetorical balance of phrases, the lack of tentativeness in the Gibbonian conclusions seem to point to a man of the world, not to a slippered recluse. Gibbon said: 'The captain of the Hampshire grenadiers... has not been useless to the historian of the Roman empire.' His knowledge of the military life, in other words, illuminated his vision of an empire sustained by a great army. As a politician he knew what he was saying when he declared, 'All taxes must, at last, fall upon agriculture,' and described corruption as 'the most infallible symptom of constitutional liberty.' His statement that 'the principles of a free constitution are irrecoverably lost, when the legislative power is nominated by the executive' has more relevance to the present age than to Gibbon's own. Gibbon was not merely writing about the irrecoverable past.

What, in fact, was he writing about? In his own words, the 'vicissitudes of fortune, which spares neither man nor the proudest of his works, which buries empires and cities in a common grave.' But there is more than the blind goddess who seems to rule over history: there is human strength and human weakness, and the principle that 'all that is human must retrograde if it does not advance.' The Roman Empire did not advance, any more than did the Napoleonic Empire waiting to be born a few years after Gibbon's death. Any empire reaches a plateau of achievement with which it is well content. It has brought certain barbarians into the circle of civilised rule, and it considers that the uncivilisable barbarians outside constitute no menace. Complacency is the sin, and it enervates the protective armed forces. A civilised people will deign to use some of the uncivilised barbarians as a mercenary instrument for quelling unrest on its colonial borders. It thinks that the barbaric energy can be controlled and, when not controlled, ignored. France in 1940 was astonished to find that the barbaric Nazis who had never read Voltaire and André Gide could capture the capital, the city of light, through ingenious energy alone. America was astonished that it could not conquer a barbaric enemy in Vietnam. Britain was astonished when the Japanese threatened India.

Gibbon is at his most readable when he is dealing with the threat of Attila and his Huns to the Christian empire that was so big and unwieldy it had to split itself in two. Rome had become the merely nominal capital of a Western empire whose rulers were mostly in Ravenna. The Eastern empire had its very nearly impregnable centre in Constantinople. Aetius, a great general sometimes called the last of the Romans, had used the Huns, as he had the Goths and the Visigoths, as a mercenary force. The Huns, seeing what they were paid to protect, disdained being a mere instrument of civilised order and, under a great and implacable leader, sought to capture what they had been hired to defend. Attila failed to take Italy, but not because of Roman strength. The legend that Pope Leo turned him back is probably a less acceptable reason than the fact of dysentery and malaria in Attila's hordes, as well as the logistic problem of carting loot back to the Danube. Attila did not make the Roman Empire fall, but it was barbaric energy, not yet civilised into luxurious complacency, that forced the gates of Rome. Gibbon (in Chapter 31) is worth quoting very nearly in full on the arrival of Alaric and his Goths:

'The last resource of the Romans was in the clemency, or at least in the moderation, of the king of the Goths. The senate, who in this emergency assumed the supreme powers of government, appointed two ambassadors to negotiate with the enemy. This important trust was delegated to Basilius, a senator, of Spanish extraction, and already conspicuous in the administration of provinces: and to John, the first tribune of the notaries, who was peculiarly qualified by his dexterity in business as well as by his former intimacy with the Gothic prince. When they were introduced into his presence, they declared, perhaps in a more lofty style than became their abject condition, that the Romans were resolved to maintain their dignity, either in peace or war; and that, if Alaric refused them a fair and honourable capitulation, he might sound his trumpets, and prepare to give battle to an innumerable people, exercised in arms and animated by despair. 'The thicker the hay, the easier it is mowed,' was the concise reply of the Barbarian; and this rustic metaphor was accompanied by a loud and insulting laugh, expressive of his contempt for the menaces of an unwarlike populace, enervated by luxury before they were emaciated by famine.'

Alaric demanded all the wealth of the city 'and all the slaves who could prove their title to the name of *Barbarians*. The ministers of the senate presumed to ask, in a modest and suppliant tone, "If such, O king! are your demands, what do you intend to leave us?" "YOUR LIVES," replied the haughty conqueror.'

This was some decades before Attila's attempt on the Roman Empire, and Gibbon's record, both vivacious and depressing, is of the dismantling, by rough people of non-Italic blood, of a gorgeous apparatus of rule and civilisation in search for loot. Meanwhile a new and nonsecular empire was preparing itself in the ruins of a dying Rome – the Church of Christ, first admitted by the superstitious Constantine, and not much regarded by a rationalistic Gibbon.

Gibbon, adept at the plain historic record, is not above the occasional speculation. It is with no hint of pious outrage that he imagines the later conquests of the Sons of the Prophet:

> 'A victorious line of march had been prolonged above a thousand miles from the rock of Gibraltar to the banks of the Loire; the repetition of an equal space would have carried the Saracens to the confines of Poland and the Highlands of Scotland: the Rhine is no more impassable than the Nile or Euphrates, and the Arabian fleet might have sailed without a naval combat into the mouth of the Thames. Perhaps the interpretation of the Koran would be taught in the schools of Oxford, and her pupils might demonstrate to the circumcised people the sanctity and truth of the revelation of Mohamet.'

He might well have liked the prospect of Islamising 'the monks of Magdalen' – 'decent easy men, who supinely enjoyed the gifts of the founder', whose 'dull and deep potations excused the brisk intemperance of youth'. Gibbon, physically indolent himself, seems to relish the energy of the barbarian and the infidel. His speculation of the prevailing of Islamic energy is no longer as fantastic as it must have seemed in his time, or even in the early years of this century, when G.K. Chesterton made England Islamic in *The Flying Inn*. The point is, I think, that Gibbon is always relevant to whatever age it is that reads him.

Was there, in Gibbon's view, ever a time when men were happy? Yes, he says: 'If a man were called to fix the period in the history of the world during which the condition of the human race was most happy and prosperous, he would, without hesitation, name that which elapsed from the death of Domitian to the accession of Commodus.' But it is in the very nature of such felicity not to endure: it is an interlude in the long chronicle of decay – entropy, we say nowadays. 'All that is human must retrograde if it does not advance.' And by 'advance' he does not, I think, mean solely the technological innovation that might have saved Napoleon's empire; he means the development of both a moral and a historical cycle in which achievement leads to decay and decay to resumption of strength (Vico's *ricorso*), the consciousness that man is a unity bound by a single law of survival and no empire may speak of peoples 'beyond the pale'.

Gibbon, naturally, has his detractors. Some of these maintain the sad outrage of the critics of his own day, who deplored his unenthusiastic treatment of the rise of Christianity. Evelyn Waugh, whose Augustan style appears to owe something to Gibbon, seemed angry that Gibbon should regard the legend of Helena and the finding of the True Cross as a piece of nonsense drawn up 'in the darkness of monasteries'. In his novel *Helena*, which follows the legend and ignores history, he places Gibbon as a literal gibbon, gibbering at the end of its leash. It is too easy a gibe.

Gibbon has the faults of his age – a too ready appeal to reason, a statuesque prose which one sometimes longs to see deliquesce into the demotic, and apparent lack of human concern in his recording of the antics of the emperors (where are the slaves? where are the ordinary honest craftsmen?) and a loftiness of perspective all too appropriate to an England which thought highly of itself. We have to look at the *Memoirs* to find the imperfect and suffering man ('I saw and loved... I sighed as a lover, I obeyed as a son'), conscious of transience. I must quote in full, as a reasonable peroration, what I have only picked at:

> I will not dissemble the first emotions of joy on the recovery of my freedom, and, perhaps, the establishment of my fame. But my pride was soon humbled, and a sober melancholy was spread over my mind, by the idea that I had taken an everlasting leave of an old and agreeable companion, and that whatsoever might be the future fate of my History, the life of the historian must be short and precarious.

In his instance, all too short. But long enough for the creation of one of the most astonishing works of all time.

New York Times, 28 February 1988

The Literature Industry

When I first began to write I stood in great awe of publishers. When I first began to publish the awe was replaced by gratitude. Here were men and women prepared to risk money in order to give my scribbles to the world, or the infinitesimal portion of the world that reads books. It seems to me strange that such power and generosity should be housed in tiny offices with unwashed windows. When I signed my first contract – so eagerly that I dropped the pen – a London fog sat heavily outside the modest premises and, on the desk along with the contract, sat a bottle of celebratory sherry.

The circumstances were the same as for Henry James and Joseph Conrad. My advance on royalties was the same, too. In the contract I promised to give to my publisher first refusal of my next two books, and the subsequent contracts would similarly imply a relationship which, so it was hoped, would be lasting. There was much talk in those days of reciprocal loyalty and even the suggestion that a lasting friendship might grow out of what was not altogether a commercial bond. The relations between author and publisher were cosy, even domestic.

There were exceptions of course. Byron, infuriated by the sharp practice of Murray, wrote, 'Now, Barabbas was a publisher'. Macmillan was too snobbish to invite the best-selling H.G. Wells to dinner: 'Began life as a counter-jumper, you know. Damned fellow might steal the spoons.' But generally an author had a sense of feeding with his regular manuscripts a cottage industry that offered him humble sales to match humble advances. And always there was that bottle of sherry on the table.

I speak of London publishing, which, in the year that I saw my first book in print, still had a gaslit Dickensian quality about it. In New York, as I was to discover, publishing was big business. There, I already knew, manuscripts did not proceed from copy-editor to printer with little change: manuscripts were processed. Max Perkins, the great editor (great? Can an editor be *great*?), made the unwieldy monsters of Thomas Wolfe into publishable commodities. Publishability meant commercial viability, and once an editor had Perkinsian power he grew closer to the cash values of literature than to the aesthetic.

Prescription was in order: cut out that passage – it's dull; begin with this sex scene; your readers want action, not philosophy; the whole thing's 200 words too long. Once it was decided that a writer of books did not really know how to write them, having to leave the job of editing to a man who had never written a book in his life, the age of the saleable commodity had already arrived. We don't want literature, my friend: we want a bestseller.

The old cottage publishers never expected to make much money out of books. They loved good writing, even if the general public didn't, and they were honoured by serving the art. Such amateurishness could not easily survive. The increased costs of the physical act of getting a book on to the market militated against the promotion of the best (of its nature not highly popular) and enforced the cultivation of the mediocre. Most people are mediocre, and want to see their mediocrity mirrored in print.

This is not to deny that, by some inexplicable quirk of the mass mind, the very best can occasionally be very popular, but the publishing world was surprised to see Umberto Eco's *The Name of the Rose* heading the bestselling list, not at all surprised to find it eventually superseded by something by Harold Robbins or Jackie Collins. Once American publishers, with European publishers quick to follow, began to see their *raison d'être* in the purveying of mass commodities, their houses became heavily staffed and highly impersonal. There was a heavy turnover in personnel, so that talk of an author's loyalty even to an editor became a sad joke. Great names subsisted, honouring dead founders, but loyalty to a great name had to be loyalty to an abstraction. There was no longer a greying head of the firm, somewhat shabby, with golf-tees in his pocket and that bottle of sherry ready to come out of the cupboard. Soon not even the great abstract name meant anything. Takeovers are endemic in the publishing business, and an author can literally end up not knowing exactly whose money is behind his advance or royalties.

Some authors desperately need the personal touch that the old-time publisher could give. Writing is a lonely occupation and writers are naturally prone to self-doubt; professional companionship to them is not the friendship of other writers, who are given to jealousy or disdain, or both at once, but that sense of a continuity of understanding, appreciation, constructive criticism that has more to do with devotion to an art than concern with the cash register.

Typescripts, or computer printouts, no longer go automatically to the cosy family firm that, out of a loyal belief in their worth, has kept their predecessors in print. Books are now auctioned, and the highest bidder hopes he can make sales match the exorbitant advance. The impersonality of the whole proceeding is mitigated, for the author, by money, but money, strangely enough, cannot easily compensate for the author's sense of being reduced to a commodity like soap or peanut butter.

It is perhaps no wonder that the future of literature seems to lie in its reduction to an industry as domestic as the packaging of More-cambe Bay potted shrimps. I knew a young author in San Francisco who produced a series of novels in which the characters of the Popeye cartoons were turned into figures of theological allegory. He could not sell these to a commercial publisher but he could turn out 1,000 or so copies on an IBM machine. These he sold on the San Francisco streets and registered a profit, despite his many remainders. Eventually he died of an overdose of drugs, but that does not invalidate his procedure.

When Dante Alighieri and Geoffrey Chaucer wrote, printing had not even been invented: copying was the trade of the professional scribe. Despite the lack of a copy-editor and a contemporary Max Perkins, to say nothing of a literary agent, their works managed to survive into the Gutenberg age. Today's literary works do not manage to survive at all. They are remaindered heavily and sold to paperback firms with a massive, and destructive, turnover.

There is a smell of well-oiled efficiency about all this, but the efficiency is often more apparent than real. At least two novelists sent typescripts of books that had 10 or so years previously been best-sellers to reputable publishers under the guise of pseudonymous submissions. They were not merely turned down flat; they were never even met with a whiff of recognition. Every New York and Boston publisher rejected John Kennedy Toole's comic masterpiece *A Confederacy of Dunces*, which, when the author had committed suicide in despair, was given a National Book Award.

Books, being works of art, are delicate, and they are also highly personal things, and the impersonality of the contemporary publishing business is not well suited to handling them.

Modern industry being what it is, the quantitative view is considered more important than the qualitative. The books are churned out, to the detriment of the world's forests, and all one can say of 99 per cent of them is that they are compilations of words with titles, jackets and blurbs. That their life is short is gleefully acknowledged: let them die quickly so that fresh books can take their place. This was not the view of those long-dead humanists.

Observer, 28 August 1988

The Man Who Invented Himself

MICHAEL HOLROYD begins at the end: with the death of Bernard Shaw at the age of ninety-four. In primadonna style he had been making his farewells for a decade. An American newspaper offered him a million dollars for a genuine last word but presumably it did not pay for his 'There is nothing more to be said.' His nurse told reporters that he had happily willed himself to die. A photographer who might have come from *The Doctor's Dilemma* snapped his corpse. 'He preserved the same puckish expression he had borne throughout life. His beard still stuck out at the same perkily truculent angle.'

Eric Bentley, who wrote the first Shaw biography in which the subject did not collaborate, read all the obituaries and said they made him sick. 'It was praise of Shaw, but what praise, and from whom... ! Such mourning for Shaw was a mockery of Shaw...'

The truth was and is that Shaw has never been properly understood. The world was tickled by 'GBS the irresponsible clown' and there was always copy in the perverse statements of his dotage. In an introduction to the one-volume collection of his plays that a popular newspaper put out in the thirties as an inducement to taking out a year's subscription, Shaw made reference to the fabulous bandersnatch that the publicists had made of him and presented himself as a 'classic writer of comedies' who extracted the bad teeth of British society with 'plenty of laughing gas'. This was a fair statement.

He was a great dramatist and a remarkable critic. Many of his quirks were attributed to his Irishry. He told G.K. Chesterton: 'I am a typical Irishman; my family come from Yorkshire.' But much of Shaw's idiosyncratic quality seems to derive from a rejection of country and family. Like Joyce, he flew against those nets.

In *John Bull's Other Island*, he throws a bright set of stage lights on the vices of the Irish – the watery romanticism, shiftlessness, self-important vindictiveness and a life-denying poetic imagination, fuelled by potcheen. No Irishman could do anything if he stayed in Ireland, except blow people and pigs to pieces and then laugh like a horse about it. His lifelong loathing of alcohol was a reaction against a drunken father and drunken uncles and his other abstinences – from tobacco, meat, unclean textiles and sub-Moore amorous sloppiness – can be seen as a revulsion from Irish squalor. Mr Holroyd's secondary title affirms that love was what Shaw was after, during his first forty-two years, but the nature of that love needs careful and idiosyncratic definition.

By any definition, he lived in a loveless Dublin household. His mother did not seem to know what even ordinary Irish love was: it was certainly not a commodity lavished on his father. Her son followed her in opting for the emotions stimulated by art. She became a singer and when her teacher, the remarkable Vandeleur Lee, sought a better fortune than Dublin could provide by taking his talents to London, she went with him.

The young Shaw learned the love of music from Lee. That love had much to do with the Dublin adoration of the singing voice. Joyce learned it too. Shaw pretended to have read Joyce's *Ulysses*, praising it for what he considered its exemplary exhibition of Dublin squalor, but he never seems to have noticed that Joyce's contribution to English prose consisted in making it approximate structurally and sonically to music. This was strange, because Shaw's own achievement in the medium did much the same thing. It is important, as Michael Holroyd makes clear, to take Shaw seriously when he speaks of the operatic foundation of his plays (not just *Man and Superman*) and the swing of his prose is overwhelmingly an auditory experience.

From Mr Holroyd's account of the early life of Sonny, as the boy Shaw was called (Joyce, incidentally, was known as Sunny Jim), it is evident that his peculiar genius was neither genetically transmitted nor nurtured in the home. School did nothing for him either: he was a lonely boy who read books. When he followed his mother to London, he disclosed a talent that nobody at first wanted. It was a talent founded on a passion for sound, whether musical or rhetorical, and a reformist zeal which, only in his late thirties, fused into the capacity to forge highly entertaining works of theatrical didacticism. Before he was a playwright who thought he had failed, he was a novelist who knew he had; he then became a brilliant and controversial critic of music and drama. He was not, of course, ever a rich one – journalism is not an enriching trade – and, up to early middle age, he never had much money.

He was, ironically, becoming moderately prosperous by his own efforts when he married the Irish millionaire Charlotte Payne-Townshend. He never courted money and he seemed eager to give much of it away. His passions were idealistic rather than commercial – the reform of British society and of British artistic taste, as well as the implantation of a certain very un-Irish logicality into British heads made thick by beer, beef, pudding and respectability. The youth who had never been properly taught became a great teacher.

You could talk of Bernard Shaw and GBS, but you could never fill out the G to George, his father's detestable name. The reformist anger was native to Shaw. The diverting eccentricities – most of which were the end-results of relentless logic – and the consistent long-term optimism were manifested by an invention called GBS. This, as might have been pointed out in passing, is the first inversion of the opening chord of *Das Rheingold* in German nomenclature. Wagner was a master Shaw acknowledged, along with Ibsen and Samuel Butler.

He needed those mentors, for he could himself originate very few ideas. His task was to disseminate and make acceptable, through wit and paradox, the revolutionary notions that were coming mostly out of Europe. He no more invented the Life Force or the Übermensch (though the translation to Superman was his) than he invented vegetarianism or rational clothing. As the great self-taught orator of the Fabian Society he relied on the plodding but necessary researches of Sidney and Beatrice Webb, who would discuss public sanitation at a performance of Tristan.

If he invented nothing except himself, he at least had the capacity to fuse passions which looked disparate into a holistic philosophy that can be called Shavianism. Behind all life was the *élan vital* which owed something to both Butler and Bergson, and, if this was at work in the biosphere, it ought also to apply to politics: hence the Fabianism. The Life Force knew what it was doing; but it was slow and had to be helped – strenuously.

Michael Holroyd's first volume of the tripartite life is a record of almost incredibly hard work. It was work on behalf of humanity. The monster egoist was a farcical mask. Shaw was one of the great altruists of all time.

The persistent image of bloated self-regard was always false. Shaw was overweening only to teach salutary lessons through shock. When he said that he despised Shakespeare, this was meant as a cat-o'-nine-tails for the thoughtless bardolators. It is the great virtue of Mr

Holroyd's biography that it uncovers the serious man, the doubter, the sufferer, unafraid to look absurd since absurdity was a door to self-understanding and a tool of the Life Force. And if GBS was heartless, Bernard Shaw raged at the wrongs and fatuities of the world.

W.B. Yeats, having seen *Arms and the Man*, had a nightmare in which GBS appeared as a sewing machine, shining and rattling but smiling perpetually. Too many have seen this coldly mechanical side of Shaw, believing the man to be bloodless (not enough beefsteaks) and even sexually impotent. Mr Holroyd gives us what facts he can about the erotic life, which was tolerably intense. Shaw was something of a sex-object, despite the gangling thinness, the pallor and the red beard (grown to hide a small pox scar), the anaphrodisiacal jaeger woollens. Jenny Patterson fell heavily and he apparently satisfied her not inconsiderable appetites. She grew operatically jealous when she espied the flirtatious and philandering side of him (this was undoubtedly an Irish endowment: compare Thomas Moore).

Before the advent of active sex, Shaw had wet dreams like other frustrated males. Given the chance to copulate, he did not much care for condoms. ('French letters 5/-... extraordinarily revolted me'). He recognised the Life Force at work in the Female: its end was less sexual gratification than the duty of breeding the Superman.

His own fertility was never in doubt: he seems to have been responsible for at least one pregnancy, though that miscarried. The handsome women of the Fabian Society are set before us like an intellectual harem; their broodingly intense photographs decorate the text. Shaw eventually preferred actresses – Florence Farr, Ellen Terry, in the next volume Mrs Patrick Campbell – but romance in powerful love letters, not French ones, was more satisfying, and more hygienic, than the rank sweat of an enseamed bed. Sex was irrelevant to the human personality. His marriage to Charlotte was not intended to have much sex in it. He knew the power of it and what it was after: now let us get on with some work.

It is only later that Shaw the dramaturge emerges. Having, as a drama critic, told the public what it needed and lectured the great actor-managers on their duty to art, he set out to provide examples of what the new drama ought to be like.

His early plays failed not because the public failed to understand them: they understood them only too well and did not care for the schoolmasterly nagging at the wrongs of British society – slum land-lordism, prostitution, the folly of war, above all the hypocrisy of the middle class which happened to be the playgoing pubic. He swore to abandon the theatre but, to the eventual glory of the stage, did not. *The Devil's Disciple* did well in the United States and permits this volume to close with a more than philosophical optimism as well as Shaw seeming to get married in a fit of absent-mindedness – that, of course, is GBS talking. We end the book with the knowledge that it is worthwhile going on living until we have read Volumes II and III. I think that Mr Holroyd's totally revealed achievement may well complete the trio, or conceivably the quartet, of great twentieth-century literary biographies. Richard Ellmann's lives of Joyce and Wilde are undoubted masterpieces, and so may be Leon Edel's one-volume redaction of his Henry James biography. James was half-Irish; the others were, like Dedalus, all too Irish. There is a lesson here somewhere. In *Back to Methuselah* it is prophesied that, with the extinction of the Irish race, also the Jewish, the world will become so dull that the rest of humanity will commit suicide. Two races seem to have taught the world everything worth knowing (Shakespeare, as Mrs O'Flaherty asserts, was born in Cork). Get an Irish genius out of Ireland and he will coruscate to such an extent that he will raise grave problems for his biographer.

Mr Holroyd cannot be as witty as Shaw, but he gives us qualities as valuable as wit – chiefly unobtrusive elegance and extreme factuality. I am puzzled by one thing and disappointed at another. I should have liked more (since I have mentioned James) of Shaw at the first night of *Guy Domville*. I cannot understand how Robert Browning could have been present at the Shelley Society's production of the banned *Cenci* in 1891, since he had been dead two years. Perhaps this supposition of posthumous life is an aspect of the Shavian infection, since Shaw refuses to die.

Though the world got him wrong the world could not ignore him. He appeared in a Disney cartoon and on the first record sleeve of the songs from *My Fair Lady*. Instantly recognisable in dress, features and brogue, he was a living presence in my youth. As a boy at Malvern I asked for his autograph and he said: 'You could never afford it.' In my old age he is still there, beard wagging, pronouncing nonsense in which the ore of wisdom is embedded.

Guardian, 16 September 1988
Review of *Bernard Shaw* (volume 1) by Michael Holroyd
(London: Chatto & Windus 1988)

Bunn in the Oven

I REMEMBER, and to a whole generation it must be prehistory, not just ordinary ancient history like the mid-Sixties, Kingsley Amis saying on black and white television that Jenny Bunn, the heroine of *Take a Girl Like You*, was intended to be 'a good person.' There was talk in those days, perhaps inspired by the eulogy of Henry Fielding in *I Like it Here*, of Amis's debt to the moral values of the eighteenth-century novel, and the virtue of Jenny (not *virtue*, as the sneerers at Richardson used to say) was held up, rightly, as estimable and, if provincial, none the worse for that.

Her eventual seducer, Patrick Standish, could be thought of in eighteenth-century terms as a lower sort of Lovelace, but the new novel, which is about their early married life, presents him as seeing affinities between himself and Tom Jones. A former Latin teacher who has become a publisher he is, however, less innocent than Fielding's hero. The former fornicator is now an adulterer and also a devourer of magazines with names like *Titter*. The period is the mid-Sixties, different from now mainly in that things were cheaper, there were 20 shillings to the pound, and Parliament decided that it was in order to be homosexual.

The point of the novel is that Jenny Standish's sexual morality is right, as is most of her thinking. She knows what Patrick is up to with the rather posh lady a couple of apartments away and she calls him not a sinner but a bloody fool. Living in London, just south of the river, she becomes tougher in response to metropolitan looseness but she loses none of her provincial sense of right and wrong. She remains a good person. Admirers of Mr Amis will see confirmed what I said in reviewing *Stanley and the Women* – that the author is no misogynist, just an altogether justified enemy of a certain kind of woman, and Jenny is not that kind.

Patrick Standish works for a publishing firm. Amis has here an irrepressible chance to satirise the book world but, if he is kinder than one would expect, this is because shying at milkless coconuts is less important than the serious business of moral affirmation. There are a couple of admirable bookish parties attended by hideous writers, but the first is to establish that Patrick is still a womaniser ready to tussle with his boss's wife and the second for him to drive Jenny into the arms of another man so as to justify his own infidelities. Jenny sees through him, just as she seems to see through the pretensions of literature: her compass-point is never deflected.

The business about Parliament getting ready to make it all right to be homosexual (the term 'gay' has not yet come in) affects the neighbours of the Standishes. Though the general feeling of the poofter community is that legality will rather take the fun out of things. Eric, who has a safe job to do with sailors' pensions, lives with a bulky former TV bit player named Stevie, whom he refers to as 'she.'

The impossibility of the female sex, as outlined both by Jake and Stanley in their respective novels, is here transferred to a *yin* personality in a *yang* body. Another neighbour, Tim, has difficulties with girls rather different from Patrick's: he is not sure whether he is or not homosexual. A night out with Eric and Stevie convinces him horrifyingly that he is not and ends with Eric sticking a knife into Stevie, who has been provoking jealousy by making up to Tim. Eric, on bail while Stevie is in hospital, seems to make the point that a relationship can survive, indeed has to, despite throat-cutting, and grotesquely and obliquely affirms the value of marriage. Jenny, whose marriage began with a miscarriage, is going to have a baby unlikely to be lost at the end of the story. This, Patrick says, has saved them both. Jenny is happy:

> She was going to have him all to herself for at least three years, probably more like five, and a share of him for ever, and now she could put it all out of her mind.

The plot is very sound, very well-knit, no loose ends, everything related to everything else. But, as with Dickens, there are things more important than plot. There is, for instance, acuity of observation. The Standishes' cat Frankie, who runs away but eventually comes home to symbolise marital continuity, jumps on the stool near the toilet when Patrick is taking a leak and sticks his nose towards the lever of the cistern: 'This was standard practice, designed to show how starved of affection he was. If he strained to put his head as close as he could to where his stony-hearted master's hand was going to be the poor lonely creature might just cop a quick stroke or so to cheer him through the morning.' The habits of cats are as well observed as those of pub landlords (there is a pretty horrible one here) and there is no fear, as in a novel by Graham Greene, that the dumb creature will be shot or poisoned. One has faith in Amis's compassion.

There are some wonderful little portraits, like Patrick's partner in adultery, Wendy, who drinks to 'the moments in our sad little lives that make us real. Frighteningly few, those golden moments.' And, of course, there is the style of the *récit*, which always catches the torn edges of the strain of getting through the day, and the cunning of the dialogue, which is far more true to life than anything a tape-recorder could pick up.

My Italian wife has made the point to me, more than once, of the difficulty of translating Amis. In this novel Jenny hears an upper-class Englishman talking about the Reds in Spain and is late in discovering that Red is as in Tottenham Court Road. Amis's novels continue to be made out of the English language, chiefly out of its quotidian distortions. As long ago as *Lucky Jim*, Bertrand turned 'hostelry' into 'hostelram.' *Girl, 20* is still remembered for its corm beef and tim peaches.

The future will learn about the state of English today not from the linguists but from the novels of Amis. To say nothing of the customs and morality that go along with the language. Above all the morality. Back to Fielding.

Observer, 25 September 1988
Review of *Difficulties with Girls* by Kingsley Amis
(London: Century Hutchinson, 1988)

A Strong Whiff of Kif from Tangier

PAUL BOWLES is a distinguished American Writer who has done most of his writing abroad. Born in 1910, he comes at the end of a great wave of expatriate American literature. He ran away from a brutal father and an education that seemed to him parochial and philistine in order to breathe the air of Gertrude Stein's Paris, and he ended up in Tangier.

His novels and stories are nowadays more easily found in French and Spanish than in English. Novels like *The Sheltering Sky* and *Let it Come Down* had a considerable American vogue in their day, when Americans at home were fascinated to read about Americans abroad, but fashion changed and the great fictional theme became the turmoil and contradictions of urban America – from Bellow's Chicago to Tom Wolfe's Bronx. Bowles for a time seemed to be the *parrain* of the Beats – Burroughs, Ginsberg, Kerouac – and he certainly smoked *kif* with them. But he was absorbed into Morocco while they merely exploited its drug and sex possibilities.

His most interesting later work had been the transcription into English of tales told to him in Moghrabi Arabic. Occasionally he has denied being a writer, professing, which is chronologically true, to be primarily a composer. His music is not now much heard. As for his songs, I am always around to accompany if not sing them. They are charming and show a fastidious concern with the pitching of vowels and the accommodation of prosody to musical rhythm. Pierre Boulez and Luciano Berio would find their melodies too tonal and their harmonies old-fashionedly Ravelian, but, as a young musician, Bowles was the protégé of Aaron Copland and Virgil Thomson.

If he had, like other American composers, submitted to the discipline of Nadia Boulanger in Paris, he might have made a large musical name. But he remained something of a dilettante, better at incidental music for the stage than at knotty quartets or loud symphonies. His music is cool; some would say cold. It expresses his temperament.

It was the coolness of Bowles's prose that impressed its first readers, particularly when it dealt in nightmare or atrocity. There is a description of a man cutting off another man's penis, and then gouging a hole in his belly to accommodate the floating member, which is positively refrigerated. The coolness could be diagnosed partly as a Puritan trait inherited from the *Mayflower*, partly as a symptom of sexual insufficiency. Tangier still is a great centre of pederastic activity, but it is doubtful if Bowles ever felt the lure, as the Beats did, of willing brown bodies ready to be sodomised for a couple of dirhams. His marriage to Jane Auer tells much of the sexual story, for she was openly lesbian and the *ménage* was *blanc* from the start to finish. She was also an alcoholic and a drug-taker, unstable and dangerous when she tried to import her inversion to a land where homosexuality was strictly for males. Her passion for a souk girl named Cherita led her into a morass of filthy magic and harsh servitude. Jane had literary talent but she was too mixed up and too self-destructive to achieve more than sporadic success. Bowles dutifully pursued her from psychiatric clinic to drying-out ward, remaining cool despite his own distress. This book is the portrait of a stoic.

Though coolness if normally associated with extreme rationality, it was irrationality, the ambages of the unconscious, that fascinated Bowles. Tangier was a good place to get in touch with the darker layers of the mind, possessing what used to be known as a drug culture. Bowles at first got no kick from *kif*, since he was a non-inhaling smoker, but *majoun*, which is a kind of jam with a cannabis base, provided the liberation of the imagination which made his first novels magical. But this concern with the irrational has to be antedated to his youthful discovery of music. Music says nothing to the reason: it is a kind of closely structured nonsense. It is a turbulence of the *id*, so Freud thought, and it has to be approached with ruled bar-lines and carefully penned notes. Music led Bowles very early on to surrealism. He was at school when he first discovered *transition* and read the *Surrealist Manifesto* of André Breton. Bowles, writing verse like 'A fresh mist drowns plantlice / as sprucetrees dribble resin', actually got into *transition 12* when he was only 18. Such a success was bound to Europeanise him prematurely. He never really came to terms with his native culture.

So he must be considered an odd man out in American letters, also a curiously transitional figure in cisatlantic modernism. Gertrude Stein helped him, in her eccentric way, but he was young enough to absorb something of the next modernist wave. He met Isherwood in Berlin; we learn now where Sally Bowles got her name. But his musical talent drew him to a radicalism which made him neither traditional nor modernist – merely unique. He became fascinated by Hispanic rhythms, both in Latin America and Iberia, and was led to a deeper fascination with the folk music of North America, which, with no help from the newly independent 'modernising' regimes, he collected on tape. This ended with his getting the tales of Mohammed Mrabet and Driss Ben Hamed Charhadi on tape and thence on to printed paper. He ends as a lonely aloof figure, still living in Tangier, not inhospitable but unavailable by telephone, handsome and still cool in old age, above all stoical.

I recommend his 1982 book, *Points in Time*, a non-fictional study of Morocco, a work which, as one of his British critics said, 'seems to insert a needle into a country's heart and draw off its life-blood for us.' Whether he described a sunset or a decapitation, Bowles sustains his old coolness, the bar-lines neatly drawn, the notes exactly penned. It was not a financial success, and America virtually ignored it. Neither critics nor publishers like books hard to categorise. Bowles himself evades all categorisation.

Observer, 23 July 1989
Review of *An Invisible Spectator: A Biography of Paul Bowles* by
Christopher Sawyer-Lauçanno (London: Bloomsbury, 1989)

The Life of Graham Greene

IF, AS is all too possible, the life of Graham Greene is turned into a television series, the incidental music will be ready to hand – the *Pacific 231* of Honegger and *The Walk to the Paradise Garden* (from the opera *A Village Romeo and Juliet*) by Delius. These two works seem to be the only ones to have answered moods of the great novelist – the striving, grinding, relentless part of his temperament best satisfied by dangerous travel, and the compassionate, tender, near-sentimental that informs his emotional make-up.

But the non-literary arts in general do not seem to have meant much to him, except for the cinema. The architecture in his books is confided to police stations that look like the threats of weak men, decaying tropical bungalows, seedy tenements and the like. Pictures are usually photographs with regretful associations. But when pictures move they enchant him. Perhaps his most notable technical achievement has been to apply the technique of the cinema scenario to the novel, and his novels have, inevitably, nearly all become films – though rarely very satisfactory ones. This is really a tribute to his literary powers, for only mediocre books become great films.

Greene has sought in his writing a kind of verbal transparency which refuses to allow language to become a fictional character in its own right, but his artistry is of a highly literary kind, acknowledging the presence of Henry James, Ford Madox Ford and Joseph Conrad among his masters. Norman Sherry, Greene's own choice as quasi-official biographer, is a Conrad specialist, and, with Sherry's looking for a subject 'after a ten-year stint on Conrad', there was an acceptance of discreet flattery in the handshake Greene offered to seal the assignment. But there was also a recognition that here was a biographer who does his work the hard way. Sherry had rigorously followed Conrad's path round the world, and he was ready to do the same for Greene, though the latter warned him that he wouldn't be able to get into Saigon.

Greene has always been almost fearfully reticent about such

elements of his life as have not been alchemised into fiction. In old age he proved himself willing to unbutton and show scars as well as muscle. His courtship of and marriage to Vivien Dayrell-Browning are set out fully with the aid of intimate letters not previously made public (for the breakdown of that marriage – which seems in prospect tragic – we must wait for the second volume). His conversion to Catholicism is seen to be in the first place a way into Vivien's heart, though the subsequent course of his faith transcends such mere accommodation. The love story is touching. For Greene it was a genuine *éducation sentimentale*. Vivien said that the Greenes were 'a very cool family. I never noticed any great affection between them. I can never imagine any child sitting on his mother's knee, being told a story or anything like that. They were not demonstrative.' She taught her lover how to hug and blow kisses. She devised a kissing code for letters: 'White stars and red stars. A red star is much more passionate than a white one. The most passionate kiss on paper would be enormous with rays coming out and dark with ink.'

Photographs show how beautiful Vivien was. Greene addresses her as 'Lovely and adored by Pussina Love-Cat'. Yielding to the feline terminology she introduced into their discourse. Greene was Tom or Tiger or Tyg, Tig, Wuff or Wufth. It is all very charming, and apparently it could not last. One divines in Greene an attitude proper to a creature of great saintliness, the adoration of the sinner. Throughout his books there is a kind of nostalgia for sainthood, but the flesh gets in the way. He has been, by several accounts, a man not easily given to sexual fidelity, and none of his novels glorifies marital love in the *Angel in the House* manner. The Greene of popular mythology is a desperate wanderer in sinful places, solitary but not celibate. He occasionally meets innocence, but it is a displaced rose among plantains of evil.

Evil came into his life early. At Berkhamsted School, where his father was headmaster, he met it in a boy named Carter who, with his accomplice Wheeler, 'turned Graham's life into a hopeless misery'. Carter was mature enough to perceive the division of loyalties in the headmaster's son and put pressure on him to side with 'the forces of resistance'. The language of the mature Greene, recalling the juvenile torture, has a force which must seem excessive unless we accept, with George Russell, that in the lost childhood of Judas Christ was betrayed. 'The sneering nicknames were inserted like splinters under the nails.' He could sympathise with his rebellious schoolfellows, despite the family loyalty: 'Inexorably the others' point of view rose on the path like a murdered innocent.' Eventually he was to side with the rebel, the dissident, even the heretic. None of his fictional heroes is an establishment figure.

The conviction that evil exists, an ultimate entity not to be confused with mere wrong-doing, lies beneath Greene's acceptance of Catholic theology. If the devil exists, God must also. But it was to be quite a time before his fiction became informed with those Catholic principles which, to free thinkers, have been a lot of fuss about nothing and, to cradle Catholics, a somewhat factitious intrusion of absolute values into narratives that deliberately breathe the banality of the popular shocker. The literary ambition was in Greene from the beginning, but it found its first outlet in journalism – a subliterary genre very much in the service of the banal. Greene was an efficient journalist and, if real literature had not got in the way, could have climbed high on the sub-editorial ladder of *The Times*. He was a brilliant editor of the short-lived but admirable *Night and Day*, which closed when Greene libelled Shirley Temple ('dimpled depravity' etc) and, through the innocent candour of a good critic, involved the enterprise in financial ruin.

Sherry recounts how he went to visit Greene in Antibes and was told by the author 'in his precise and practical way' that there was no heating in the hotel he had elected – only 127 francs a day – and he'd better bring a hot water bottle. There are hotels in Antibes fully heated, though they cost more, and one gets a hint here of money being important to Greene, even in a vicarious connection. No writer forgets his early struggles, and, that desperate libel judgment apart, the young novelist suffered from scant rewards for painful literary endeavours. On the strength of the success of *The Man Within*, he resigned form *The Times*. The success was not repeated in subsequent novels. With *Stamboul Train* moreover a libel suit loomed. Unlike the later one preferred by the guardians of Shirley Temple, this was a matter of a man seeing himself in a fictional character. J.B. Priestley took umbrage at Greene's portrait of a popular author; he and Greene shared Heinemann as a publisher; Heinemann preferred to take the part of one of their best-sellers rather than that of a 'literary' author of doubtful prospects. It was part of the pain of Greene's apprenticeship. But, as if pain were not always ready to strike from without, Greene seems to have sought it with a kind of gloomy relish. How else explain that incredible jungle-trek he made, with his cousin Barbara, through the Liberian jungle, or, later, the Mexican trip which was to yield the genuine masterpiece of *The Power and the Glory*?

Norman Sherry, having made those trips himself, is qualified, with the help of the appropriate Greene books, to depict the anabases in full colour. The great novelist joins the men of action, reminding his readers that books aren't made out of other books but out of the sweat and fatigue of actual involvement in life. With his black carriers, in whom he found real incorrupt innocence he learnt that the true jungle was civilisation. The title of his book *Journey Without Maps* speaks the truth: Greene, striding through head-high elephant grass with Barbara exhausted in a hammock behind, encountered fever and devil-dancers, and Sherry guesses that a kind of family competitiveness helped to fire it. Graham's brother Raymond, a successful doctor, climbed the Himalayan mountain Kamet in 1931. The African jungle was a fair, if flat, analogue.

Raymond's successes are neatly balanced by the failures of one of the other three brothers, Herbert. Perhaps, in Grahamian terms, they cannot really be called failures. The Greene cousin Tooter described Herbert as 'financially utterly untrustworthy, he gambled and got everyone else gambling'. Graham deplored his bounderdom as early as 1926: 'My eldest brother's 'broken out' again. His is a case where I can't help feeling that suicide far from being sinful would be meritorious. It's fearfully depressing and hopeless for my people.' It was a good thing that he was not a Catholic apparently, which seems to imply a curiously relativist approach to morality. 'I think in his case the sin is in not shooting himself.' In 1938 Graham wrote to Hugh Greene (the future Director General of the BBC): 'Did you see Herbert's front page news story in the Daily Worker, Dec. 22, "I was a Secret Agent of Japan"?' Here is a case of an admirable fictional character having the effrontery to operate in real life. That his seedy experiences were useful to his younger brother there can be no doubt. Not being an exemplar of sin, Herbert could be taken as a mere rogue acting outside the covenants of the social system. When Graham expresses his abhorrence in the terms of fraternal outrage, he is really on the side of Ida in *Brighton Rock*. This ought to be considered unworthy.

Sherry spends much time on *Brighton Rock*, which we take as the first genuinely Greenean novel in that it makes the morality of social expediency confront the theological dichotomy of good and evil. It is

based on a principle which many, including myself, regard as dangerous to merely doing the right thing. T.S. Eliot gave authority to this
view in his essay on Baudelaire, in which he pronounced that most
people we know, including poets and statesmen, 'are not men enough
to be damned'. The young gang-leader Pinkie, though a mere boy,
is man enough. 'Hell lay around him in his infancy.' This must have
been a difficult book for Greene to write, since its milieu is remote
from that of a Berkhamsted headmaster's family. If he touched earth
in Africa, he hardly did so in England. The 'literary' writer is not,
without great implausibility, able to plant arcane references in a story
about race-course gangs and decent holiday rock-suckers. We do not
need Professor Cedric Watts to tell us (in Sherry's footnote) that
'the pseudonym Kolley Kibber' – under which the murderee Hale
operates as the donor of five-pound notes to readers of a popular daily
paper who recognise him – 'is adapted from the eighteenth-century
actor-manager and Poet Laureate Colley Cibber (1671–1757)'. The
literary Greene finds a kind of safe anchor in such references. And
yet the curious power of the novel, which persists fifty years after
its first appearance, lies in its fusing of theology and the theological
overtones of literature in a narrative about sordid low life. We hear
too much about Greeneland, but there seems to be no other name for
this transmogrification of dear safe breezy Brighton.

As 1939 approaches, Greene visits Mexico to confirm that Pinkie's
religion is proscribed, along with the wine that is potentially the blood
of Christ. He hated the place but found heroism among the perse-
cuted adherents to the faith. In the Prologue to *The Lawless Roads*,
which preceded the remarkable novel *The Power and the Glory*, Greene
relates the Mexican hell to the hell of his boyhood. Evil is eternal.
Carter 'who practised torments with dividers' (Pinkie too remembers
dividers, though it is hard to associate him with geometry lessons), is
still around, along with the Judas Wheeler. In the novel, good and evil
very curiously interpenetrate. In the antagonism between Carter and
Greene, 'there was an element of reluctant admiration, I believe, on
both sides. I admired his ruthlessness, and in an odd way he admired
what he wounded in me.' And so the atheistic lieutenant and the
whisky priest are drawn into a sort of empathy through the recognition of opposed rigours. Greene is now ready to make some of the
dangerous statements which, in the eyes of simple-minded Catholics,
gravely impair his orthodoxy. 'The greatest saints have been men with
more than a normal capacity for evil, and the most vicious men have

sometimes narrowly evaded sanctity.' I should be grateful for some historical examples.

Greene returned from Mexico fearful of arrest because of the Lord Chief Justice's vicious moralising over the Shirley Temple case. But he met nothing worse than the shock of 'the grit of the London afternoon, among the trams, in the long waste of Clapham Road, a Baptist Chapel, Victorian houses falling into decay in their little burial grounds of stone and weed, a coal merchant's window with some fuel arranged in an iron basket, a gas showroom'. He wondered how a world like this could end in anything but war. The connection is not clear. The contrast between the genteel mass in a Chelsea church and the memory of a Mexican woman dragging herself up the aisle on her knees is all too clear. 'We do not mortify ourselves. Perhaps we are in need of violence.' Another dangerous statement. We look forward to many more in the second volume of this exemplary life.

Norman Sherry has done justice to his subject, not an easy one. The second volume cannot be shorter than the first which is very long but not too long. A long life and a triumphant literary career. As for the man within, we need not delude ourselves into thinking that we will ever get the whole truth. A man's soul is for the gloom of the confessional, not the bright light of biography.

Daily Telegraph, 8 April 1989
Review of *The Life of Graham Greene* (volume 1, 1904–1939)
by Norman Sherry (London: Jonathan Cape, 1989)

Joyce as Novelist

I MAY in the past have made claims to be a kind of Joyce populariser, in that I have celebrated his humanity rather than his ingenuity in all the available media, but I have never considered myself to be a Joyce scholar. Joyce scholarship has become so much an intramural discipline since the days when I began to read him that there is very little a mere scribbling outsider can contribute to it. I can only take a kind of gloomy pride in one qualification only – that of being so old that I have known Joyce's work longer than most reputable scholars. Indeed, I lived my adolescence contemporaneously with the composition of a book called *Work in Progress* and achieved legal maturity before its publication as *Finnegans Wake*. My reading of the earlier work is hard to separate from a period of growing up not dissimilar from that recorded in *A Portrait of the Artist as a Young Man*.

I was nurtured in a city closer to Dublin than to London – Manchester – and in a culture more Irish than English. My family was Catholic, had begun as indigenously Catholic, and, in a Protestant land, had sustained its faith by Irish marriages under the aegis of an Irish priesthood. Until the Emancipation Act of 1829, English and Irish Catholics had been debarred from higher education, and intelligence and initiative were unable to find an outlet in any of the professions save one. This was the field of popular entertainment, in which my family worked. The musical background of Joyce was of a kind familiar to a Manchester Catholic. Opera meant the touring Carl Rosa company rather than Covent Garden. The songs sung around the family piano were Moore's *Irish Melodies* and arias from *The Bohemian Girl* and *Martha*. *Finnegans Wake* is, among other things, a compendium of the songs that Joyce's family sang or heard at the music hall.

Joyce did not always remember the family songs with the right exactness. Buck Mulligan sings: 'Won't we have a merry time / Drinking whiskey, beer and wine / On Coronation Day.' This is wrong. My stepmother put it right. It should be 'We'll be merry /

Drinking whiskey, wine and sherry / All be merry / On Coronation Day.' When a copy of *Ulysses* eventually got into the family house, my musical father was puzzled at the transcription of the song about little Harry Hughes, supposedly sung by the tenor Stephen Dedalus. He pointed out that it was wrongly placed in the bass stave and that the lowest note was A, impossible to a tenor. I have had ever since to justify these solecisms by suggesting that Stephen temporarily takes over Bloom's baritone voice, that the song is sung by Stoom or Blephen, or conceivably perhaps both.

Joyce made his primary appeal to me as a failed professional musician who had taken to literature as a *pis-aller*. This remains my own situation. The structure of *Ulysses* still seems to me to be closer to that of a symphony than to a work of literature, just as the typical Joyce declarative sentence seems to be composed on a melodic principle. The impact that Joyce made on me as a young man was partially musical. The absence of a strong visual element in me and him could not be attributed to weak sight. After all, the near-blindness of Aldous Huxley didn't militate against an encyclopaedic knowledge of pictorial art. It seems that one is born with a partiality to one sense rather than another. Joyce as an auditory man was not permitted to be a visualiser as well. Moreover, it is somehow typical of the kind of Northern Catholic education I shared with Joyce that training in the visual arts should be neglected. The eye is an inlet of sin. The only pictures in *A Portrait of the Artist* are pornographic ones, stuffed up the bedroom chimney. There is fine comic irony in Joyce's title. The portrait is, so to speak, an audiograph. The pictorial implication suggests a totally false trail.

I first read *A Portrait of the Artist* when, at the age of fourteen, I was beginning to lose my faith. The book had been suggested to me by my Liverpool Irish history master, who had lost his own faith some years before but was too prudent to assist me with the loss of mine. Whether it was his intention or not, Father Arnell's sermon on hell drove me back shivering to the arms of the Church, beating my breast. I maintain that no non-Catholic can meet that novel with the right response. Or perhaps there is a deeper irony in Joyce's method than scholars have been willing to descry. Stephen Dedalus sets out at great and eloquent length the principles on which proper art should be conceived. The artist must avoid equally the temptations of the didactic and the pornographic. And yet that massive section of *A Portrait of the Artist* which deals with eternal damnation is thoroughly didactic in both the Joycean and traditional senses – it arouses loathing and it teaches a heavy lesson. One has to be innately agnostic to take it as art. I have read no other book which so aroused fear that I had to burn my copy.

The head of one of Oxford's colleges, noticing the first volume of my memoirs, which inevitably paints a Catholic upbringing, said that it was inferior to Joyce's *A Portrait of the Artist*. There is a confusion of genres here. The content has been remembered but the form forgotten. And yet that content is so memorable that the non-scholarly reader tends to ignore those elements that make *A Portrait* a work of art and not merely a selection of juvenile reminiscences. What makes this book a novel is what makes a poem a poem – or should I specify a symbolist poem? There is a cunning manipulation of images of earth and air, and ascent up from the mud – and, for that matter, the subterranean fire – to a creative empyrean, the slow sprouting of wings. Old father, old artificer – the improbable name Dedalus is justified, and a conflation which can make sense only to a Catholic is adumbrated. For if Dedalus is the father, the son must be Icarus, whose waxen wings melt, who falls as Lucifer fell. In other words, *non serviam*.

As I have said, I am not a Joyce scholar, but a working writer aware of market forces: in other words, I write for a living in a way that Joyce never did. I call myself a novelist who is forced to write other things on the side: the situation is more Fitzgeraldian than Joycean. I've produced, to date, thirty novels, which is considered too many, but no writer can write too much if his living depends on it. I was led to the writing of fiction by an admiration for Joyce and a sense of community of temperament, sensibility, taste, faith, and the need for exile. I suppose the only two writers who have meant much to me, Shakespeare apart, have been Joyce and Gerard Manley Hopkins. Trying to write verse in my youth, I followed Hopkins; trying to write prose, I followed Joyce. It was following Joyce that warred against turning myself into a novelist. *Ulysses*, as one of the five greatest novels of the century, ought strictly to be a novelist's model, but, as we all recognise nowadays, it represents the end of an artistic impulse, a fulfilment rather than a new beginning.

Of course, in my youth *Ulysses* possessed an extraneous glamour in that it was a book one read about rather than read. It was banned everywhere, it seemed, except in France and Nazi Germany. My history master imported from Berlin the two-volume paperback

Odyssey Press edition of the book into Manchester. This he gave to me. It was, I think, as good an edition as one could find in those days. I would have it still if the Luftwaffe hadn't bombed Manchester in 1940 and 1941. Previously we had known *Ulysses* in baffling extracts meant to show, and castigate, the unacceptable avant-gardism – chiefly in books like Collins's *The Doctor Looks at Literature*. Since three instalments of *Work in Progress* were available, and delightfully baffling, my generation expected *Ulysses* to be of the same substance. It was hard to reconcile the imputation of obscenity with unintelligibility, but we knew that the puritanical could always find the scabrous if they looked carefully enough. To read *Ulysses* was naturally thrilling, since it was an illegal act, but it was also disappointing. It was not sufficiently like *Anna Livia Plurabelle*. On the other hand, it was not sufficiently like an orthodox novel. It had added something to the European fictional tradition, but it had also taken something away.

The opening chapter works well, but only as a kind of etiolated version of the Edwardian novel. The brazen bells of religion keep chiming, and we do not know why until we realise that the presiding discipline is religion. We wonder why the progress of a narrative should be oiled or clogged by an exterior symbol. More worrying is the fact that we can see so little. Compare it with a passage from a genuine Edwardian novel:

> The two brothers had ordered red mullet, which lay scattered about their plates in mingled hues of cornelian, rose and tarnished copper. Their wine was Lacryma Christi of the precise tint to carry on the scheme of their colour. Jenny and Irene were drinking champagne whose pale amber sparkled against the prevailing lustre, just as Jenny's fair hair set off and was at the same time enhanced by Irene's copper brown. As a group of revellers the four of them composed into a rich enough study in genre, and the fanciful observer would extract from the position of the two men a certain potentiality for romantic events as, somewhat hunched and looking up from down-turned heads, they both sat with legs outstretched to the extent of their length. The more imaginative observer would perceive in the group something unhealthy, something *faisandé*, an air of too deliberate enjoyment that seemed to imply a perfect knowledge of the limitations of human pleasure... That senescent October moon which a year

ago marked the end of love's halcyon would have been a suitable light for such a party.

And so on. We would accept nowadays that that is not the way to write narrative. We do not welcome the omniscient observer, we deplore the *faisandé* phrasing, but we worry that the Joycean technique cannot accommodate such a description of red mullet. The passage, by the way, comes from Compton Mackenzie's *Carnival*, a novel praised by Henry James. Admittedly in his dotage. It must be said that that tradition still holds: the majority of novels published these days are closer to *Carnival* than to *Ulysses*. For that matter, such a continuation of techniques which, somewhat debased in Compton Mackenzie, are brilliantly deployed by both James and Conrad, is integral to the writing of fiction. The tyro will find in *Ulysses* various useful technical devices – the interior monologue, the extreme descriptive compression, above all the avid ear for realistic dialogue (compare, or rather contrast, Thomas Hardy) – but he will not learn how to write a novel.

Joyce's aim was to eliminate from fiction those elements which fiction can hardly do without. He called the sensational the journalistic, he deplored the element of coincidence which drives the Dickensian plot. But he displayed both these elements in the 'Nighttown' episode of *Ulysses*, where they are justified by hallucination and magic. The fact is that a novel can be defined as a fictional composition in which a particular double swathe of time is engaged – time in which something sensational happens. Without a major event of a kind rarely encountered in ordinary life, without a measure of coincidence, a novel is hardly possible. *Ulysses* contradicts totally these conditions; therefore it is not a novel. Or, if it is a novel, it is a novel that maintains its movement by means extraneous to the novel. We know what these means are – the means of symbolism, which is more proper to poetry than to prose fiction.

Examine *Ulysses* in terms of the traditional novel, and you will find that it fulfils some of the desiderata once the Odyssey gets started. Bloom unwittingly gives a tip for the winner of the Ascot Gold Cup, receives a letter from Martha Clifford, contemplates masturbating over it in the bath, sees Stephen three times, arranges to see Mrs Purefoy in the lying-in hospital. These minor incidents lead to a pogrom, an oblique and onanistic revenge on the Citizen who arranges it, a meeting with Stephen of a more intimate nature than previously, and the possibility of a further meeting. In other words, one event breeds another, as in the traditional fictional programme, but the major outcome of the narrative will take place at some other time. We are justified in expecting the real story to begin on June 17, 1904. There is a wilful evasion of all the properties we expect from a traditional narrative, and when Joyce is faced with a situation all too traditional his evasion becomes manic. I refer to the meeting between Stephen and Bloom in Horne's hospital, when the entire action is obscured by the most thoroughgoing symbolism we have so far met.

If we want a story, we shall find it somewhere else: in Homer. Joyce's own narrative alludes to him, however, only in the most facetious manner. Certain stage props of the *Odyssey* appear, but they merely decorate the action. Bloom's 'knockmedown' cigar, one of the 'prime stinkers' of Barney Kiernan's pub, does not put out the eye of the Cyclops. The moly which protects Bloom in the house of Circe is probably three things implausibly combined: the potato in his pocket against rheumatism, the Molly always in his mind, the pale flower of his ejaculation on Sandymount shore. If the Oxen of the Sun are blasphemed against, it is in the most jocular way imaginable, and there is no blasting of the blasphemers. 'Loud on left Thor thundered, in anger awful the hammerhurler' – it's a minor response from the God of fertility. Nobody is struck by lightning.

Why is the Homeric matrix there at all? The usual response is: to relate quotidian urban banality to myth, thus elevating the one while abasing the other; to turn Bloom into a classical hero. The truth is that the template of the *Odyssey*, and the symbolism which is engendered, is there for two reasons. If much of the movement is relegated to interior monologue, that monologue must be given a shape to prevent it from deliquescing into mere inconsequent vapour. Not only the Homeric parallel, but the other symbols that spring out of it, control the direction of the flow. But the main purpose served by the parallel is the shunting of action, which includes emotional impulses, points of self-discovery, even resolutions of the narrative, to an invisible siding. If we have to assume that Bloom has conquered the suitors, it is only because we know that Odysseus has done it on his behalf.

I'm aware, naturally, that Joyce's triumph is to make a compelling narration out of drab ordinariness, and that this had never been done before (except possibly in Gissing's novel, *The New Grub Street*). But, from the angle of the genuine working novelist, which Joyce was not, it's clear that most of the problems of the novel have been grossly evaded. *Ulysses* was, from one angle, all too easy to write. To confine the action of the book to a single day in a single town meant a limitation of the action which would have shocked Fielding or Dickens.

A novel is not a novel unless it admits the possibility of the change consequent on some kind of emotional impact. There is, in the classical novel, a kind of watershed: things flow one way and, after a variety of climaxes, they flow another. The major difficulty of the novelist is to present the moment of change without making it too blatant: the reader sees change, but it not quite sure where it began. This is in conformity with human life as we know it. The difficulties which Joyce set himself are purely of a superficial technical order, some of them embarrassingly ludic.

I would like to say something about my own early career as a sub-Joycean novelist. You may take me as an example of a writer made so desperate by Joyce's achievement in *Ulysses* that I delayed entering the field. Clearly, *Ulysses* raised and solved new fictional problems which had no general application: what Joyce discovered he discovered for himself only. To write novels after *Ulysses* meant ignoring everything in that work except a new attention to dialogue and *récit*. If Joyce taught nothing else he certainly taught a rigorous attention to language – an aspect of the traditional British novel which is generally despised. Hugh Walpole told Henry James that it was character that counted; one could forgive slipshod prose and improbable dialogue as well as careless construction if – as in Dostoevsky – the personages strode off the page and lived. James wrote a long letter to Walpole lamenting this attitude. Joyce never said anything about style; he merely disclosed to Frank Budgen that he had spent a day worrying over the order of words in a sentence. After Joyce, a novelist had to learn a new fastidiousness in handling his verbal material.

Prepared to learn, I embarked on my first novel in my late thirties. The title was *A Vision of Battlements* – a reference to one of the symptoms of migraine as well as the locale, which was Gibraltar. The fact that I had spent three years as a soldier in Gibraltar, while Joyce had never visited the Rock, granted me the courage of a certain superiority. For Gibraltar is necessary to Joyce's symbolic scheme in *Ulysses*, being a place of caves proper for the nymph Calypso. Joyce had learned all he could about it from books, and his particular knowledge of Gibraltarian families like the Opissos impressed other Gibraltarians when I read parts of his novel aloud to them. Indeed, one of the extant Opissos complained of Molly's attitude to his grandmother. But

Joyce committed a desperate error in his portrayal of Molly Bloom as a daughter of the Rock garrison. We cannot believe in a Major Brian Tweedy who married a Spaniard and begot a girl whose speech is low Irish. Molly's first language has to be Andalusian Spanish, but her approach to Spanish in the book is that of someone who has tackled it through Hugo's Spanish primer. As a young lady on the Rock she would have either spoken a near-patrician English – if her father was really a major, which I doubt (a sergeant-major seems more likely) – or the Gibraltarian patois, unidiomatic and full of Iberian vowels. Joyce's realism falls down badly here. Despising him, I felt better able to tell the truth about life in wartime Gibraltar.

If Joyce could take his classical template from Homer, I could take mine from Virgil. I followed the *Aeneid* closely. I called my hero Richard Ennis ('Ennis' being fairly close to Aeneas). As a new Aeneas, he is committed to the building of a Utopian postwar community blazoned by the British Army's Bureau of Current Affairs. This is as fanciful as anything in Joyce. He is a sergeant in the Army Vocational Corps, concerned with teaching conscript soldiers civilian trades. The AVC flash on his uniform enables him, in the opening lines of the novel, to tell the ignorant that it means *Arma Virumque Cano*. The story follows Virgil in making Ennis conduct an affair with a Gibraltarian widow, sees her marry a rich Gibraltarian named Barasi (an anagram of Virgil's Iarbas) and then fall in love with a member of the Women's Royal Naval Service named Lavinia (another Virgilian name). He meets the Sybil in the form of an Army schoolmistress who tells fortunes with the Tarot pack. He visits hell in the shape of a corrupt and broken-down La Línea over the border. All this was considerable fun, but it did not solve the main narrative problem. The characters had to function under non-Virgilian steam. When the novel was eventually published, no reader noticed the framework taken from the *Aeneid*.

The second novel I attempted took its mythic structure from Wagner's *Ring*. In calling the book *The Worm and the Ring* I was spelling out its provenance. The theme was the lack of ambitions in a Midlands grammar school, with the headmaster named Woolton for Wotan, the chemistry master Lodge for Loge, Freia the goddess of beauty as Miss Fry, a Latin teacher. The gods and heroes were the teaching staff, the dwarfs the pupils. All this was established on the Joycean example, but the temptation to follow Joyce in other ways was irresistible. The 'Oxen of the Sun' episode is both deplorable and admirable. Every author wants to have written it. When I sent my Siegfried, the German master, to Paris to bed the hockey mistress, I presented their liaison as a history of French prose in reverse. After an evening in the bistro in the style of the Oath of Strasbourg, they couple in a *hotel de passe* in Silver Latin. All this went too far. Blame Joyce.

You see the situation in which a post-Joycean novelist finds himself. He cannot write *Ulysses*, and he is forced to pretend that *Ulysses* does not exist. He feels ashamed at having to revert to a more orthodox tradition. He has to do this anyway in order to earn a living. That Joyce produced a work *sui generis*, touching the traditional novel only in the superb rendering of ordinary life, is confirmed by the fact that he ceased to be a novelist after its publication. *Finnegans Wake* is not usually considered to be a novel, or, if it is, only in a Pickwickian sense. But it joins *Ulysses* in possessing recognisable characters. The hero in particular is one of the most massive in all fiction despite the fact that he is invisible and so much of his inner life is hidden. The eccentricity of the technique of the book which contains him is jus-tified as a series of obstacles which he is powerful or cunning enough to overcome. A hero who can survive the 'Oxen of the Sun' episode is genuinely heroic.

If in *Ulysses* Joyce clothed Bloom in fantastic garments which the reader tries to strip off, in *Finnegans Wake* he hides Earwicker from us by a device which is so simple as to be shameful. It is a trickery of paranomasia which anyone can learn. It is termed oneiric, a language of dreams, but it is better thought of as contrapuntal. We are back to music. The 'Sirens' episode of *Ulysses* has, by the unmusical, been taken as a triumphant conflation of the sister arts. In fact, and I believe this to have been Joyce's intention, it demonstrates that the two arts have little to say to each other. *Finnegans Wake* at least attempts to fulfil that dream of all novelists who envy the capacity of music to say more than one thing at the same time. The initials HCE warn us that something musical is to be attempted. H is the German for B natural, by the way, and *Tristan and Isolde* ends in the key of H major. BC and AD are played as a theme that transcends time, and the FACE of the cad in the park has a GBD pipe stuck in it.

Joyce's method can best be clarified in the form of a series of mad examination questions. For example: 'If one is drunk the whole year round, what would be the names of the months?' Answer: 'Ginyou-very, Pubyoumerry, Parch, Grapeswill, Tray, Sawdust, Siptumbler,

Actsober, Novitner, Decentbeer.' Again: 'If Charles Dickens is a cook as well as a novelist what works may he be said to have written?' Answer: '*Charred Limes, Grate Expectorations, the Cold, Curried Sausagy Shop, Our Muttonial Fried, Halibut Twist, Pick Weak Peppers,* and *Snackelius Knucklebone*'. If Shakespeare were a cat? He wrote *The Tompist*. If he were a jobbing printer? He wrote *Pamphlet, Prints of Penmark*. If he were an American? He would have written *All's Swell that End? Swell*. There's no limit to punning, if, like Joyce, we draw on foreign languages. If Joyce does that sort of thing better than I do, it's because he has had more practice.

The astonishing thing however about the dream that is *Finnegans Wake* is the solidity of the basic cast of actors. Mr Porter, if that is his offstage name, has to play Earwicker and also Finnegan, as well as a host of guilty personages, some of whom stutter. But he is easy to recognise under the disguises. In respect of this solidity, Joyce shows himself to be more traditional a novelist than D.H. Lawrence. To Lawrence human identity is not important. One has to excavate deeply beneath it to discover a divine or animal substance, actually both, recognisably living through its commitment to life. The surface of clothes, regularly discarded, or cigarettes, discussion of *Pelléas et Mélisande*, holds the characters to life as we know it, but surface is not, as it is in Joyce, an aspect of identity. Curiously, we have a better idea of the outward appearance of Earwicker than of Bloom. We see Kevin and Jerry and Izzy and Ann. More than that, we're aware of the nature of the daily life that is transformed into universal dream.

Joyce was no Freudian, and the dream was not presented as a mass of data for the clarification of a neurosis. But from this data one can reconstruct the plot of an orthodox novel. This plot is driven by guilt – the guilt of sexual incapacity in the marital sphere, compensated by spurts of unlawful desire in the filial. 'Incest' is too terrible a word even for a dream to utter, and the three inner notes of the theme – C E S (or E flat) are reordered to make 'insect'. Although Earwicker, or Porter is of Scandinavian Protestant origin, this is a very Irish Catholic story. Much of the poignancy of the narrative, if we may call it that, lies in the dreamer's attempt to sublimate his fleshly cravings into the impulses of universal history. Out of an unlawful erection a lawful one may be made. Balbus is building a wall, and we know why he balbutiates. Lust is cleansed into the founding of a city.

I know that these aspects of *Finnegans Wake* do not appeal to scholars in the way that the pains of more particular exegesis do.

Much critical labour has been expended on dragging the book away from the fictional zone I'm sure it inhabits. If it is not fiction, what is it? And if it is fiction, it exhibits the same evasions which disfigure, or glorify, *Ulysses* or *The Blue Book of Eccles*. For there is no resolution of the narrative except through myth. It's interesting to note that genuine though frustrated admirers of Joyce regard the two great books as quarries from which can be excavated the materials of true fiction. We've seen at least two dramatisations of *Ulysses*. A film was made of *Finnegans Wake*. Some twenty years ago I made a television adaptation called *A Night at the Bristol Tavern*. This began in full evening light, with the pub at its Saturday busiest with the twelve Sullivani on their settle, the four evangelists round their table, gigantic Earwicker behind the bar, the children running in and out, Earwicker's fond but tortured eyes on his daughter, the Slav-featured Ann dragging the children off to bed, Sackerson, or whatever his name is, washing the glasses. With the closing of the pub and Earwicker's retirement to bed, the calendar on the wall showing February 1132, the branches of the Eggdrizzle tree tapping at the window, the true story began but the television producers lost interest. Joyce's dream story is too spatial to be good narrative.

It would seem that one part of me is looking for the wrong things in Joyce. I blame my career as a novelist, a career which Joyce never had. César Franck wrote one symphony, and this does not make him a symphonist. In the works of Conrad, Henry James, Ford Madox Ford we find a strenuous engagement with a genre, the raising of fresh problems with each new novel, evidence of commitment to a form and not merely a single vagrant example of it. And yet Joyce's single novel – if we ignore the mixed fictional-autobiographical-historical-mythical formula which is *Finnegans Wake* – towers above the work of all his contemporaries and successors. Was it ever possible to regard it as the forerunner of a whole new mode of art? Apparently not, for Joyce has no followers. In that sense, he is nobody's master. Joyce Cary, a fellow Irishman, used his technique of interior monologue in the Gulley Jimson novels, but he merely sounds like a feeble imitator. Samuel Beckett had to free himself from Joyce's influence by turning to another language and cultivating the vacuum instead of the plethora. Flann O'Brien was stifled by *Ulysses* and had to end up by diminishing Joyce into a Dalkey bar curate who wrote pamphlets for the Catholic Truth Society. Speaking for myself because I happen to be here, and not because I consider myself worthy of that august company, when I start a new novel in order to earn my bread the horrible example of *Ulysses* glooms from the shelf.

Ulysses belongs to an experimental period in all the arts, and we have to wonder why experiment, the urge to make it new, was necessary at all. Was it not better done as others used, to follow the plain omniscient time-bound narrative method of Fielding, Smollett, George Eliot, Dickens, Thackeray? This is the way things have turned out in the post-Joyce epoch. The novelists who make money have never doubted that the plain story-telling technique good enough for the Victorians is good enough for them – though they have profited from Joyce's candour in the bedroom, if not in the privy.

The fact seems to be that experimentation in the novel, with rare exceptions, is directed towards destroying the form. The great general public, in its undoubted wisdom, wants the straight arrow of uncomplicated narrative without the fuss of psychological penetration, the bending of time, the mythic component. Fiction is, like suntan oil and the scuba suit, an appurtenance of a holiday. Some years ago I remember watching on television a discussion between the late J.B. Priestley and the late Lord Boothby. Boothby, a greatly admired statesman, said: 'There are only three novelists worth bothering about: Jack here, Monty Mackenzie and Willy Maugham. All the rest are bloody awful.' This is pretty much the attitude of the British politician, to say nothing of the Royal Family. The general public accepts that the novel is for a pleasant read, not for a deeper engagement with life. It may be wrong, but we ought perhaps to feel uneasy that works like *Ulysses* are the province of scholars and that a ring of fire – that sometimes, mercifully, is extinguished – is made to surround them.

If we had a regular international conference to examine aspects of the James Bond novels, there's no doubt that great subtleties of symbolism could be made to emerge. To be less facetious – but am I really being facetious? – closer scholarly attention to Ford Madox Ford, without doubt the greatest British novelist of the century, would be more profitable in terms of the genre itself. But the fascination of James Joyce lies in the manner in which he exceeds the bounds set by his chosen form. He seems closer to Dante or Rabelais or Blake, even Shakespeare, than to Ford or Conrad.

I noted at the beginning that my own attraction to Joyce had more to do with temperament, auditory endowment, and above all race and religion than with the fictional revolution that he represents. Race, I think, is important in a way that does not apply to the half-German Ford or the wholly Polish Conrad. The alleged madness of the Irish is not just a matter of affectionate jokes. In his *Back to Methuselah* Shaw prophesies a time when the Irish and Jewish races will be wiped out in an ultimate holocaust and the rest of the world will commit suicide through boredom. *Ulysses* and *Finnegans Wake* are mad works in the sense that the Irish are mad. The madness fascinates. It is a spasmodic madness, not a steady state. Only Sir Hamilton Harty, saved by his residence in England, was able to compose an Irish symphony. Irish operas are pure music-hall. Except for George Moore, who was really a Frenchman, the Irish novel does not really exist. Joyce was an admirable writer of short stories who planned *Ulysses* as a brief narrative about the day of a certain Mr Hunter. In the story 'Grace', the ascent from inferno to paradiso is parodied; Homer was to receive a much swifter comic treatment in the story which eventually swelled considerably. *Ulysses* remains a short story of great length. But length is less an inherent attribute than an applied one. If the later chapters of *Ulysses* had been as brief as the earlier ones, the total work should be easily pocketable. The comic expansion is mad, and it is Irish madness.

When I say more boldly what I've already implied, that Joyce is a Catholic writer, I mean it less in the narrow sectarian sense (if the Catholic church can be diminished to a sect) than in the wider sense of a civilisation, a massive culture from which the Reformation wantonly separated itself. The novel is usually considered to be a Protestant form, despite its beginning and its fulfilment in Cervantes. Certainly, the English novel, from Richardson to E.M. Forster and beyond, celebrates the Protestant virtues of individuality, pragmatism and middle-class morality. Joyce can, and does, parody this tradition, but he is far closer to the Catholic Middle Ages than to the revolutionary epoch of Protestant mercantilism. He attempted to drown his Irishry in Europe, producing finally an international language that can be called Eurish, but the mere fact of his being an Irish Catholic, impervious however to the siren songs of Irish nationalism, automatically made him a European. He attempted a very early revolt against the Southern Europe that produced Dante by acclaiming Ibsen as his master and by learning Ibsen's own Dano-Norwegian. In *Finnegans Wake* the Master Builder or Bygmester relates directly to Ibsen, but Southern Europe gave him both Bruno and Vico – heretics admittedly – and the philosophies of both grant him a structure.

When Joyce was told that too much of his last great work was trivial, he demurred, saying that some of it was quadrivial too. The education that the three children of Earwicker receive is safely medieval, though it ends with a kind of Freudian revelation. The deeper medievalism of Joyce lies in devices like arithmology, to say nothing of sacramentalism, which makes us seem to be eating the bread of narrative while in fact ingesting the flesh and blood of a deeper reality. But I would merely assert that this lapsed Catholic, a heretic inimical even to baptism, had genuinely exchanged one priesthood for another and had turned his back on a logical absurdity not in order to embrace an illogical one. If you don't become a Protestant you have to remain a Catholic.

W.H. Auden said of the novelist that his task was 'to be dirty with the dirty' and, finally, 'to suffer dully the wrongs of man'. It was the dullness and not the dirt that Joyce objected to. 'Novel', unfortunately, has only two rhymes: 'grovel' and 'hovel'. Joyce raised the form above these associations to its destruction and to its glory – and we, his admirers, followers, have, like the saintly hero of the blessed Thomas Eliot, to mourn and rejoice at the same time.

Previously unpublished. A version of this piece was given as a speech at the Princess Grace Irish Library, Monaco, in 1990.

Can Art be Immoral?

'THOSE WHO find ugly meanings in beautiful things are corrupt without being charming. This is a fault. Those who find beautiful meanings in beautiful things are the cultivated. For these there is hope. They are the elect to whom beautiful things mean only Beauty. There is no such thing as a moral or an immoral book. Books are well written or badly written. That is all... The moral life of man forms part of the subject-matter of the artist, but the morality of art consists in the perfect use of an imperfect medium ... No artist has ethical sympathies. An ethical sympathy in an artist is an unpardonable mannerism of style ... Vice and virtue are to the artist materials for an art.'

And so on. You will recognise these doubtful aphorisms as part of the preface to *The Picture of Dorian Gray*. When I say 'doubtful' I suppose I'm subscribing to the hypocrisy of the period which Oscar Wilde tried to define and which tried to kill him. The post-Paterian aesthetic frightens us vicariously. Believe in art for art's sake and you will end up in Reading Gaol. The philistine British public is still so scared of art that it sends its political representatives on holiday armed with detective stories. If we want to be strict about morality, the most immoral books ever written are those of the late Dame Agatha Christie, who killed people for sport. This is not the general view.

I see that in my very title, like Wilde himself, I use terms which I'm always too inept or usually too frightened to wish to define. I don't know what art is, and I'm uncertain about the meaning of 'immoral'. I practise an art, thought I have adversaries who deny this; my life is moral in that I've so far evaded prison in a democratic country. On the other hand, I've engaged in the international sport of cheating the State of lawful revenues, travelled second class in a first-class compartment, committed fornication, blasphemed, used obscenities, been drunk, above all, lied. Treat every man according to his desert, says Hamlet, and which of us would scape whipping?

When we all gleefully accept that we're immoral, evidently there's something wrong with the accepted view of morality.

And, of course, morality is whatever the community, abetted by the State, says that it is. It is contingent, expedient, and changes with the wind. During the Second World War we saw how fickle were principles of right and wrong. It was right to eat bread in a time of moderate plenty, wrong to eat it during a shortage. It was right to kill Germans then; now presumably it is, except on Italian holidays, reprehensible. It's clear to all of us that the principles of morality which custom, community, and the State enforce are no more than bows towards expediency. Things which were a dirty business during the war and for the rather more gruelling ten years after – exportation of currency, dealing on the black market and so on – now seem quaintly laughable. There has to be a deeper morality that is impervious to the merely contingent. This may or may not coincide in certain areas with the State's version of behaviour, but it carries a gravitas that looks beyond the merely expedient.

You'll remember that the late Graham Greene, on being converted to his own idiosyncratic version of Catholicism, began to perceive that there was a secular morality and what might be termed a theological one. He wrote a novel, eventually turned into a film, entitled *Brighton Rock*. In this a young gang leader, Pinkie, espouses not wrong but evil. He is a Catholic, as idiosyncratic as his author, who sees the logic of eternal punishment but hardly of eternal bliss. Evil to him is an eternal verity. He's pursued because of his evildoing by a jovial Guinness-swilling highly secular lady who believes in right and wrong. Being a late product of the English Reformation, she's never heard of good and evil. Greene seems to deride her while granting the theological gangster Pinkie a measure of respect. T.S. Eliot wrote an essay on Baudelaire in which he said that 'the worst that can be said of our malefactors is that they are not men enough to be damned.' Baudelaire apparently was man enough to be damned. So is Pinkie. There is, in the Greene-Eliot ethic a certain nobility attached to the conscious awareness of transgressing God's laws, which may not be the same as man's. God is not concerned with right and wrong, only good and evil.

These terms have always been difficult to define. 'God' is a dangerously ambiguous, perhaps even multiguous, word. When we say that God is good, we could mean that he is good as the taste of an apple is good, that there is a fundamental goodness beyond morality. Nobody would commit a sin if he did not expect a satisfaction to come out of it – an awareness of goodness. But goodness is action as well as a passive state of wellbeing consequent upon an action. Goodness as action is, I should think, the manifestation of concern with the capacity of a living organism to fulfil itself according to a fundamental principle of free will. Interference with this capacity is the opposite of good, and that opposite is termed evil. To kill, to injure, to rape – these are clearly evil, though the state merely calls them criminal. The State, in fact, has to be wary of employing theological terms at all, since it must always be ready to condone the injuring or extinction of putative enemies. The morals of war constitute a total ethical volte-face. I think the term 'evil' first made its appearance in popular journalism at the time of the My-Lai massacre in Vietnam, when *Time* magazine had to use the term to describe a destructive event which served no purpose but itself. Gratuitous acts of destruction represent the full rich cream of evil. To kill without motive is so pure an act that it seems to take on the quality of an art-form.

And yet the term 'evil' has to be employed when certain acts are committed that do not seem to contravene regular secular principles. To make a derisive noise during the performance of a Mozart quartet is a breach of etiquette rather than a criminal act. But, in the sense that a piece of music is, metaphorically or perhaps literally, a living organism, an injury has been done to it, and that has to be termed evil. I consider that any interference with free will is evil. But what we do when free will is itself directed towards evil? I suppose we must answer that free will must be instructed in the obligations of free will. You see how difficult it is to say anything useful or even intelligible about the nature of morality.

You will have noticed that Oscar Wilde said something about 'the morality of art' without saying what he meant by the high-sounding expression. Evidently he had in mind something about a closed system of conduct on which rigorous judgments can be made. This is pushing the term 'morality' too far, but it may be useful to consider how it is possible to make judgments on art at all.

Art has been defined as the disposition of physical material to an aesthetic end. This begs a fundamental question. What do we mean by 'aesthetic'? Etymology doesn't help. The Greek *aisthánesthai* means merely to perceive, and it is perception, not pain, that is wiped out by an anaesthetic. Art is concerned with the creation of beautiful objects, but this is only one aspect of aesthetics, which finds beauty in nature and gets terribly mixed up with biology. For the beauty of a woman, or any other kind of animal, cannot be separated from biological utility. When nature is beautiful, we know that its beauty is attached to its own brand of utility. Even when we find beauty in human artefacts like aircraft, sailing ships or intercontinental ballistic missiles, we're uneasily aware that a purely aesthetic judgment is out of place. Art is concerned with the creation of beauty for its own sake. Oscar Wilde's last words in that preamble to *Dorian Gray* are: 'All art is perfectly useless.' When art wants to be useful, then we're probably justified in saying that it's not art.

If art is not useful, what is its use? The creation of an artefact which shall be beautiful presupposes that the Platonic term beauty which Wilde doesn't attempt to define at least has a meaning. It's not a meaning that can be expressed formulaically, although certain aestheticians have tried. It's most easily thought of as the objective correlative of a state of feeling. I say that a thing portrays beauty when it induces a feeling of elation which is unrelated to the biological or the utilitarian. The orgasm produces elation because that is nature's bribe to ensure the continuation of the race, even though that bribe is thwarted. The elation of health, or its recovery, or financial success, the winning of a difficult game doesn't call into being the praise or near-worship of an artefact. The elation is probably the elation of a kind of metaphysical discovery, and that discovery is very frequently a sense of unity which only the arts can convey. This unity is the contrived coherence of what, in daily life, is not coherent. Coherence can only be brought about by selection, and selection connotes limitation. The essence of art is cunning limitation.

I suppose that the art with which most visual artists are concerned most typically exhibits the necessity of limitation, since the pictorial art is enclosed in the prison of a frame. Within that frame elements of the visual world are so arranged that a fragment of experience looks like a unity of experience. A pattern is imposed on, or grows out of, a selection of physical objects. A photograph will show us physical objects, but we feel that the frame is arbitrary. This is not so with a painting, and of course a photograph can contrive to accept the creative limitation of a painting. Beauty does not lie in the subject matter but in the organisation of the subject matter. This probably applies to all the arts.

I have to confess to great personal limitations when it comes to the pictorial aesthetic. One has to accept the choice that nature makes for us all, confining us to one sense or another. Though my earliest ambitions were pictorial, and my first publications were of cartoons in great daily newspapers, I was always hampered with Daltonianism or colour blindness. This represents a kind of local patriotism, since I was born in Manchester and John Dalton made his numbing discovery there. In my early youth I turned to music and literature – essentially auditory arts. My problem is to find a rough and ready aesthetic which will apply equally to the auditory and visual arts, and the motor ones as well. I don't think it's possible for anybody to practise an art without knowing why he is doing it. This entails having a pliable aesthetic.

Oscar Wilde, like his master Walter Pater, saw that all the arts try to attain the condition of music. This is presumably because the arts are happiest when they are dealing with form at its purest, its most remote from representation. This means its safest, for when the arts represent persons or objects they are drawing close to the possibility of moral judgment. There's an instinctive desire on the part of the artist to keep well away from that area. I don't think we well understand what music is trying to do. Certainly the musician himself was once confused by the fact that musical sounds, the mere raw material, can be pleasant in themselves. If I sit at the keyboard and strike arbitrary chords, it's all too possible for some auditor to remark: 'How beautiful.' You'll remember that Miss Skinner, in Samuel Butler's *The Way of All Flesh*, says: 'Give me a simple chord of Beethoven – that is happiness.' Modern composers, perhaps starting with Stravinsky and Schoenberg, discovered that true musical skill lay in contriving satisfactory patterns out of what was not in itself pleasing. To cease to draw a distinction between a concord and discord was the beginning of modern musical wisdom. Form or pattern was all. The analogy is with, say, Leonardo da Vinci's painting of an old man, bald and carbuncular, embracing his great grandson. The uglier the nude, the less like a *Sun* Page Three sub-pornograph, the greater is the possibility of outstanding artistic creation.

Probably in music we see not merely the ultimate art but the most primitive representation of essential structure – that structure out of which cultures and civilisations are made, the structure of oppositions. We live in a binary universe, created by our own brains, which depends on codes of communication made out of opposites. These, of course, do not exist in nature. Colour in nature is a spectrum; the separation of one colour from another is a human achievement.

When colours can oppose each other, as in a set of traffic signals, then communication is possible, though not for me the Daltonian. In language we have a whole set of oppositions – phonemes versus morphemes, bound morphemes versus free morphemes, unvoiced consonants versus voiced consonants, consonants versus vowels, and so on. Music is made out of tensions which are resolved only to make new tensions, ending, we hope, with an unequivocal resolution. In traditional music, the dominant opposes the tonic, and the subdominant opposes both. In modern music there is often a difficulty in finding oppositions, and that is why a great number of people stay away from concerts devoted to the music of Pierre Boulez.

Literature is close to music in that it's an auditory art. The very term literature denies this, preferring to think of it as visual – the arrangement of words, which are made out of letters, fixed on the page. Homer, whoever he was or they were, singing in a pre-literate society, would not have understood this. The development of the Greek alphabet, according to some theorists, was in the service of fixing the Homeric auditory for ever – letters in the service of sounds, not as a substitute for them. Literature then is sounds, but sounds to which meaning is attached. Not phones but phonemes. Literature at its purest, meaning its most poetical, is essentially the manipulation of phonemes already manipulated into words. Words belong to the great world which exists outside art. Literature is the most dangerous of the arts, as Oscar Wilde was to discover, because it allows the possibility of moral judgment.

Another Irishman, James Joyce, against whom, like Wilde, morality unsheathed its claws, was greatly concerned about the possibility that literature might, because it is made out of words, move out of the zone of aesthetic purity into one in which artistic, not moral, impropriety was ready to take over. He talked about proper art and improper art or, to be more technical, static art and kinetic art. Static art aroused emotions which were then cleansed or cathartised by the rhythm of the artistic medium itself. This, of course, is pure Aristotle. Tragedy arouses pity and terror, only to allay them through artistic catharsis. If tragedy were a kinetic art, instead of a static one, then the auditor would leave the presentation terribly aroused and liable to do damage, as after a football match. But Milton's phrase 'calm of mind, all passion spent' is the proper state of mind of one who has suffered the vicarious agonies of *King Lear*. He perceives torture, mutilation, death, as aspects of the pattern of human life, accepts them, dimly sees the possibility of a unity in which all things are subdued and explained by necessity, and is not only calm but exalted.

I think it might be useful to consider this theory of the static and the kinetic in graphic terms. Let's suppose that the whole process of artistic communication is contained in the middle of a line. This line is a continuum. At one end of it, it uses the materials of communication to instruct, at the other end it uses those materials to excite. In other words, there is a static area in the middle, and at one end a didactic area, at the other a pornographic area. The true artist has to avoid invading either of these two areas, but avoidance is not easy.

Perhaps for simplicity's sake I should confine myself for the moment to literature. Books are most revered, especially in America, when they are didactic, when they wish to teach. A didactic book will tell you about anything from the abacus, or the aardvark, to the zygospore. It uses language not for an aesthetic end but as a medium of instruction. It does not try to excite. It does not address the emotions, only the brain. At the other end of the continuum we have pornography, which addresses neither the emotions nor the brain but the senses. Etymologically, pornography means the representation of a harlot, a desirable but anonymous sexual partner. Because of a large accumulation of associations, because of an increase in the discovery of the fountains of human action, the term has expanded its meaning. Anything which provokes violence, usually with a sexual connotation, is these days labelled pornographic.

But pornography is generally harmless – in the social sense. It promotes auto-erotic acts, it is masturbatory. It provokes a sexual discharge, but usually in solitude. It is cathartic. It may, far more than the didactic, use the materials of art, though usually in a manner defiantly unoriginal. I don't think it is in order to make a moral judgment on it. The only possible judgment is a Wildean one: pornography is improper art; it offends against the morality of art because it arouses what cannot be purged within the rhythm of art. It provokes a discharge outside itself. In the same way, didactic writing is fulfilled outside itself: it leads to action in the same way as pornography. When it pretends to be art, it is to be condemned on the same moral grounds as its distant or polar partner.

Think again of that continuum – art in the middle, the didactic and the pornographic at the ends. The line is pliable and can be bent. More, one end can be made to touch the other. Most readers of books feel guilty if they're surrendering to sheer enjoyment. Information allays guilt: the book they read has a use. Grant the reader, as a reward, a touch of the pornographic, and he will be thoroughly content. A couple may copulate, discuss hotel management, aeronautics or Florentine incunabula, and then fall once more to love. They are mere phantoms anyway: if they all fall to their messy deaths in a defective hotel elevator, no one is going to bewail their disappearance.

I think it was André Gide who called pornography one-handed literature. He might have applied the same term to a book on cookery: stir the pot with one hand, hold the book with the other. In each case the book becomes unclean, literally stained.

Joyce, in his autobiographical novel *A Portrait of the Artist as a Young Man*, has his hero Stephen Dedalus expound very eloquently on the morality of art – meaning the closed code that forbids the pornographic and the didactic alike. Strangely, when I first read the book at the age of fifteen I was so appalled by the sermon on hell which frightens young Stephen out of sin and into repentance that I vowed never to touch it again. In other words, the novel was acting kinetically and not statically. The ghastly rhetoric of the Jesuit sermon ought to belong either to the didactic or the pornographic zone, but, not being addressed to the brain, it cannot be didactic; not exciting the sexual instinct it can hardly be pornographic. What then is it? If we expand pornography to signify any appeal to the flesh – not a pleasurable appeal, far from it – and if we expand the didactic to mean any appeal to reason and emotion combined, then the sermon inhabits a double area. Of course, in a work that so diligently tried to obey the aesthetic propounded within it, that sermon should not be there. But the novelist always has the problem of trying to cope with the inclusion of material that leaps outside the confines of the static aesthetic appeal. So probably does the painter.

I recognise that painting has an origin in magic, or so the primitive cave-drawings of our remote ancestors seem to tell us, and that in its long history it proceeds through other kinds of kinesis. A religious painting, like a religious play of the old guild cycles, has a didactic task, and the function of teaching remains as deliberate as the anecdotal pictures of the Victorians, which I personally love. But this is not what the pictorial art is about. Nor is it the task of the pure artist to depict the human form with the intention of arousing any passion other than of a kind of formal or structural love. But I can't deny that the Rokeby *Venus* or Bronzino's allegory of *Venus, Love, Folly and Time* in the National Gallery excites in a distinctly carnal manner.

And the Cecil B. DeMille canvases of Alma Tadema, another painter I guiltily admire, are near-pornographic. But I can think of only one painter whose works were confiscated by the police, along with a volume of Blake reproductions that happened to be lying around. These were painted by a man who was not a painter at all – D.H. Lawrence. He hated the Tate Gallery and everything he considered that it stood for, and he produced male and female nudes intended to glorify human love. They were not well done, and any sin Lawrence committed was against the morality of art. This was, perhaps rightly, construed by the Home Office as a sin against public morality. This kind of confiscation is rare. But in the field of literature it is not uncommon.

You'll forgive me, I hope, if I draw on my thirty-odd years of experience as a professional writer to exemplify the particular dangers that the writer of fiction faces. The first instance relates to morality of a special kind, personal injury frequently unintended, often unconscious, which carries heavy damages in civil courts. Libel is attached to a work and not essentially to its author. The fear of the unwilling committal of this tort, a tort not being quite a crime, leads writers to give up writing or when, like myself, they're tied to the craft because no other seems available, to become unbecomingly escapist. When, by total accident, I discovered that I'd libelled a former lady mayor of Banbury named Miss Bustin, I ceased to write about the present and composed instead a novel about Shakespeare's love-life. In this, somewhat vindictively, I placed an unpleasant Mistress Bustin, a puritan of Banbury and almost at once was threatened with another libel suit. The late Constantine Fitzgibbon, writing a novel about an imaginary future, placed a London nightclub in it which bore the same name as an existing one in the real present. He was sued. I doubt if even portrait-painters have this problem. Mrs Churchill would have liked Graham Sutherland to have this problem, but all she could do was to destroy the portrait of her husband that he'd painted.

Another moral problem I've faced in my time is that of meeting a charge of blasphemy. I believe it was Mrs Mary Whitehouse who was prepared to raise this spectre when I published my translations of some of the sonnets of Giuseppe Gioacchino Belli, a poet who lived in the Napoleonic era, and just after, and produced nearly 2,700 sonnets in the Roman dialect. These sonnets are of profound anthropological interest. They depict the Roman psyche through the gutter language of the Romans. I chose those of Belli's sonnets which dealt with religious subjects and was faithful in dealing with his obscenity as well as his blasphemy. The voice is not quite mine. The original voice is not quite Belli's. Belli was a respectable academic poet who served as a Vatican theatre censor. The work is ventriloquial. Who is being obscene? Who is being blasphemous? Surely it is in order to display the foul nature of the lower-class Roman mind? Surely, in a novel, if it is permissible to present blasphemy, disclaiming it oneself but attaching it to an invented or even real-life personage. The Muslims have decided that this is not so. We all know what has happened to Mr Salman Rushdie and his *Satanic Verses*. Here is some of my own verse, heavily didactic in the style of a debased Alexander Pope:

> Ladies and gentlemen, a graver theme
> Confronts us. To begin, let us blaspheme.
> Jesus, the bastard of a drunken brute,
> Was gotten on the village prostitute.
> His followers were active sodomites
> Who dragged in Judas to their dark delights.
> The heavenly kingdom was not for the just
> But just the devotees of lawless lust.
> Read this, and then re-read it. Having read,
> Do not heap hot damnation on my head,
> But add inverted commas and 'he said'.
> I may have written this, but on behalf
> Of some fictitious sneerer whose foul laugh
> A fictional believer counters thus:
> 'Your fiction is so vilely blasphemous
> You damn yourself to darkness.' The reply?
> 'Christ was a liar and he taught a lie,
> A bastard brat, son of a fucking whore,
> His words a drunkard's belch and nothing more.'
> Our world is built of opposites. Not strange
> That one mind can engender this exchange,
> And it's unjust to fasten on to me
> The fouler voice of the antiphony.
> Imagine death and take the blame for death?
> Macbeth is bad, but Shakespeare's not Macbeth.
> Turn to a later giver of God's laws

And you may libel him with greater cause.
Mohamed claimed no heavenly origin,
And to defame his essence is no sin.
'This shoveller of camel-droppings who
Craftily married and pretended to
Broadcast the Word from Gabriel's microphone
– We have his word for it, but that alone –
Raped virgins under age and robbed the poor,
Corrupted Arab, Persian, Turk and Moor,
And left a bloody legacy of hate
To doubter, heretic and apostate,
A stinking rubbish dump made white with paint,
A shaitan masquerading as a saint.'

[From *An Essay on Censorship*]

The next of my moral problems as regards literary expression goes back some years and still goes on. In 1961 I wrote a novel in which I tried to tackle an essentially theological theme – that of free will. The cult of juvenile violence had just begun in this country. Home from Malaysia, I was interested in phenomena like the Teddy Boys and the Mods and Rockers. I was especially interested to hear talk about quelling this belligerence through conditioning techniques. I think the notion of a kind of super-Pavlovian control of the reflexes came from Professor B.F. Skinner in America. To me, with a traditional Christian upbringing, such a notion was appalling. Men and women are free – free to make moral choices; other kinds of freedom don't greatly matter. I wrote a book called *A Clockwork Orange* in which I presented – implicitly, not, I think, with overt didacticism – the case for regarding freely chosen evil as somehow better than imposed good. I'd come back from speaking Malay, in which the word for human being is *orang*. *Orang* and *orange* were close, possessing in common colour, sweetness, juice, organic life. Conditioning or brain-washing meant the imposition of mechanical laws on a product of nature.

My aim was simple. To present a young thug committed to violence, rape, robbery, murder and other vices who is caught by the police, tried, imprisoned, and then given the chance to participate in a psychological experiment. He is made to watch films depicting gross violence while, at the same time, an injected substance courses through his arteries which induces nausea. In the Pavlovian manner, he associates extreme sickness with any thought of violence after the completion of this cure. He avoids sin not because sin is morally wrong, but because his body forbids it. Unfortunately, the use of music as an emotional intensifier during the showing of these films of violence produces an effect unintended by the devisers – nausea is attached to the hearing of the music by Beethoven. The young man tries to kill himself while listening, against his will, to Beethoven's Ninth Symphony. Falling from a high window, he undoes his condition and becomes the young thug he always was. But, as the story ends, he grows out of his taste for violence. He grows up.

The novel was published in 1962 to little notice and small applause. Ten years later it was made into a film which convulsed the nation. This was because it was made out of visual images, not literary constructs. Words can hit hard, but not as hard as shapes in technicolour. The film was alleged to have been the cause of gratuitous violence among the young. Parliament asked for it to be banned. The director, Stanley Kubrick, an American living at Borehamwood, was, apparently, threatened by guardians of public order. The film exists elsewhere in the world – as *Uhrwerk Orange* and *Naranja Meccanica* and so on – but not here. Kubrick committed a secondary sin in making the film; the primary sin was my own.

And yet I'd done my best to avoid the pornography of violence through the employment of verbal tricks. I wrote the novel in a weird invented language – a mixture of Russian, rhyming slang, gipsy bolo, with the rhythms of the King James Bible – in order to make the violent substance of the book difficult for the reader to reach. By the time the reader had deciphered a phrase like 'I gave him a tolchock on the rot and dratsed him with my oozo on the ochkies', the referent had, I assumed, already passed by. There was no real possibility of corruption. But in the film there was total explicitness, and for this I was blamed.

Was it possible to write a serious novel about the dangers of conditioning without showing what was to be conditioned out of existence? Yes, but it would have been cheating. Even the mildest and most innocent old lady would demand, rightly, to know what crimes the criminal had committed. It is sometimes necessary for the novelist to come close to corrupting himself. The kind of novel that cabinet ministers read on holiday – Jeffrey Archer, Dame Agatha Christie and so on – is not of the type which *A Clockwork Orange* represents. I'm not referring to content but to technique. When language obtrudes, when it refuses to be a pane of well-polished glass through which actions can be viewed, when it prefers opacity to transparency, then it belongs to a different class of literary endeavour than the popular novel. The transparent novel, in which language is not important, I call Class One fiction. The opaque novel, in which language is a character, a constituent of the action, I call Class Two fiction. It's interesting to note that two of the most remarkable novels belonging to this class in this century – Joyce's *Ulysses* and Nabokov's *Lolita* – have both earned moral condemnation, just like *A Clockwork Orange*. It seems that the novelist who is interested in language is also interested in life – too interested, say the censors.

I think there's a parallel to this process in the visual arts. When painting began to move away from the representational it was, in effect, freeing itself from the dangerous real world where moral judgments are made. In other words, Class 1 painting, Class 2 painting. And sculpture. Architecture? Music? They've always been somehow outside the possibility of moral censure. Or when moral censure culminating in censorship appears, this is always ideological, which means bizarrely impertinent. The Nazis proscribed Mendelssohn because they could hear Jewish elements even in his Italian and Scottish Symphonies – just as they could find Jewish corpuscles in blood identical with the Aryan variety, as it has to be. Israel decided that Wagner's music was Nazi. Walking round the Stadio in Rome, or viewing the architecture of EUR, I think I see fascism in the very structure. I don't know whether I'm right or not.

Painting has been able to cleanse itself of the dirty world by becoming abstract – a process which totalitarian ideologies naturally attack. After post-impressionism, we had cubism, vorticism and a yielding to the appeal of non-representational design. Literature tries to do this, though with great difficulty. The nearest literature can get to abstraction is surrealism, in which fragments of the outside world are reorganised, as in this poem from Edith Sitwell's *Façade:*

When Sir Beelzebub
Called for his syllabub....

This makes a kind of sense, but not in the covenant the reader expects to be drawn up with the writer. This covenant relates every-day logic to the logic of literature, which is not always wise. Some years ago I wrote a novel in which a former jockey appeared. I wrote: 'He got up, or down, from his chair.' The fury of the response was unexpected.

The visual confusion in the minds of some readers was so intense that it led to a kind of dementia. A covenant was being broken. Write genuine surrealism, and the reader shrugs it away as though he knew there was no covenant. Try this: 'The five-toed spider, cognac-coloured, annexes the perspex keyboard'. The perfect syntax of that mad utterance half-persuades us that there is sense there. The well-formed sentence, however insane its burden, speaks a kind of sanity. This is what Noam Chomsky meant when he formulated the classical statement 'Colourless green dreams sleep furiously'.

Whether we like it or not, we novelists are committed to a kind of waking sense. Unless, of course, we're writing *Finnegans Wake,* which recounts a dream in dream-language. Here the urge to make language behave like music is extremely powerful. Writers of verse or prose envy music its capacity to say more than one thing at the same time.

I must seem to have wandered away from my initial question – 'Can art be immoral?' The answer is yes, if art disobeys its own rules, if it ceases to proffer a static pleasure and moves down the continuum in the direction of either the didactic or the pornographic. 'The perfect use of any imperfect medium' – so Oscar Wilde defined the morality of art. No artist can concern himself with the exterior morality decreed by the State. Of its very nature art cannot subscribe to the primacy of evil, whose function is to break not make. Art is in the deepest sense ethical in the sense that it accepts the holiness of the human imagination. I see I'm quoting William Blake. There's a song sung by our Women's Institutes which is worth quoting in this connection:

> And did the Countenance Divine
> Shine forth upon our clouded hills,
> And was Jerusalem builded here
> Among those dark Satanic mills?

Most of our chanting matrons assume that Jerusalem is Zion, the fulfilment of the Christian vision, and that the dark Satanic mills are the smoky horrors of the industrial revolution. This is not true. Jerusalem to Blake meant the human imagination, seasoned with free sensuality, the dark Satanic mills were primarily churches, which taught restriction and the narrowest of moralities. They were naturally also the State, the philistine community, those forces of darkness which would import a contingent, expedient morality into the self-sufficient morality of art. Art cannot be immoral. If it seems to be immoral, it is not art.

Previously unpublished. A version of this piece was given as a speech at the Tate Gallery, London on 17 October 1991.

Getting the Language Right

HAMLET CALLS playwrights and actors the abstract and brief chron-
iclers of the time. This is not strictly true, for Elizabethan drama
usually dealt with the past not the present. The novel was waiting to
take over the function of chronicler of the present, which all too soon
becomes the past. Thus, we read Fielding and Smollett to find out
about the eighteenth century, and Dickens and Trollope have fixed
the nineteenth century for us in a manner no mere historian could
achieve. Nevertheless, the novelist often thinks it his duty to revivify
the remote past, and to that end will research deeply in the manner of
the historian. He can be accurate about everything except one thing –
and that is language. Bulwer Lytton, writing *The Last Days of Pompeii*,
is a sedulous antiquarian, but he dare not give his readers dialogue
in Latin or Greek. All he can do is contrive a kind of English which
has been termed 'Wardour Street'. Wardour street, in Soho, London,
is at present concerned with the marketing of films: a century ago it
specialised in shops which sold fake antiques – hence the application
of it to language. Sir Walter Scott's dialogue, full of odds bodkins and
gadzooks, is today risible. Can contemporary novelists, writing about
the past, do better?

I have myself written about various kinds of past in fictional form.
I have written two novels dealing with the first century after Christ.
Obviously, I cannot plunge the reader into Latin, Greek, Hebrew and
Aramaic. In using English the profoundest danger is represented by
anachronism. I wrote, for example, of the assassination of Caligula.
There is a Latin verb, *assassinare*, which seems to justify the use of
an English derivative, but the notion of assassination only came in
with Islam. The Old Man of the Mountains trained his Christian-
killers with dreams of paradise induced by hashish. An *assassinus* was
a hashish eater, hence the assassination of Caligula is an impossible concept. There are certain writers, especially the writers of film
scripts, whom this would not worry. Some time ago the great director
Franco Zeffirelli sent me a script about the Emperor Tiberius which

contained the colloquialism 'Okay' several times. Reading Gore Vidal's recent novel *Live from Golgotha*, one is tempted to believe that ancient Rome might be rendered in American slang, but Vidal is only joking here. When he tackles ancient Rome seriously no one can be more meticulous in handling a neutral kind of English which will serve for any period in time.

Americans have particular difficulty in coping with the language of the past, since they are so very much children of the present. I shuddered when I picked up Norman Mailer's *Ancient Evenings*, which deals with a very remote Egypt, fearing the intrusion of Americanisms. But, you may say, why cannot Americanisms be as legitimate as Anglicisms? Using a modern language to convey the past is false anyway, so why should not terms like 'take a rain check' or the greeting 'Hi' intrude? The answer is not easy, and there is a difference between modern and contemporary as far as language is concerned.

The problems are considerable when we are dealing with an English-speaking community remote, but not too remote, from our own day. Susan Sontag's *The Volcano Lover* is about Nelson and the Hamiltons and it does not commit a single linguistic error. When Erica Jong decided to write about eighteenth-century London in her *Fanny*, she used the resources of scholarship to get her colloquial lower class English right. No American brought up on the Declaration of Independence is likely to get the higher eighteenth-century registers wrong. When we go back to the seventeenth century, however, we face great trouble.

I know this to be true, because in 1964 I published a novel on Shakespeare called *Nothing Like the Sun*, which displeased some readers because they found much of the language unintelligible. In 1993 I celebrate the quarter-centenary of Christopher Marlowe's assassination (is this the wrong term?) with a novel entitled *A Dead Man in Deptford*. It has been suggested by some that the book increase its prospective readership by being translated into modern English. I do not see the point of this argument, since Elizabethan English *is* modern English. True, there are words that Shakespeare and Marlowe use which have died out – 'nief' for 'first', for example, and 'kibes' for 'chilblains' (and perhaps 'chilblains' itself is disappearing, along with the ailment) – and certain words have changed their meanings.

To Shakespeare a politician was a Jesuit and suburbs were not dormitory areas of some affluence but brothel districts. But the bulk of the language is common to the Elizabethans and to ourselves, especially those of us who are American. Americans say 'sure' as an affirmative and so did Shakespeare; they have also in common the past participle 'gotten'. Elizabethan London and New York have rhythms in common, as well as phonemes. Hamlet pronounces 'tropically' to pun with 'mouse trap' which Americans can still do but Englishmen not. To modern Americans 'customary' has two stresses, as it does for Hamlet, who says: 'Customary suits of solemn black'. No modern Englishman can, like an American, give that five-stressed line its full value. The Americans are a kind of Elizabethans, and their presidency is an Elizabethan monarchy. It seems to me, in writing both a novel about Shakespeare and a novel about Marlowe, that the thing to do was to avoid contemporary language rather than to work hard at installing Elizabethan peculiarities. We take for granted nowadays concepts derived from Darwin, Karl Marx and Sigmund Freud. We use terms like 'proletariat' and 'complex', as well as clichés like 'the survival of the fittest' without realising how modern they are. Shakespeare's intuitive knowledge of psychology is vast, and the Oedipus complex may be at work in *Hamlet*, but Shakespeare was no more ready than D.H. Lawrence to formulate such a concept.

Novels about the past have to be a shameless kind of compromise. *Nothing Like the Sun* filtered Elizabethan usage through an imaginary narrator who lives in the contemporary Far East and is drunk on the Chinese rice spirit called *samsu*. He is not always accurate, but his inaccuracies are deliberate. For instance, he has the young Shakespeare note the 'spurgeoning' of the back eddy under the Clopton Bridge which spans the river Avon in Stratford. This is a reference to Caroline Spurgeon who wrote a substantial book on Shakespeare's imagery and refers to the poet's use of the image of the back eddy in *The Rape of Lucrece*. If anything seems anachronistic in *Nothing Like the Sun*, blame it on the narrator.

My novel on Marlowe has as narrator a young actor named John Wilson. This is my own baptismal name, and my family always believed that it could trace itself back to that actor. At the end of the novel I disclose that I myself, John Anthony Burgess Wilson, am making a self-identification with that putative ancestor. Whether this works or not, I do not know. I do know, however, that I could not have ended the novel like this:

'Okay, Marlowe,' growled Frizer 'You're a damned traitor and a fucking fag. You're going to get what's coming to you, bastard.'

And he drove his knife into Marlowe's eye. Marlowe screamed like the siren of a fire engine before dropping his dead weight to the floor. 'Yeah,' sneered Frizer, 'I guess he got what was coming to him. He's paid the fucking reckoning.'

Previously unpublished; dated 1992.

Stop the Clock on Violence

EVELYN WAUGH said that change was evidence of life, though that maxim never noticeably softened his stiff opinions. There are beliefs we cling to and will not let go; it must be considered a kind of grace in my old age to abandon a conviction that was part of my blood and bone. I mean the conviction that the arts were sacrosanct, and that included the sub-arts, that they could never be accused of exerting either a moral or an immoral influence, that they were incorrupt, incorruptive, incorruptible. I have quite recently changed my mind about that.

This protective attitude to the arts was really a desire to justify the corrupt elements in the greatest literature of all time – that of the Elizabethan stage. It was a wish not to see William Shakespeare as a violent writer. One play of his we are unlikely ever to see on the stage again, and are totally certain never to see adapted to television, is the tragedy *Titus Andronicus*. This, with its gang rape, mutilation, cannibalism, and a final massacre, goes as far as we could expect from the most depraved porno-violence of today: that it is the work of the most highly respected writer who ever lived does not mitigate its cheap opportunism.

Even in *King Lear* the tearing out of the Earl of Gloucester's eyes seems a gratuitous sop to the corruption of the viewer ('Out, vile jelly,' indeed). Thomas Kyd made Hieronimo bite out his tongue in *The Spanish Tragedy*, but this was too improbable an act to be taken seriously; nevertheless, that play is the progenitor of the tradition of the Tragedy of Blood, to which *Lear* and *Hamlet* belong. The greatest drama of all time was soaked in blood and crippled with violence.

Of course, it may be said that without violence there can be no drama. A play, even a comedy, depends on opposition, and opposition can be murderous. Opposition has to be resolved, either in mourning or in laughter, and this is what makes plot. The bland novels of Jane Austen, or of Barbara Pym, depend on civilised opposition which can be resolved through reason; it requires immense artistic integrity to contrive a plot in which opposition sizzles without a blow being struck. Physical violence is the monopoly, at least in our own age, of the inferior artist.

I am now about to rub certain sore places. I have been allegedly as responsible as anyone in the last 30 years for the cult of violence. I published in 1962 a novella entitled *A Clockwork Orange*, which was more concerned with methods of quelling violence among the young than with the glorification of aggression. Ten years after publication, baffled reviews, and a tiny readership, Stanley Kubrick adapted the book to the screen, rather brilliantly. His version differed from the original in that he emphasised the visual, whereas I had been concerned with converting to sound – specifically, the sounds of an invented language – the clichés of mayhem and murder.

In both book and film the protagonist is, though aversion therapy, changed from an aggression-loving lout into an automaton that vomits at even the thought of violence. The question was asked: is it permissible to kill free will in order to ensure the stability of society? Not many viewers of the film took notice of the question: most were too excited by the violence to bother about the philosophy of the concept.

As we know, Kubrick, and incidentally myself, were accused of concocting a piece of violent pornography; Kubrick received violent threats from some of the foes of violence; the film was withdrawn in this country, though in no other; because no one here is free to see it, the film has accrued a far worse reputation than it merits. More than anything, a major cinematic artist has admitted to the world that art can be *harmful*. If *A Clockwork Orange* can corrupt, why not Shakespeare and the Bible? And, indeed, why not?

I remember flying back from New York to London with a couple of valuable plaques awarded by the New York Critics' Circle and being invited to defend the film on a radio programme. Note that the only approaches to the film, then as now, were of attack and defence: a cool aesthetic assessment seemed out of the question.

My argument was that action was anterior to art; that aggression was built into the human system and could not be taught by a book, film or play. If one wished to believe that a book could instigate violence, the Bible could be one's first choice, and yet this was taken to be the Word of God. Reports had come through from the United States about gangs of four, fantastically dressed in the manner of *A Clockwork Orange*, raping nuns in Poughkeepsie and beating up senior citizens in Indianapolis. I continued to deny the possibility of a mere film's stirring up juvenile mayhem, but I was not being wholly sincere: I was defending William Shakespeare.

From the film of *A Clockwork Orange* youth did not learn aggression: it was aggressive already. What it did learn was a *style* of aggression, a mode of dressing violence up in a new way, a piquant sauce to season the raw meat of kicks, biffs and razor-slashings.

A work of art has a magisterial quality about it, a justifying *élan* which grants virtue to imitation. We know, and do not wish to know, that the story of Abraham's proposal to sacrifice his son to the Lord God has been a justification of child murders, and that the multiple murderer Haigh's drinking his victims' blood had its origin in a manic devotion to the Holy Eucharist. Possibly a man may see *Hamlet* and then do what he has put off doing – namely, kill his uncle. Whether *The Silence of the Lambs* has genuinely promoted cannibalism or the mad butchery of its major villain we do not know. We all bow now, anyway, to the thesis I thought I would never accept – that art is dangerous.

At the time of the Moors Murders, when the killer Brady admitted that he might have been influenced by the Marquis de Sade's *Justine*, the late Lady Snow said that if the burning of all the books in the world were necessary to save one child's death, we should not hesitate to incendiarise (naturally, film would make a better blaze). That goes too far, but I begin to accept that, as a novelist, I belong to the ranks of the menacing. I used to regard myself as a harmless key-basher or pen-pusher.

As much of the fodder of television is film narrative, and it is unleashed on the blasé and the susceptible alike, the question of how far it is likely to corrupt has become urgent. In turning itself into a kind of movie museum, as well as a showcase for low-budget telefilm, the medium has already betrayed something of its initial function. The BBC TV of the 1950s showed plays, not films. The evening's highlight was Chekhov or Rattigan or even Shakespeare, acted live with intervals. The theatre was brought into the drawing room, and the theatre never permitted the excesses of the cinema.

The kind of detection film that now fills the odd hour before bedtime has to be violent – there is not time for psychological penetration – but the violence of the wicked is balanced by the violence of the just. Yet I doubt if the formulaic violence of such films makes any real impact: there are no human beings about, merely cops and killers.

In principle – and it is a principle I have been willing to adopt only after 50-odd years – I am for censorship in the medium, but I feel that a public sensitivity towards TV violence has established itself, one that in the senior medium of film is probably prepared to say 'Enough – no more.' Some of the cinematic excesses have frightened more than the merely squeamish, and they seem unlikely to be reproduced on the box.

Most of my TV-viewing over the last 20 years has been in France and Switzerland, with occasional sojourns in New York. TV is, as the world knows, best in Britain, but there is no vast division in quality whether one crosses the Atlantic or the Alps. World television is homogeneous, meaning crammed with harmless American sitcoms. It is given to blandness, like breakfast food, and its faults lie not in the administration of the sharp jabs of violence or the stimuli of sex as in the recognition that television is a demotic medium and may as well be vulgar as not. As a mere visitor to Britain I am appalled by the vulgarity of the commercials that pay for what comes before and after, by the debasement of speech, by humour so anally based that one blushes. One longs for the old days – the one BBC channel, the leisured presentation, the potter's wheel, *Muffin the Mule*. Now the urge to cram every minute with chromatic fodder is bound to draw on cheap violence. But I do not think there is anything to fear. The danger of television especially when its standards are virtually established by commercial interests, is that it is an agent of social degradation. This is far more frightening than the prospect of *A Clockwork Orange* getting to the screen.

Observer, 21 March 1993

Confessions of the Hack Trade

REVIEWERS ARE lazy; critics are not. Reviewers are viewed by genuine writers with a mixture of foreboding and contempt. The status and, indeed, physical condition of the reviewer is summed up in a trenchant article by George Orwell. The man looks older than he is. He sits at a table covered with rubbish which he dare not disturb, for there may be a small cheque lying under it.

He began his sub-literary career as a genuinely literary one, with high hopes, noble aspirations. But he has sunk to the condition of the hack. He has learnt the trick of reviewing anything, including books he has no hope of understanding. He earns little money and is unlikely to earn the accolade of a state award for services to litera-ture. Services to reviewing are not recognised either at Buckingham Palace or in the office of the Prime Minister. This despicable rat, gnawing away at the fringes of literature, is only ennobled by being one of a pack kept encaged by a literary editor. Or, to exalt the animal metaphor, an also-ran of his literary editor's stable. In this image the term 'hack' finds its proper connotation.

Literary editors, on the whole, are respectable members of society. They are literary men in a sense that reviewers are not. If we are prepared to speak of great literary editors, we must number the late Terence Kilmartin among them. I was never a member of the salaried reviewing team that came and went at the *Observer*, but, as a freelance writer, I did what reviewing work he requested from 1960 till the year he retired – and, of course, beyond. Thus I knew him for about 30 years and can speak of his qualities. Terry will be remembered as a literary editor only by a comparatively narrow circle of book-lovers; his achievement as a translator ensures him a much larger public for a very long time. There was a time when we considered that the Scott Moncrieff version of *A La Recherche du Temps Perdu* was the supreme English Proust. Then Terry shows Scott Moncrieff where he had gone wrong. Terry, in my view, does not await further redaction.

What is the task of a literary editor? I am not sure, not having been one, though there was a time, about 20 years ago, when it seemed that I might take over the book pages of the *Times* or the *Sunday Times* or some such paper – certainly not the *Daily Mirror* or the *News of the World*. This would have been a full-time job, and I regard my full-time job as providing material for literary editors to hand over to reviewers.

The task is a typical newspaper one of turning books into a kind of news. Of the millions of events that happen daily, some are more newsworthy than others – man bites dog, and so on. And so some books are more newsworthy than others. There was once a Victorian study of urban drainage in Eccles properly called *Odour of Sanctity* whose title suggested it might be news, but good literary editors are never tricked by titles. If there are millions of events, there are also millions of books, or so it seems. Choice of the newsworthy entails more skill than the average newspaper reader can easily imagine.

For the average reader cannot imagine the immense number of books that are published until he has actually handled them. In the 1960s I was shocked to discover how many novels are published in a year. This was when I was given the job of fiction editor for the *Yorkshire Post*, a very reputable journal, much read in the Dales and the clubs of wool and steel magnates. I had to furnish a fortnightly article in which five or six new books had to be given serious treatment and, in a kind of coda, ten or so others granted a phrasal summation – like 'All too putdownable' or, rather ambiguous, 'For insomniacs', or 'India encapsulated in a poppadom' or 'Sex on Ilkley Moor – baht more than 'at'.

When the stint began, in the January of 1960, I felt that it might be easy enough, for few novels arrived. I had forgotten that the New Year was always a slack time for publishing. As the year burgeoned, so did fiction. I was living in a small Sussex village, and extra staff had to be taken on at the local post office to cope with the flood.

The pay for the fortnightly article was very small – £6 in pre-decimal money – but the incidental rewards were considerable. Every other Monday morning I staggered to the local railway station, weighed down with two suitcases full of new fiction. The villagers, whose memories were short, assumed on each occasion that I was leaving my wife. These suitcases were emptied on to the floor of the back room of Louis Simmonds, a bookseller on the Strand. He paid 50 per cent of the sale price of each book, in crisp new notes. This was non-taxable cash, and my walk back to Charing Cross Station was usually an irregular one.

The sale of review copies remains a source of income for hacks: they would be lost without it Some really indigent hacks – I could name names but I won't – have in their time sold their review copies without reading them, need being so great. The publisher's blurb grants enough information for processing into a cautious notice. When a review is totally laudatory, lacking in 'nevertheless', you may assume that the book has not been read by the reviewer.

My discovery of the vast number of novels published in Britain alone was, to me, disconcerting because I was trying to make a primary living out of adding to that number. The competition made my heart fail. And yet there were times when my heart lifted. For so many of the novels submitted for the review were of a badness hardly credible. Yet they had got into print. Did aesthetic judgments truly operate in publishing houses? Nobody properly knows.

Given, in the batch for reviewing, a new novel by Greene or Waugh or Powell or Amis, I knew what had to be done, but there was always the possibility of some new genius turning up. One did not dare neglect anything, though there had been glaring examples of neglect in the annals of literary editorship. V. S. Naipaul told me that his first novel, now considered a classic, had not received a single review. My fourth novel failed to be noticed in several of the upmarket Sundays, and I assumed this was a conspiracy, which it probably was.

If you examine the archives of the new defunct magazine *Punch* for 1922, you will find reviews of Sheila Kaye-Smith and Ethel Mannin, but none of *Ulysses* or *The Waste Land*. In 1939 there were hardly any reviews of *Finnegans Wake*, though the late Malcolm Muggeridge contributed a manifesto of total bewilderment to I forget what paper. Total bewilderment was not in order. *Finnegans Wake* had been appearing in pamphlets under the general title of *Work in Progress* all through the 1930s, and there were learned articles of exegesis around. But statements like 'I find this a mass of total gibberish' are often excused in a mere reviewer. The situation is different for a critic.

Indeed, it is highly exceptional for a reviewer to behave like a critic, though, with the heavier periodicals that no longer exist, the two vocations could be regarded as identical. We have T.S. Eliot's volume of *Selected Essays*, which were nothing but reviews reprinted from his magazine *The Criterion*. When I was an undergraduate, this tome, along with Williams Empson's *Seven Types of Ambiguity*, was a *vade mecum*. Being by Eliot, it was assumed to be reliable. In it were definitive judgments on Marlowe, Shakespeare's *Hamlet*, the influence of Seneca on the Elizabethans, the Metaphysical poets. Some of the summations have, over the years, proved to be of very dubious validity. For instance, Eliot said that the Elizabethans took the five-act division from Seneca. But Seneca's plays had no act division; they were more likely to take it from Plautus. The epigrammatic serves well in a review but not in a critical essay. Marlowe's genius was presented as comic in the sense that it went back to some ancient dark native tradition, but of this tradition we were never told, nor could we ever find it. *Hamlet* presented the problem of an emotion being in excess of any possible cause, and we still puzzle over what precisely Eliot meant. The trouble always was that Eliot could do no wrong. In his poem 'Gerontion' he uses the phrase 'In the juvescence of the year came Christ the tiger'. 'Juvescence' is wrong; it should be 'juvenescence', but Eliot would not be told. That solecism is in the *Oxford English Dictionary* and it has to be taken as an authentic form. I have been frequently whipped for whipping Eliot.

In the early days of reviewing, the days of the *Edinburgh Review*, despite the immense length of articles which granted the space and time for genuine critical exposition, the tradition of insufficient thought and attention and, more than that, the transmissible disease of waspishness and sheer malice seems to have been fully established. As Byron put it:

John Keats, who was killed off by one critique,
Just as he was really promised something great,
If not intelligible, – without Greek
Contrived to talk about the gods of late
Much as they might have been supposed to speak.
Poor fellow! His was an untoward fate: –
'Tis strange the mind, that very fiery particle,
Should let itself be snuffed out by an article.

It is doubtful if any writer was ever so snuffed out. A bad, meaning thoughtless, review can induce deep depression and sometimes a silence, which in a sense *is* death, in sensitive authors. This happened to the playwright Christopher Fry, who gave up producing verse plays when consistently attacked by malicious reviewers. One must, I suppose, ponder a little on that term 'malice', since it is doubtful if it can arise from the mere close perusal of a text. A text is not a person, though it may exhibit some facets of a personality. Reviewers prefer the personality for their target, not a text, and this relates them to their colleagues in the gossip columns.

I still smart from a review excreted by the late Geoffrey Grigson. In noticing a volume of essays I had published, he said: 'Who could possibly like so coarse and unattractive a character?' This, I think, was unjust and impertinent. Unfortunately, it is the sort of thing that the baser literary editors prefer to the impersonal weighing up of a text. Terry Kilmartin was not one of these base promoters of malice. When he made mistakes it was rarely in the region of confusing gossip with serious, or semi-serious, appraisal of literary artefacts. He was balanced, and he did not even commit errors of taste, except on one occasion, when he headlined a review of a book on the position of women in the Roman Empire with 'Lays of Ancient Rome'.

With myself he made an error of judgment which still hurts a little. This sprang out of my own error of judgment when reviewing for the *Yorkshire Post*. I had become somewhat uneasy about throwing my reviews into what seemed like a great silence. Readers never responded to my reviews. I received only one letter from a *Yorkshire Post* reader, and that was a horticultural lady who responded to my incidental statement that British orchids had no smell. 'They do, you know,' she wrote, and instanced many odorous varieties.

This has nothing at all to do with literature. I got into the habit of throwing untenable judgments at my presumed readers, saying, for instance, that Barbara Cartland was much influenced by Molly Bloom's monologue at the end of *Ulysses*, or that one could descry the impact of D.H. Lawrence on Charles Dickens. Angry at the unangry silences, I determined to arouse some interest by reviewing a book of my own.

There was a precedent for this: Walter Scott had reviewed *Waverley* at great length in the *Edinburgh Review* and had not been trounced for it. There is something to be said for allowing a novelist to notice his own novel: he knows its faults better than any casual reader, and he has at least read the book. I published a novel entitled *Inside Mr Enderby*, which I'd issued under a pseudonym, and I reviewed this at some length in the *Yorkshire Post*, pointing out how obscene, how fundamentally unclean the work was, and warning readers against it.

A gossip columnist in the *Daily Mail* picked up my act of immoral import and gleefully reported it. I was attacked by the editor of the

Yorkshire Post on Yorkshire Television and promptly, and perhaps justly, dismissed. But at that time, I'd written for *The Observer* an article appraising new books by V.S. Naipaul, Iris Murdoch and Brigid Brophy. This would not be published, since I was now untrustworthy and might conceivably be all these authors, and more, masquerading under the name Anthony Burgess, a name that was itself a masquerade. This tremor of distrust was not typical of Terry Kilmartin. The distrust, anyway, did not last. Journalists are quickly forgiven, and this may be taken as one of the signs of the essential ephemerality of journalism. As a character in *Ulysses* says, 'Sufficient unto the day is the newspaper thereof'.

But to return to this theme of malice. In his essay on the reviewer, Orwell made a very astute remark, to the effect that most books make no impression at all on the reviewer, and hence an attitude to the book must be contrived. One must fabricate a feeling towards something that arouses no feeling. Hence the conjuring of an attitude towards the author her or himself which, since the book has wasted one's time, might as well be one of malice. I personally show malice very rarely; my general attitude towards any book, however bad, is one of vague sympathy. As one who writes books himself, I know how much hard work goes into authorship; hence the sympathy, which is probably not good journalism. But I can well understand why some reviewers develop an attitude, when given a book which they may not well understand or become bored with reading.

I published a novel about contemporary Russia at the time of my disgrace, and this was reviewed at some length in the *New Statesman* – I will not say by whom – and considered as a literary demonstration of my homosexuality. In those days it was still a crime to be homosexual, but I do not think that malice motivated my reviewer – perhaps rather the opposite, indicating the reviewer's sexual tropism. Perhaps, perhaps not.

This review came at a very opportune time. People rarely fall in love with me, or fell at the time when I was young enough to be fallable in love with. But at this time a lady dentist had interpreted, much in the manner of Katisha in *The Mikado*, my affability, a natural attitude to a dentist, as lovability, meaning a willingness to engage in an adulterous relationship. She proposed that we make love in her surgery using the dentist's chair, and for all I knew various surgical instruments, as adjuncts to the act. It was very difficult to demur, since I was engaged in a fairly lengthy course of NHS treatment.

But my lady dentist regularly read the *New Statesman*, and thus she discovered from the aforementioned review that I was homosexual. I was able to tell her that I had fought against this aspect of my personality but without success. She understood, or professed to, and the dental surgery retained its clinical purity. This was the only time when a review proved useful, indeed salvatory. I offer this anecdote to prove nothing.

Nobody really understands why reviews do so little for books, while theatrical notices can, at least in New York, make or break a play. There was a time when Arnold Bennett could promote high success with a review in the *Evening Standard*. This has not happened since his day. The quite incredible success of *A Brief History of Time* by Stephen Hawking owes nothing to its reviews, though much to the newsworthiness of his physical condition. Its unintelligibility – as well as the physical condition of its author – is certainly a factor in its high sales record. Because, and this is particularly true in America, if a book is not easy to read it becomes a part of the furniture: the money paid out for it has not been wasted on an ephemeral and enjoyable object.

T.S. Eliot said that a genuine writer at the age of 35, is *nel mezzo del cammin di nostra vita*. This entails, presumably, relegating the craft to the young and ill-read, the trendy, the alternative comedian. It is because of the pain that ignorance causes that some of us keep on with the work of reviewing even in old age. Of course, old age means forgetfulness, which looks very much like ignorance. But it is through being reviewed that one learns how much ignorance resides in the reviewer. And alone with ignorance, carelessness.

When in 1960 I produced a novel that dealt with London's underclass, I was rebuked by a young Oxonian reviewer for using the term 'kinky' – terribly old-fashioned. In fact, during the time of erotic leather gear, the word was coming back and I was a little before the trend. These annoyances are mere gnat-bites, but the multiplicity of gnat-bites feels like the onset of malaria.

Let us go back to the ringmaster of the reviewing animals and clowns. How does the literary editor decide what is to be reviewed and what not? One way of answering the question is to consider a definition of literature as the arrangement of language to an aesthetic end. It is, I think, true to say that the novels of Lord Archer, Dame Barbara Cartland and the late Dame Agatha Christie do not fall into the category of literature in this sense. Such writers are sometimes praised, though distractedly by people who should know better, because they get on with the action and do not let words get in the way of it.

In a sense it is quite impossible to review a novel by Frederick Forsyth, because it achieves perfectly what it sets out to do. *The Fourth Protocol* is perfection, as our last Prime Minister affirmed by reading it at least twice. The perfection depends on limitation. It does not dare the properties which we find, say, in William Shakespeare – complexity of character, difficulty of language, the exploitation of ambiguity.

Levels don't come into it, only categories. Lord Archer belongs to Category A, Mrs Woolf to Category B. Category A tries to soft-pedal language and bring the narrative as close to the cinematic as possible. Category B regards language as a narrative character. Here is the beginning of critical wisdom, and it has to drift down to the mere reviewer. The literary editor has to contrive a balance between the needs of the lover of literature and those of the mere reader of books. Increasingly the latter establish a priority.

Book reviewers ought to be read, forgotten, and then used, along with reports of trade deficit and child abuse, to light the kitchen fire. But, to their shame, they survive in bibliographical archives. American scholars make sure of that. I cherish, as I cherish chronic dyspepsia, some of the reviews of my work that have been put together by my own American bibliographer. I will cite examples of malice that are engraved on my heart, such as it is. 'Why are Mr Burgess's books so loud?' – obviously a woman reviewer. 'It seems a pity that Mr Burgess's book is so bad' – another. 'There is too much sex in this novel, and we are all sick of Mr Burgess's scatology'. 'I yawned on the first page and would have yawned on the last, if I had ever reached it.' 'Mr Burgess would writer better if he wrote less.' So it goes.

Should one fight back? Hugh Walpole used to do this, engaging in a kind of fisticuffs with Rebecca West, but he always got the worst of it. He also did what, in the persona of Alroy Kear, Somerset Maugham made him do in his novel *Cakes and Ale*. He would write to a reviewer to say that he was sorry he did not like his latest novel, but, if he might say so, the review was so well-written and contained so much good critical sense, that he could not forbear to drop him a line to say so. He does not want to be a bore, but if the reviewer is free any day next week, he, Alroy Kear, would be honoured if he's accept a luncheon invitation at the Savoy.

As Maugham puts it, 'no one can order a luncheon like Alroy Kear, and by the time the reviewer has eaten half a dozen oysters and a cut of some baby lamb, he has also eaten his words as well. So that it is not surprising that, in his review of Alroy Kear's next book, he has found a vast improvement in all departments of his novel-writing technique.'

A writer who, in his spare time, conducts the craft of reviewing, is in a position to strike back. But to do so, as to indulge in reciprocal backscratching, is inglorious, totally unworthy. The editor of the *Yorkshire Post*, a year after he'd sacked me from my lucrative post of fiction reviewer, produced a book on the Balfour Declaration and the birth of the state of Israel. I reviewed this book with unqualified praise in *Country Life*. The author was overjoyed and rather astonished. He was grateful for my magnanimity and invited me to lunch at the Reform Club. I was able to write back that he could keep his lunch: I liked his book and continued to dislike him. This is what is known as total objectivity of approach. Books are objects, not adjuncts of personality.

Objectivity of approach is a reviewer's right, privilege and duty. What he thinks of a book is something that subsists between the book and himself. Nor can he be told what to think and write. British literary editors are admirably disinterested in this respect. The *New York Times* sent me a rather boring spy novel by John le Carré, saying 'As a special privilege, we are prepared to allot you 2,000 words to assess what is clearly an important book.' I sent 400 words, which was about what the novel was worth. I was regarded as insulting the literary editor's taste and acumen: the author himself, of course, did not matter.

No, if one is to continue with the detestable craft of reviewing, detestable but necessary, one must maintain integrity. A book, however bad, has to be accorded sympathy, since it is so difficult a thing to produce; there is no agony like the agony of writing badly. The good literary editor appreciates this, and it is a good thing for him to be confronted daily with the worse agony of trying to write well, or at least translate well. The thrill of the new book, clean and shining, fresh from the binder, sustains both the reviewer and his master. Like the thrill of the sexual encounter, it does not last, but it can be renewed. And there is always the hope of a masterpiece. That's why we go on.

Literary editors live in a world of dilemmas. Journalism lives on compromise. I give a hypothetical example of the pain of choice. Two books came to me, not in my capacity as a reviewer, on the same day. One was a biography of the British film producer David Puttnam, responsible, among other things, for *Chariots of Fire*, an Oscar-winning masterpiece. The other was the record of a symposium on the so-called bad quarto of *Hamlet*. I had no doubt which was the more important book. The Shakespeare scholars had come up with new facts. They had worked out what this traditionally disgraceful pirated version of Shakespeare's tragedy represented. It was a blaze of light on the dark world of scholarship.

But who, among the readers of the upmarket Sunday papers, would really care? Most, having seen the film *Chariots of Fire*, with an easily scratchable itch of curiosity about the state of the British cinema industry, would see this biography of Puttnam, despite it being ill-written and pedestrian, as – I use quotation marks – 'relevant'. It's clearly not the responsibility of literary journalism of an unspecialist kind to deal with the arcana of Shakespeare scholarship. And yet one regrets this.

In the same way, the reviewer himself must not pretend to too much learning, or use words not found in the *Shorter Oxford*. He may not even quote Latin. Reviewing, one is always holding back, trying not to displease too much, serving the ephemeral.

I revert to this business of the plethora of books – in Aldous Huxley's novel *Point Counter Point* it's referred to as 'a bloody flux, like what the poor woman in the Bible had'. There are so many, and one wonders why. One reason, of course is the need to keep the book technicians occupied. I write fairly regularly for a highly prestigious Italian newspaper called *Il Corriere della Sera*, published by Mondadori. Visiting Mondadori's printing works, I saw a new edition of Suetonius and a new Mickey Mouse compendium – Topolino in Italy – being printed. They were on the same rolling sheet; presumably later they would be surgically split at the spine. The total indifference of the machine was what appalled. Let anything be printed so long as printing goes on.

The true horror that's implicit in the plethora is the disposability of books, like so much garbage. Books have to appear, but they have to be destroyed to make room for more books. Keeping a book in print is damnably difficult We used to have the naïve conviction that if a book had value it would keep itself alive, would defy the burners and shredders and recyclers and, being the precious life blood of a master spirit, continue to circulate and nourish the body of civilisation. But this is not so. Lord Archer's books are alive, while his superiors breathe briefly, then gasp, then perish.

One of the tasks of the literate is less to conserve great books, or worthy books, than to resuscitate them. I remember some years ago, appearing on a highly elitist television programme in which passages from books were skilfully elected by actors and then named and allocated by a team of *litterateurs*. When a comic passage was read out and I did not know it, I said, for want of something better to say, 'Oh, that's from the novel *Augustus Carp Esq.*' Immediately the proceedings were held up while Robert Robinson and Sir Kingsley Amis cried simultaneously: 'What, do you know that book?' There had been a silent and secret underground of admirers. This had the effect of getting the book briefly back into print. We must do this for A.E. Ellis's *The Rack* – a novel, on its appearance, hailed as superior to Thomas Mann's *The Magic Mountain* (it was about a tuberculosis sanatorium). It appeared in 1961, but not even its publishers remember it. How about the novels of Rex Warner, William Sansom, H.G. Wells, for that matter, which some of us urge on to a new public through laudatory prefaces? They breathe again briefly, then sink back into oblivion.

Meanwhile the flux continues – biographies, accounts of life in Provence, books of herstory as opposed to history, thigh and hip books, manuals of Kurdish cookery, brief histories of time. The literary editor, faced with the daily avalanche, has to choose, and often he chooses wrong. And ultimately it doesn't matter. What we read today tomorrow we burn. At the beginning of World War Two, Louis MacNeice wrote:

Die the soldiers, die the Jews,
And all the breadless homeless queues.
Give us this day our daily news.

Or, if you like, Sunday news. The procession of what, by definition, is forgettable goes on, duly forgotten. Books, being part of the news, join the polluted stream that flows into oblivion.

Yet I ought to end on a less cynical note. Nothing in my life, except the love of a good woman, has been more important than books. The writer is impelled by his desire to achieve the honour of being numbered among the master spirits who have produced them.

Pride and humility conjoin in the writer's life. The literary editor and his reviewers are ancillary agents of the conviction that nothing is as important as the box of organised knowledge which is acronymised into B.O.O.K. It may be a mad conviction, but it's the madness that sustained our civilisation in the past and despite the new technologies and the homogenisation of values, is unlikely to be superseded by new models of communication between souls, if souls may still be said to exist. We have our uses. I rest my case.

Originally given as the Terence Kilmartin memorial lecture at the Dartington Ways With Words Festival, and later published in the *Observer*, 30 August 1992

Index